DOING FAMILY THERAPY

The Guilford Family Therapy Series
Michael P. Nichols, *Series Editor*

Recent Volumes

DOING FAMILY THERAPY:
CRAFT AND CREATIVITY IN CLINICAL PRACTICE
Robert Taibbi

NARRATIVE SOLUTIONS IN BRIEF THERAPY
Joseph B. Eron and Thomas W. Lund

IF PROBLEMS TALKED: NARRATIVE THERAPY IN ACTION
Jeffrey L. Zimmerman and Victoria C. Dickerson

LEARNING AND TEACHING THERAPY
Jay Haley

THE REFLECTING TEAM IN ACTION:
COLLABORATIVE PRACTICE IN FAMILY THERAPY
Steven Friedman, Editor

REWRITING FAMILY SCRIPTS:
IMPROVISATION AND SYSTEMS CHANGE
John Byng-Hall

INTERNAL FAMILY SYSTEMS THERAPY
Richard C. Schwartz

NORMAL FAMILY PROCESSES, Second Edition
Froma Walsh, Editor

CHANGING THE RULES: A CLIENT-DIRECTED APPROACH TO THERAPY
Barry L. Duncan, Andrew D. Solovey, and Gregory S. Rusk

TRANSGENERATIONAL FAMILY THERAPIES
Laura Giat Roberto

THE INTIMACY PARADOX:
PERSONAL AUTHORITY IN THE FAMILY SYSTEM
Donald S. Williamson

HUSBANDS, WIVES, AND LOVERS:
THE EMOTIONAL SYSTEM OF THE EXTRAMARITAL AFFAIR
David J. Moultrup

MEN IN THERAPY: THE CHALLENGE OF CHANGE
Richard L. Meth and Robert S. Pasick, with Barry Gordon, Jo Ann Allen,
Larry B. Feldman, and Sylvia Gordon

DOING FAMILY THERAPY

Craft and Creativity
in Clinical Practice

ROBERT TAIBBI

THE GUILFORD PRESS
New York   London

©1996 The Guilford Press
A Division of Guilford Publications, Inc.
72 Spring Street, New York, NY 10012

Printed in the United States of America

This book is printed on acid-free paper.

Last digit is print number: 9 8 7 6 5 4 3 2 1

Library of Congress Cataloging-in-Publication Data is available from the Publisher.

ISBN 1-57230-108-2
ISBN 1-57230-181-3 (pbk)

To Rosemary, Jenni,
Chris, and Julie

Preface

I still have vivid memories of my early days in this profession — not of the successes, nor even the failures, but the anxiety, the overwhelming sense at times that I had absolutely no idea what I was doing. Not because I didn't know anything, I did; my head was filled with theories — about depression, marital conflict, behavioral problems, communication — on and on, an endless stream. I had no problem speaking to my supervisor or around the lunch table with my colleagues — about etiology and goals, about this diagnosis or that — but, in the heat of a session with clients, I often found myself lacking any real sense of how to put my ideas into operation, how to turn the information in my head into something I could say or do that might be helpful.

What I usually wound up doing, it seemed, was winging it — impersonationing the latest Master Therapist I had seen in the film at last Friday's staff development meeting, using the hand gestures and voice of my father, which I unconsciously adopted from his assorted lectures to me as I was growing up. Any time this deadly combination didn't seem to be working (which was quite often), I resorted to Plan B, the "William Buckley Maneuver" — firing question after question from notes I had on the clipboard. What the clients answered was less important than the sense that I had absolute control over the conversation. Clients usually left these sessions feeling like they had just been interrogated by the police in a murder investigation, and what was surprising to me at the time was that they usually didn't come back.

Over the years I've realized that I wasn't unique in feeling both overwhelmed and incompetent; each year's new crop of students and "green" therapists brings with it variations on the same theme. In spite of the advances we've made in our knowledge about what works and what doesn't by way of helping people, and in spite of whatever support I can muster as a supervisor, newcomers to the field continue to feel as though they are either flying by the seat of their pants or are becoming pathologically rigid. Too often they struggle with trying to translate the theory in their heads into the seemingly surefire, effective moves of the experts.

The difficulty, of course, is that learning and doing therapy isn't a clear-cut, fixed process. Unlike a mechanic in the garage, there's no tried-and-true, one-size-fits-all way to turn concepts into practical operations. Therapy, after all, doesn't deal with things but with people, making it both an art and a science. The therapist is part of the process, not apart from it, and change often comes about less from what interventions the therapist uses than from the relationship with the family he or she is able to establish.

The challenge that arises from all of this is that in order to do family therapy therapists must learn to be both competent in the craft and creative in their approach. They must try to be aware of what they are doing, but at the same time always move themselves and the family beyond their own limits—the family toward change, themselves toward an integration of heart and head into a personal, effective therapeutic style. This is not an easy task, especially in these days of managed care when more and more eyes are peering over one's shoulders.

My hope is that this book can serve as a bridge between knowing too much and becoming confused, and knowing too little and becoming immobilized; between focusing too much on skill and becoming rigid, and focusing too much on one's own personality and feeling incompetent. My hope is that like Goldilocks therapists will find what is "just right"—discover enough about their values and skills to know what they want to keep; learn enough about the basics of family therapy to feel that there are always therapeutic options, opportunities to repair mistakes, and ways to give families what they expect and need most. Most of all my wish is that therapists will come to experience and value the power that lies in the smallest of psychic spaces between themselves and others.

I appreciate all the colleagues and clients who over the years have helped me to see both the fragility and strength inherent of each of us. All the case examples in this book are based on real families with real problems; however, identifying characteristics have been changed or composites were made of the clinical examples to protect confidentiality. My thanks to the families who have allowed me to be part of their lives.

Contents

DOING FAMILY THERAPY

ONE

Family Therapy:
Welcome to Oz

They shuffle into your office without saying a word—first appointment and nobody is happy. The six-year-old boy immediately goes for your desk chair; the mother, a large woman in a faded green dress, nails him before his butt hits the seat—"A.J., that's the lady's seat. Come sit over here." She rocks back and forth on the chair without standing up and stretches out one of her massive arms toward him; her tone is moderately firm. A.J. hesitates for a moment, then shrugs his shoulders and sits next to her with his head down. She reaches over and rubs his back.

The father is sitting across the room from the mother, and he has pulled his chair back so that it's almost in the corner. In contrast to his wife, he's as thin as one of the chair legs. He looks like he just got off work. His work boots still have mud on them, his uniform looks dusty. The name on the pocket says Earl. He doesn't look up at you, but surveys his fingers, then begins to pick at some dirt under one of his nails.

Next to you is the daughter, a blond-haired, attractive girl, 13, maybe 14. She's chewing gum and jiggling her foot, looking straight ahead, staring, it seems, at the molding behind the couch.

"So," you say, "thanks for coming. Glad to see you were all able to make it." You smile and try to make eye contact with everyone in the room. No one meets your eyes except for the mother, who is now sitting at the edge of her seat.

"Momma, I got to go to the bathroom." A.J. tugs on his mother's sleeve and wiggles in his chair. The mother takes a quick glance at him, raises her index finger to her lips, and pats his knee.

"Momma, I got to go bad."

"A.J., sit still!" You're startled by the loud thud of a command from the father, who is now staring at his son.

A.J. ignores him. "Momma, Momma." His voice is getting whiny;

he's tugging at his mother's sleeve again and has shifted from wiggling to bouncing up and down on the seat.

"Now, you can just wait a few minutes, A.J., while we talk to this lady." The mother's voice has that strained sweet tone to it; she reaches over and starts rubbing his back again.

"Damn it, Loretta, why didn't you get him to go before we came?" snaps Earl.

Time to get to work. "Earl, it seems—"

"Because he didn't need to, that's why." Loretta glares and stretches out her neck and words at the same time toward her husband. Then she turns back to A.J., and her voice shifts back to its saccharin tone, "Go ahead, honey, if you need to go. Just ask the lady if it's all right."

"He can wait!" Earl slams both hands down on the arm of the chair.

"Momma—"

"A.J., shut up!" Earl hooks his hands around the chair arms, threatening to get up.

You try again. "Earl, how—"

"The boy's got to go, Earl!"

"Hold it, everybody," you say, raising your voice. Things are starting to get out of control.

"Listen, you're the one who dragged me down here to talk to some stranger," says Earl, flicking his hand toward you, "all because of your precious little boy who—"

"Well, Earl, I sure as hell don't want him to turn out like you!" Loretta, with some effort, is on her feet, screaming, waving her arm. "Like you, Earl!"

"Momma, I got—"

"Okay everybody," you croak, "let's—"

"I don't need this shit!" Earl stands up and kicks the chair back against the wall. "And I don't need you, bitch." In a flash he swings the door open, stomps out, and slams it shut.

"Momma, I got to go."

The daughter keeps staring at the molding.

SWEPT AWAY

This, of course, is one of the family therapist's worst nightmares. The family that breaks into a fight before you even get the fee set. The family that stages a mutiny and gangs up on you—"Do *you* have children?" "Are you telling me that I should let him run around 'till three in the morning?" "We tried being nice, tried talking to him, but it doesn't help." "You don't understand, young man, I have bad nerves." And worst of all, perhaps, the family that just won't talk.

Individual therapy always seems easier. One on one, no distractions. The client coming to you, the expert, as the one who can help him or her sort out issues, causes, solutions. As you listen deeply, soaking in both what is said and not said, as you both talk together, exploring the past, the present, the emotions, and the reasons, his or her internal world slowly unfolds, layer by layer. Through the quiet intimacy of the therapeutic relationship, the vulnerable and fearful parts of the client's psyche become defined and known; by becoming known the client's view of the world is changed.

Family therapy is a different world all together. Like Dorothy, you're swept up and suddenly dropped down into a realm that seems strange, bewildering, intimidating. Even though it's your office, you're the outsider. Six people talking at once, each wanting your attention, each testing the limits ("Psst, Johnny, hand me that basketball"; "I want to go to the bathroom"; "Can I go get a Coke from the machine?"), everyone talking at once, blaming someone else or waiting for you to blame them, wanting you to tell them what to do, how to fix the problem, five minutes after they hit the door. A group of people with their own history and culture and language. Secret signals—the biting of a lip; a quiet laugh; the shaking of a head; the clenching of a fist; the subtlest of twitches, jerks, and grunts—pass among them and around you, setting off a chain reaction that can spiral out of control before you have a chance to glance up from your notes or catch your breath.

That is how it seems to go in family therapy—too much happens too fast. The sigh that just hung in the air and seemed so poignant in individual therapy is now quickly swallowed up by the stepfather's smirk or overrun by the belching of the 10-year-old in the corner. The intimate conversation between the caring but frightened mother and her lonely and awkward adolescent daughter that you worked so painstakingly toward for months is suddenly dissolved when the four-year-old decides she can't handle it and insists that she is going to throw up right there and then.

And then there are the stories—he said . . . , she said . . . , they said . . . —today, last Friday, 30 years ago. Stories of the past, stories about people long dead yet strangely alive and powerful, stories that show just how bad things can get or how good they can possibly be, stories that have no point at all except to take up time and grab a bit of that much desired commodity, attention. The heap of facts, figures, and perspectives from all corners of the room that can quickly drown the best family therapist if he or she isn't careful.

Yes, family therapy can be tough. It requires a flexibility, a creativity, an ability to fly by the seat of your pants that exponentially increases with the number of people in the room and their level of distress and conflict.

What can make this all the more difficult, especially for those new to the field, is the bewildering array of approaches from which to choose. Over the years, as family therapy has moved into more and more problem areas and gathered under its belt more and more experience, it has become more and more complex. The number of theories is overwhelming — structural, strategic, narrative, contextual, intergenerational, psychodynamic, paradoxical, solution-focused — and the list goes on and on, supplemented by a vast array of adjunct techniques and contexts, such as NLP (neurolinguistic programming); hypnosis; EMDR (eye movement desensitization and reprocessing); the growing sensitivity to the impact of multiculturalism, racism, sexuality, class, developmental issues, and a whole host of environmental stressors.

How do you decide which approach is best — for you and for your client family — when they all claim to be right? How do you not only keep track of all the things going on in the room, but at the same time also keep track of what is going on inside your head? How do you keep from feeling overwhelmed when you already feel overwhelmed? Why bother with it all? Why not just keep it simple, you think. Go ahead and just see Mrs. Jones by herself and leave Tommy to the guidance counselor at school.

Faced with the bewildering array of novel interventions, hot new techniques, and the latest therapeutic trends, it often seems impossible to stay informed, to find a solid footing that you can stand upon. But they are there — basic, practical ideas and techniques that form the core of the family therapy approach. These tools and concepts are like the ballast on a ship and can keep you steady when you begin to lose your balance in the swirl of a family session. They form the core, the anchor that family therapists use; you can learn them and return to them whenever you begin to feel overwhelmed. One of the goals of this book is to familiarize you with these tools.

But the other goal of this book is to go beyond survival, to help you not only get through your sessions, but to help you realize the power of family therapy and see that you can do it well. This means worrying less about following the chapter and verse of a particular theory and drawing instead upon your own creativity and flexibility. This is the key to good family therapy; utilizing your own strengths, style, and values. Working with families in this way not only helps the family by giving them most of what you have to offer, namely, more of yourself, but in the long run keeps you energized and sane.

This is different from what unfortunately is often the end product of formal education and the learning process. Rather than being encouraged to discover him- or herself, the new therapist often only winds up discovering others and imitating them — at best an ill-fitting suit of therapeutic style that hampers rather than encourages the true expression of one's personality. Or the therapist is pressured to quickly give blind allegiance to a particular school or theory—you become a structuralist, an object relations person, a staunch believer in constructivism. Rather than building a theoretical approach around your strengths, you squeeze yourself into a theory and leave important parts of yourself out. Gradually, to no one's surprise, you become what you call yourself, and the left-out parts of your personality are forgotten.

If staying anchored means learning to rely on a basic core of concepts, staying creative means realizing that there isn't only one approach to any family. This is the pragmatic, individualized side of family therapy that we'll be focusing on together, the awareness that there's always more than one way to skin a cat. Through numerous case examples we'll look at options—the multiple ways of tackling a family and their concerns—so that you can learn to map out alternative routes that not only fit your skills and the family's resources, but can keep you both moving when a particular path seems blocked.

This book is divided into three parts. In the first section we'll be mapping out the terrain of family therapy, the basic skills that keep you afloat, the obstacles and dangers, and the ways to handle them in the beginning, middle, and end stages of treatment.

In the second section we will be looking at a variety of cases and problems. Here's where we'll talk about applying the basic skills, exploring clinical options, and beginning to sort out your own preferences and style. Through this process you'll be able to learn to think creatively and make use of your intuitions.

Finally, in the third section, we'll return to some practical tips for dealing with the pressures of the work, especially in agency settings, ways of staying emotionally healthy over the long haul, ways of managing the daily wear and tear of the work. We'll also step back and explore work in the larger context of your everyday living, the need for work and therapy in the light of your beliefs and values, what it means to have a calling, what it takes to have sense of integrity.

Along the way there will be exercises for you to try, to help you see how the concepts of the chapter may apply to your personal and professional life. These exercises will give you a chance to further define your strengths, skills, and values.

But before we begin this exploration we need to talk a bit about the basic ingredients, the starting points for becoming a good family therapist.

THEORY—SOMETHING TO HOLD ONTO

Too many theories can overwhelm you, the wrong kind can constrict you, but have none and you are set adrift in a vast ocean of facts and observations. A theory of therapy gives you something to hold onto. It can be as simple or complex as you like, and what a theory says is less important than what it can give to you and allow you to do.

Theories fulfill several important functions. First they are, by definition, tools for organizing. They are the peg board upon which we hang what we see and hear; they show us where to look and what to listen for. Events that once seemed random are now seen as connected. A father's hunting trip with his son is no longer just a family folktale, but, when hung on the theory, an example of role modeling, an attempt to resolve unresolved issues of the past, or a way of avoiding growing tension within the marriage. A daughter's unexpected running away from home is not the ridiculous ending to a stupid argument about what shoes to wear, or the senseless, impulsive copying of a TV movie that was on the night before, but an understandable, even predictable, response to the brother's life-draining depression, the mother's debilitating fear of going outside, or the parents' angry denial of the girl's claims of sexual abuse. Behavior and words suddenly have meaning and merit; they become linked to a whole family of concepts that not only explain what has happened, but tell what can happen in the future, and most importantly, describe ways to change it.

With the theory's ability to organize our information comes the additional benefit of directing and containing our anxiety, which potentially can make us ineffective. When we fear becoming overwhelmed in the process of the session—by the conflicting stories about what happened last Thursday, the building emotions of Dad's anger or Mom's sadness—we can lean on our theory to tell us what to ask or do to gather the information we need. As we read the intake sheet we use our theory to help us start filling in the blanks, formulating a hypothesis that we can take into the initial session with us. The theory becomes then not only a tool, but a support, an internal security blanket, or a place we can always return home to. With it we have courage to walk into the unfamiliar world of the family; we feel prepared, rather than confused and apprehensive.

The practical support that theory provides is enhanced by the sense of belonging that comes with it as well. By allying yourself with a particular theory, you not only have a name for what you do and how you think—a structural/strategic therapist, a cognitive behaviorist—you also become a member in a club of like-minded therapists. The concepts and language of the theory act like a secret handshake that separates you from those in the field who are different and draws you to those who are similar. This can be a powerful anchor in the shifting array of confused and confusing family situations.

But the benefits of theory are not only yours. These same theoretical concepts and language can also be passed on to others, most notably clients, who can, like you, use them to reorganize what they see. Through the filter of your theory old behaviors are suddenly seen with new eyes, and new, more neutral words replace those laden with anger and blame: "No, Johnny isn't acting like a brat, Mrs. Smith; one of the characteristics of hyperactivity is that it is harder for him to sit still like Tommy does, and he may have trouble following complicated directions"; "Did you all see what just happened, the way that patterns works? Mom says something, Dad disagrees, and Mary starts to whine. Every family has patterns; this is one of yours."

The therapist needs to do more than brainwash the family with theory, of course. This has always been a running criticism of therapy from those inside and outside the field, namely, that therapy and therapists often wind up converting their clients to their pet theories, rather than helping them solve their problems. The classic example is the person who after years of psychoanalysis is as unhappy as ever but can now talk about the "projections" that he is making or the way his "id impulses are always at battle with his superego." It may be great sport to mock what others do, but a therapist with some understanding of why people do what they do—a theory of behavior—can help people transform the words into ameliorative action.

By seeing their problem in such a new light, by talking to themselves with different words, the family can discover, with the help of the therapist, alternative ways out of the mental ruts in which they were constantly spinning. Now new, more creative solutions become possible— Johnny isn't a bad kid who needs to be punished, but has a biochemical disorder that makes it hard for him to do certain things; I'm not really going crazy, I just need to talk to someone about my sadness; our relationship isn't lousy simply because we're both stubborn, but because our needs have changed over the years. The theory opens new doors to the solving of problems, the process of healing.

Organizing, naming, and supporting are qualities that all theories share, but because it's the template you'll use everyday in your work, in order for a theory to do all it should for you, it needs to fit you.

This means that you shouldn't just settle on a particular theory just because it's what you were exposed to in school. You shouldn't choose one because it intellectually appeals to you, is popular with your colleagues, or even seems to work with certain problems. The best theory for you is the theory that meets you halfway. It should fit your personality and strengths, your view of the world—the way people are, the way problems are solved. When there's that kind of a match, a close fitting of the basic you and the theory you embrace, it supports you rather than you supporting it. Such a theory enables you to move freely, rather than awkwardly; it underscores your natural instincts and intuitions. It suits you and empowers you.

PHILOSOPHY—LOOKING AT THE BIGGER PICTURE

Good theories also fit our personal philosophy. These are our values and notions of what life is and the role people and problems play in it. In order to make a good match between our theory and ourselves, we need to first step back and look at the landscape and decide what we believe.

This is easier said than done. Unfortunately, this ground all too often remains uncharted and shrouded in fog because we don't take the time to figure it out, don't know the right questions to ask ourselves, or don't have the words to articulate what we feel. Rather than doing the hard work of our own discovering and defining, we're often inclined to take the shorter path and grab on to what's already in front of us, namely, the personal philosophies of others—those of our parents, friends, or spouses, or those we read in books or learn in class.

This works fine until it doesn't work, and eventually it doesn't work. The problem is that we're trying to walk in shoes that don't quite fit, adapting ourselves to something that's made for someone else. At some point there's a strain—who we are and how we live grow ever wider apart. We begin to feel bored or empty, we have a "crisis" in our career, in our lives; nothing seems right, something seems to be missing, we itch for change, but don't really know what we want to change. All we know, in fact, is what we don't want.

We see examples of this strain in people's lives everyday: the man who enters his father's business and 15 years later feels as though he is merely going through the motions, the woman who married at an early age out of peer pressure or family expectations and has what everyone considers a "good life" finds herself facing each day with an overwhelming sense of emptiness and despair. The feelings they have tell them what they don't want, what they no longer believe, what they may be ready to give up.

Having only this handful of negatives, a list of what-not-to-do's, can be a good start to discovering what we do believe and want, but it's a frightening one. There's little that's positive and solid enough to hold onto, and the anxiety we feel can cause us to cling tighter to what we already have—the job we hate, the marriage that is collapsing, the spiritual life that has become a hollow shell of habit. Out of despair or frustration we may grab hold of another philosophy, another's philosophy, one that may not fit us any better, but which at least makes us temporarily feel better simply because it is different.

Rather than holding tighter or switching we need to ask the basic questions, walk around the landscape of our lives in order to discover what's already there. What enabled Dorothy to survive in the strange land of Oz, to make the tough decisions and find courage, was not only her memory of home, but the philosophy and values of home—the clear sense

of good and evil, fakery and truth, values of commitment and friendship—
that were deeply embedded within her. Similarly, in order for you to survive in the land of family therapy, in order to be able to fly by the seat
of your pants, you first have to know where your pants are.

Before you can find that theory that meets you halfway, that underscores what you already know, you need to know what you know, you
need to name the values and core beliefs that run your life. Then when
you hear the philosophies and theories of the families in your office, or
read those in the books of fellow clinicians, you can measure them against
your own. You may find that you can offer that family another system
of beliefs that is more humane, positive, loving; you can more clearly decide whether the new clinical ideas will support what you believe and give
you what you need.

And when you feel disillusioned by the grind of the work, pessimistic
about your ability to help, or burned out by simple wear and tear, you can
go back to your philosophy to reignite your creativity. Just as our theory
helps us fill in the holes in our clinical understanding and points in the direction we need to go, our personal philosophy helps us fill in the holes during our times of confusion and doubt, and points us back to what we know
is right for us. Our personal philosophy not only gives us a running summary of what we believe, but a continual vision of what we can become.

How do you discover your philosophy? You can begin by asking yourself some of these basic questions:

> What is the most important thing in life?
> What is the purpose of life? What is the purpose of *your* life? What
> can only you give, create, do?
> What is the meaning of relationships, of families? What is our respon-
> sibility toward others?
> Why do relationships change? How much can people change? How
> do we know when change is necessary?
> What are the limits of relationships? When should relationships end?
> What does commitment mean?
> What is the relationship between doing for yourself and doing for
> others?
> What does it mean to love someone or something?
> What should parents most teach their children? What are the limits
> of the parents' responsibility, involvement?
> What is the role of emotions in our lives?
> What is the purpose of work?
> How much of our life is controlled by our past?

These are big questions that you may or may not have ready answers
to. In thinking about these questions you may think of others that seem

even more important. What particular questions you ask is probably less important than starting the process of asking them.

And as you listen to others, as you read, including this book, step back and sort out for yourself what fits and doesn't fit, based on your philosophy, intuition, or beliefs. Don't be afraid to change your mind nor to hold to what you believe to be important.

COURAGE

Theory and philosophy together create a foundation upon which skills develop; the mix of all three—theory, philosophy, skills—forms the nucleus of good therapy. But there is limit to how much theory and philosophy can support us, how far skills can carry us. The final ingredient that the good clinician needs is courage.

Few of us would list therapy up there among the world's most dangerous professions—there are no high-speed chases, ducking of bullets, balancing on the edge of rooftops, or handling of dangerous heavy machinery. Instead we sit around on blue couches or wingback chairs, sipping coffee, asking how the past week went, looking reflective, occasionally furrowing a brow or patting a client on the shoulder—hardly the stuff of drama and danger. But risk, and the courage needed to face it, is there nonetheless. Courage doesn't necessarily come from the facing enormous challenges on the outside; courage comes from dealing, no matter what the source, with the fear and anxiety that lie inside.

This fear is powerful. It's fear, after all, not foolishness or ignorance, that usually keeps our lives stuck and stagnant. In families it's the interlocking of fears—each family member's struggle to maintain what is known—that compounds itself to make any change ever more difficult. Your success and failure as a therapist come less from knowing what to do and more from pushing hard enough to propel the family members out of the constraints that they naturally place around their lives.

Doing family therapy doesn't mean taking foolish chances, but having the courage to steer yourself and the family toward the anxiety of change. This is the everyday courage that doing therapy demands, pushing yourself beyond the foundation that theory and philosophy can provide or the confidence that practiced skills can create. It's the courage of not only putting your own philosophy into practice, but of helping others to define, refine, and eventually live theirs. It's the simple courage of honesty and approaching challenges, the willingness to try something in order to move ahead, even if you aren't exactly sure where it will lead.

This kind of courage in therapy enables you to do the work of therapy—namely, leading families to the edge of change and helping them look over the brink. This means confronting the mother who appears so fragile and makes others, including you, believe that she can't handle confrontation, talking to a child about the terrible things that happened to him or her without getting lost in your own grief and anger, or saying nothing at all so that the person across from you can finally say what he or she has been holding back for a long time. It means talking about what's difficult, moving against the family's natural inertia to stay put and keep things the same, resisting the temptation and tension that pulls on you to become one of them. It's acknowledging both the gift of seeing much of your own life in the life of others and the danger of becoming confused over who you are trying to help.

Good therapy requires control, but not being controlling; constantly dealing with the unpredictable, while just as constantly predicting that the unpredictable will come; fostering intimacy while keeping clear limits on that intimacy; being committed, but being willing to stop when it seems an end has been reached or will never come. Good therapy is a seeming hodgepodge of contradictions and qualifiers that requires that you walk a thin line between too little and too much, between reaching out and holding back. Courage is the stuff that glues the contradictions together, keeps you steady on the line, gets you moving until the skill, knowledge, and self-trust can take over. Without it the families you see are penned in, confined to the narrow range of your own comfort.

These three, then—theory, philosophy, and courage—are the prerequisites for journeying through the land of Oz that is family therapy. We'll be talking more about them as we explore more of the technical aspects of treatment and discuss specific case examples. Keep them in mind as you move through this information. In the next chapter we'll be reviewing some of the basic family therapy concepts.

LOOKING WITHIN

Following discussions of major topics you will find a number of exercises and questions designed to make the material more personally relevant, and help you to ground the concepts within your own practice.

It may be tempting to just read these exercises and not actually do them. Try not to. If, after starting, an exercise seems too redundant or irrelevant, go ahead and move on to the next. But if the exercise stirs your curiosity, or better yet, your anxiety, give it a try. You have nothing to lose, and you may be surprised at what you find.

1. A short imagery exercise: Go to a quiet place for a few minutes where you know you won't be disturbed. Sit comfortably in your chair. Take a few deep breaths, and for a few moments just concentrate on your breathing. Begin to feel relaxed.

See if you can see in your mind's eye a meadow. It is a bright, warm, sunny day; the grass is green, flowers are in bloom and the air smells sweet with their fragrance, a slight breeze blows. And there you see yourself, walking along, feeling relaxed, the sun warm on your back. As you are walking you see ahead of you the edge of a wood. You decide to walk toward it.

As you approach the wood, you begin to hear in the breeze the sound of a name, the name of a person of the same sex as you. As you near the edge of the wood and peer into the darkness of the trees, you are aware that someone is there in the shadows, the person whose name you heard. You become curious; you begin to wonder who this person is, what he or she is like. Then you listen and can tell that this person is coming toward you.

A person emerges from the trees. Notice how he or she looks. Imagine yourself starting a conversation with this person. Imagine asking all the questions that you were curious about, finding out all you want to know that will tell you just what this person is like. Take as much time as you need talking to this person.

When your conversation is over, the person waves good-bye and walks back into the wood. You turn around and begin to walk back down the meadow, thinking about all that you have just heard. When your fantasy feels over just sit for a few minutes and relax.

It is important to hold within ourselves (and help create for families) a vision of what we can be. This imagery exercise is designed to get you in touch with your ideal self. This may have been easy for you to do, or you may have had some difficulty. Perhaps you had sensations or recalled memories, or heard dialogue, but had trouble creating the images. Don't be concerned. You can try again another time, and will probably have a different response.

Be aware of the person you saw, not only of his or her appearance, but of his or her personal qualities, dreams, attitudes toward others, toward life. Notice the gap between the way you see yourself now and the person you imagined. Is there anything that surprised you? Is there a particular quality that you most would like to develop? What would it take to do it?

2. Look over once again the philosophical questions presented above. Try writing down the answers to as many as catch your interest. See if you can develop a concise (a couple of sentences) personal statement of life, values, and work.

3. You don't need to take karate lessons or Outward Bound courses to increase your sense of courage. Simply begin by taking small risks, not just in your work, but elsewhere in your life. Practice approaching your fear—walk up to that neighbor on your block that you've seen a few times and start a conversation, ask a question in a group even though you know it sounds stupid, try something physically different even though you feel clumsy or know you're not good at it. A half-dozen times during the week, as you become aware of approaching the edges of your own anxiety, go forward, do whatever is scary, then pat yourself on the back. The goal is not to be without fear, but to be able to act in spite of it.

TWO

Family Therapy: The Basics

Your partner starts to object to your wonderful idea, and before he or she has spoken you know what's coming next. In fact, without thinking much about it you probably could predict just how the whole conversation/argument would run, all the twists and turns of logic and emotion, down to his or her squinty eyes, your deep sigh, and that infamous closing line, "Go ahead, you're going to do what you want anyway!"

When you call up your parents on Sunday the sense of déjà vu is intense. You imagine that if you felt lazy, you could probably just make a tape recording of yourself and play it over the phone next week. No one would notice the difference.

And God forbid you should make a mistake and sit in someone else's chair at the dinner table one night—World War III will break out right there in the dining room before the seat could get warm.

For all our talk about being our own person, in reality we spend most of our time engaged in never-ending ping-pong matches with others, where what we do and they do is always a series of set and predictable reactions to each other. With those we are closest to—our family, our friends, our colleagues—knowing each other well means having each others' game moves down pat. We can see that slam argument coming 10 minutes before it arrives, sense out of the corner of our emotional eye the sarcastic remark that always zings past us before dropping off the edge of the conversation, know that a slight head fake to the right means our partner is about to cry. We can anticipate and respond to each other so reflexively that most of our interactions run completely on automatic pilot.

When this social volleying is compounded over and over with the people we interact with all day, we wind up finding our everyday lives filled with blocks of routine (morning wake-up/prework time, the work block, the dinnertime block, postdinner, and bedtime routine), handfuls of predictable social patterns ("Hi, how are you?" "I'm fine"), and unspoken rules and deals that essentially are designed to merely keep the game going as it is ("You don't mention my drinking, and I won't talk about your mother").

It would seem that these routines and rules are enough to flatten life, to make it deadly boring and uncreative, but, of course, they don't. On the contrary, it's precisely because of these predictable routines that we can run on remote for huge stretches of time and free up the mental and emotional energy within us that we need for innovative thinking, creative problem solving, and deliberate action. And the slightest deviations in this regularity—the boss failing to respond to our "Good morning" greeting, our partner forgetting our anniversary (or was it really forgetting?)—help us realize that being creatures of habit keeps us from being perpetually anxious and insecure. All in all, it's the repetition and structure in our social world that save us the trouble of having to reinvent our lives each morning when we wake up.

But the downside of our dependency on routine and reaction is that these interactional patterns can become unbelievably tenacious, as the dinner table melee makes clear. Both internal habit and group momentum create strong pressure to keep the pattern going, to stay in the game and counter the shots as you have been all along. If your moves radically change or, worse yet, if you stop playing, confusion and anger break out, everybody starts emotionally tripping all over each other, and it all threatens to fall apart.

These ideas about the power of the game and pressure of the group have seeped into the popular culture to become everybody's common knowledge. From self-help books that lay out the basic his and her moves and countermoves that make up our intimate relationships, to the sixth-grader coached in health class about the 15 ways to handle the peer pressure of drugs and "Just Say No," we learn that we all too easily fall into social and emotional ruts and that change comes from going against the tide.

These ideas form the basis of family therapy—that problems and their solutions lie in the patterns and connections among people; that the patterns are usually stronger than any one individual; and that the ping-pong match continues, even though the participants may not even be aware that they're playing. It's a different perspective than the more vertical and linear psychodynamic approaches, moving down as they do into the individual, moving back in the past. In contrast, family therapy's view is horizontal, kinetic, circular—focusing on the spaces between people; their round-robin of behaviors; the way the patterns are started and stopped, and kept going.

How you think shapes *what* you think you can do. Thinking in terms of circles and interpersonal connections, rather than lines and individual pasts, changes the shape of therapy. If the patterns are circular, then where you start isn't all that important, since circles are notorious for not having starting points. Whether you talk to the parents, then see the child, or see the child and then the parents, work on the marriage, or help the parents set up some structure theoretically doesn't make any difference: The pieces and the parts and the patterns will all eventually emerge as you look for them and gather them together.

Everything is, after all, interconnected, and changing any one pattern or behavior within a pattern (e.g., getting that sixth-grader to say "no") can and will ripple across to affect the others (the friends who are pressuring him or her). This makes change in itself valuable for itself; the act of change can start the chain reaction that can break apart the patterns in which the problems and emotions are suspended. Precisely what the change is or where it is, is often less important than the presence of some type of change at all.

The implication of this way of thinking is that there is less need to worry about doing it right. It's easy when seeing an experienced colleague in action, or seeing one of the masters—Salvador Minuchin, Jay Haley, Virginia Satir, Carl Whitaker—at work on tape or in person, to feel that he or she has figured it all out, has made that perfect match between the particular problem and the proper solution. And so you carefully watch his or her every move, transcribe word for word his or her response, practice getting just the right inflection in your voice, asking the questions in just the right order. In your mind you keep a running chart of problems and their matching strategies. If you can just do what they do, think how they think, you too, you feel, can be, if not a master therapist, at least competent.

But no matter how effective they seem, their way is not the only way. The basic goals that power family therapy are less delicate and precise than what may appear through the work of the experts, their intent more broad, more general—to disrupt the patterns, or stop the patterns, or make the family aware of the patterns so they can stop them themselves and create brand new ones. The good family therapist is less a meticulous detective or brilliant strategist and more a shrewd and insightful anarchist, the unfailing resistance fighter.

This doesn't mean, of course, that as a family therapist you're left to bludgeon problems with only a blunt theory; your work includes a range of techniques, and it takes skill both to choose those that better suit the particular problem and family and to remain sensitive to the family's anxiety and needs as the dysfunctional patterns begin to come apart. What it does mean is that family systems theory gives you more room to move around, to adjust what you do to best utilize your greatest skills and strengths and the family's motivation.

This flexibility and freedom that you have as a family therapist reduces the need to battle with the client over where to start or who has the problem. Even though it seems that individual therapy offers you, as the clinician, greater control over the session process, this is more than offset by the presence of other family members in the room who can demonstrate their game moves right before your eyes, as well as add information that the individual may not so readily provide.

MAPPING THE GROUND—STARTING ASSUMPTIONS

Before looking more closely at the basics of family therapy, we need to look at the ground on which it's built. These are the assumptions, or, rather, *your* assumptions, about what therapy is all about. Before the therapy starts it's important to be clear about what you believe the therapy to be, to know your own bottom lines and givens because they eventually form the parameters, the outline of the map that you use in navigating through the work of family therapy. Your answers to some of the questions raised in the last chapter may have revealed to you many of yours. The following are mine—once again, measure them against your own.

Therapy is one option among many for creating change and solving problems. I once worked with a woman individually who was struggling with a number of problems in her marriage. She gained some insight, was able to change some of the patterns within the relationship itself, but for every step forward she felt she was taking two back. Depression set in. I was considering hospitalization because her symptoms were getting steadily worse. Then one Monday she came for her appointment feeling totally different. She felt great, much less anxious and depressed; she had a much clearer sense of what she wanted and was willing to do even though she hadn't made any drastic changes in her relationship. She had had a life-changing experience.

Over the weekend, she explained, as she was lying on the couch feeling miserable and hopeless, she found herself actually contemplating suicide, imagining going upstairs, getting sleeping pills from the bathroom, taking the bottle, and lying back down on the couch where she would fall forever asleep. But even as these thoughts ran through her mind, others tied to her religious beliefs rose up as well. She remembered all the messages of all those childhood Sunday school classes, the power of God, the presence of Jesus always there to help, to love her. Suddenly she was overwhelmed by the sense of comfort and security, and she felt that God was right there in the room at her side. She knew deep inside herself that everything would turn out all right if only she would recommit herself to life and love.

And so she did. This brief but powerful religious experience helped her to change, and even on follow-up a year later she was doing well. I've known other people over the years who have had just as powerful, if not quite so dramatic, religious experiences as this woman, people who have simply prayed or sought advice from their minister or spent time alone in what for them was a sacred place. I've been amazed by others who joined a support group and after three meetings were already on the road to resolving a long-standing problem; people who found hope or inspiration in a magazine article or book; or a person who in a casual conversation with a neighbor about her grandson found some moral in the story that became the seed for a new perspective; people who hadn't looked for change, but found their view of life different simply by driving out West and looking up toward the sky from the bottom of a canyon.

It's all too easy for us as therapists to get tunnel vision, to feel evangelical about our work, to project our own inner dependency and need for help onto the lives of others and feel that they too need what only we can give them. Therapy, we quickly come to believe, is the best and main path to personal change and problem solving. But it's only one option among many. Keeping that in mind helps us present what we have to offer more fairly and responsibly, helps prevent us from seeming arrogant, reduces the pressure we may feel at times to provide the only salvation there is.

Therapy is a service. When therapy is presented as the only way to solve personal problems, when it begins from a one-up position, when it's forced on the client by the therapist, it runs into trouble. To say that I am offering you a service that you can accept or not means we can sidestep some of the open resistance that comes from the use of power. Change, after all, is hard enough already; we don't need to make it all the harder by being rigid or condescending.

But, you say, what about all those court cases, those families that obviously need to come but never would if not made to do so? We're back to values. I still say that I am offering a service that the family can choose to accept or not. If the court orders the counseling, the court is the one with the initial agenda, and I make that clear to the clients. They can still come or not, and if not I will be happy to tell the court, and the court can decide on the consequences. If clients have a another idea for solving the problem, they can try it because there are other options; their problem will be convincing the court that this will truly work, and I may help them think that argument through.

If they decide to stay with me we will negotiate what we will work on. Since everything is connected, I'm not too concerned if a client doesn't immediately want to deal with the problem that the court wants him or her to deal with; I just don't want the client to waste my time by coming simply for the sake of telling someone else that he or she showed up.

As a therapist I cannot foster intimacy or trust if my job is to be the enforcer. I prefer to leave that role to someone else.

People change at different rates / people must be ready for change. This, of course, sounds like the biggest excuse in the whole world; this is what the critics of counseling complain about — that if counseling doesn't accomplish what it sets out to do the clinician can always argue that the client "wasn't ready," "wasn't motivated"; the rationale becomes a built-in excuse for failure. Maybe. But there's also a growing realization that certain deeply ingrained patterns of behavior — of abuse, or violence, or dependency, for example — are not so easily given up. Substance abuse counselors will tell you that the relapse rate after first detox is high, and that some clients have to go through the process several times before they "get it" — before they're ready to make the commitments that recovery demands.

The same is true for many of the clients that we see, especially in agencies. A large number of the families that show up for therapy don't only need to change the patterns and the problems layered within the patterns, but they often also need to learn a different approach to life. Many see themselves as pushed along by crises; their stance is always a reactive one — "It always happens to me" — toward the events in their lives. Often going beyond the symptoms means helping people see that they can be proactive, can actively initiate and seek out what they want from life and those around them.

These needs are generally lumped into issues of self-esteem, assertiveness, and personal responsibility. While the clinician has the responsibility to help clients see the broader fabric of their lives, seeing therapy as a service means that many will only get as far as focusing on the immediate crisis and then leave.

Many others will find that therapy doesn't give them exactly what they thought it would, that what they want isn't what others (the court, the therapist) may want for them. Some will never fully understand how therapy can work, how talking in a room with a stranger about something that already happened can make a difference in the behavior or feelings of themselves or others out there in the outside world.

Still others just won't like the clinician — his last name sounds too funny, her clothes are too sloppy, the way he looks at you after he asks a question, or the way she sounded so rushed on the phone. Any or all of these reasons are enough to derail the process. The client quickly decides that other options or counselors would work better, becomes minimally involved, or simply drops out.

From the clinician's side of the desk this is quickly tagged as resistance, but that's not always fair. The fact of the matter is that there are too many things going on in- and outside of therapy that pull on the client that the clinician either isn't aware of or underestimates. For many clients, especially those new to therapy or overwhelmed by environmental stresses, therapy all too easily gets pushed to the bottom of the list; it isn't half as important to the client as it is to the clinician.

The bottom line of all this is that just as therapists need to be careful that their own grandiosity or projections don't make them believe that therapy is the only right and real solution to life's problems, they also need to accept that they themselves are not omnipotent. The power that any one therapist has extends as far as what he or she can do within the session; in order to feel empowered this has to be the focus, namely, concentrating on the session processes and learning to a large extent to let go of the outcomes.

The best of therapists needs to accept that he or she is incapable of controlling all the factors in the client's world that work against therapy, that not every client will be cured, that through no particular fault of anyone, client or clinician, not every intake will ultimately result in healing or even completion of modest goals. To expect otherwise is to put unrealistic pressure and expectations on ourselves and our clients. Other aspects of our lives are generally not so tidy and conclusive, and there is no reason to believe that therapy, which is only a more condensed form of life, can or should be much different.

The therapeutic relationship is important. When I ask clients at termination what they remember most about their therapy, or, looking back, what they thought was most helpful, I'm always surprised how so many times it's not anything big and therapeutic that I thought I did to them that made a difference. It's usually the small things that were important—the two-second phone call when the client went into the hospital to see how he was feeling, the pat on the back on the way out after the third session, the way I played with the three-year-old, the story I told about my father's birthday as we were walking into my office, a follow-up letter after a missed appointment. These little gestures of humanity and concern become the glue that holds the relationship and therapy together; they convey to the client that here is respect, caring.

We learn this early on in Counseling 101 and it continues to remain true. Just as the little things can undo therapy, it's the little things that often keep it alive and make it valuable to the client, little things that come through the relationship itself. A therapy relationship has the potential to be very different relationship than the client is used to. It can be more committed or caring or confrontative than others in the client's life, and while this can be frightening for many, arousing old habits of distrust and avoidance, for many others it can be healing enough.

Most of all, the therapeutic relationship has the potential to be simply more honest, where people say what they mean and mean what they say even if they change their mind and say something different five minutes later, where words match emotions and behavior matches thoughts. It's an honesty that begins with the clinician.

It's with these assumptions that I start family therapy. They form for me a framework around what I do, and they help me stay clear about the limits and responsibilities of my power. Again think about your own — your own ideas about change, about your role and responsibility to the client, about the limits of your own power or the power of therapy to solve problems, about the whole notion of client resistance and what you should do about it. Try to be as clear as possible about what you believe.

THE BASIC SEVEN

Once your assumptions are clear the work can begin, and that work begins within your own mind. As you talk to the members of a family, as you gather information, as you watch how they behave while they are with you, you begin to envision how this family can be different, how the family would look, sound, and operate if the problem that they most face was not there, if the patterns that held their lives together were changed. It is this vision, this positive vision of what can be, that is the guiding light for the therapist, and when shared with the family, for them as well; it can empower them, point them in the right direction, and most of all give them hope.

But the vision-making process gets muddied when you have to deal with too much activity in the room; when the family unravels problem after problem, with no end in sight, and shifts the burden they feel directly onto your lap; when the family is paralyzed by emotions that quickly evaporate the new and fragile sense of promise and that paralyze you as well. Family therapy, like tennis, piano playing, accounting, baking, and building, has its fundamentals, its basic concepts and skills. This core of ideas and skills are what you can turn and return to in order to recenter yourself and the family.

Being able to recenter and return is important. I remember studying meditation many years ago; I was taught to use a one-word chant as my focus. The teacher stressed over and over that whenever I "caught" myself lost in meddlesome thoughts, I didn't need to feel concerned or guilty or worry about doing it right; I merely needed to stop and return back to the chant. In the beginning it was easy to wander off into the forest of my own plans and worries — the argument I had had with my wife that morning, the list of items I needed to get at the hardware store, the upcoming deadline on the report at work—without even being aware of it, and it seemed that I was returning to the chant more than I was actually saying it. But with practice I was more and more able to stay with the chant before wandering off.

So it is with family therapy. When you find yourself lost in the family, overwhelmed by their words, their questions, and their emotions, don't panic, don't kick yourself for messing up, simply return to the basics and get recentered. In the beginning you may find yourself seemingly always going back, but with practice your forays forward into the thick of the family will be increasingly longer and farther. And even with a lot of experience, you'll sometimes get overloaded, and then it's good to know you can always go back and start again.

What follows are family therapy basics. Each of these is one vital part of the foundation; together they interlock to form the backbone of both systems theory and good family therapy. Keeping these basics in mind can guide you through the most difficult sessions, help you stay on track. Once you feel comfortable with them you can use them as the basis for improvisation. Mix and match them the way a good chef mixes and matches his or her favorite ingredients to create your own style, your own unique approach to a particular problem or family. In this chapter we will map them out; in the second section we'll talk more about the creative variations.

1. Determine Who Has the Problem / What Is the Problem

"I just haven't been feeling myself lately."

"The teacher says my son is acting up in class at school, and he has been giving me a hard time at home. I want some counseling to help him straighten out."

"The judge ordered me to come here for counseling until you say I don't have to. I don't think I need to come; my ex-wife is the one with the problems."

"My husband and I think our daughter has a problem with her attitude, but I think the real problem is that my husband is rarely home."

People come to you because of problems, and, as brief, solution-focused approaches and managed care have emphasized, it's vital that you know exactly what the problems are. This means having a clear knowledge of just what the client is talking about—what does "not feeling myself," "acting up in class," or "a problem with attitude" mean? By helping clients refine what they're saying, they not only begin to create a clearer picture of what is wrong, but you can begin to create a clear positive vision of what can be.

But you also need to be clear about who has the problem. Sometimes, especially when the client is a self-referred adult, the client in the room and the client with the problem are one and the same, and it's all pretty simple — "I feel depressed; I'm here so you can help me"; "My kids are running all over me; I need to learn how to handle them better." Other times, however, it's not quite so easy. Often the only person with the problem is the person who is seeing a problem in someone else: the mother who thinks her son should find new friends, but the son thinks his friends are just fine; the father who thinks the mother should be tougher, but the mother feels she has a close relationship with her daughter and the father is just jealous; the wife who wants her husband to stop drinking so much, but he says that he only has a beer now and then and it isn't a problem for anyone but her. If only this other person would change, they say, I would feel better.

When they all show up in your office, with everyone pointing a finger at someone else, it's important to pair problems and people carefully. The mother and teacher who are having problems with the boy may be the only ones having a problem; that is, the boy and father may not. The man referred by the court doesn't have a problem, except perhaps with the court order itself; so far the only person with a problem is the judge or probation officer. The father has a problem with his daughter, but the mother has more of a problem with the father.

When the problem behaviors seem so obvious — the husband is falling down drunk every night, the little boy is fighting everyone in the neighborhood, the teenager is refusing to go to school — it's easy for you to get caught up in everyone's concern and to join forces with them in trying to convince the I.P. (the identified patient) that a problem really does exist. It's an awkward role that you need to avoid. You're stepping out of the service role, rapidly becoming an enforcer, and the I.P. generally starts to respond to you with more and more resistance. From his or her point of view, he or she simply doesn't have a problem, at least not the problem that everyone is so concerned about, and your siding with the others only makes you more quickly dismissed.

Rather than wrestling with the I.P. over the problem, you can leave the I.P. alone and help the other person with what he or she can do about his or her problem. Thank the son for coming in, set up a time to meet with the mother alone to talk about parenting, and have her sign a release for you to talk to the teacher so that they can both coordinate how they will handle the boy's behavior. Let the reluctant, court-referred client know that you'd be happy to tell the court that he doesn't see a need for coming and that they need to consider some other option. Tell the man that you're not sure whether he has a drinking problem or not, but suggest to the wife that she attend an Al-Anon meeting or offer to help her figure out what she can do if the drinking continues.

If the person defining the problem — the probation officer, the social service worker, the teacher, or generally some other representative of an agency or institution — isn't present at that first meeting, invite him or her come in. That person can explain the problem as he or she sees it and, ideally, help the I.P. see that he or she has a problem as well. If you don't settle down in class and pay attention, says the teacher to the boy, you'll be left back. If you don't stop arguing with me at home, says the mother to her son, you won't go to your aunt's this summer. If you don't get counseling to help you control your anger, says the probation officer, not only will you possibly be sentenced to jail time, but you could lose custody of your daughter.

Your job in this type of confrontation again isn't to take sides, but to clarify just what the sides are. The boy, it turns out, is actually very upset that his mother seems to be spending all her time with the new baby, or he feels like his teacher is always on his back and never gives him credit for what he does well. The man agrees that maybe he does have a problem with his temper, but he's gotten a lot worse since he lost his job, and he feels like no one is willing to help him get into job training.

There are now two, or more, problems — the parents' problem and the kid's problem, the agency's problem and the client's problem, the husband's problem and the wife's problem — to work on. That's normal in family therapy, simply because there are many people, each with his or her own version of reality. In order to manage them all you start by drawing lines of responsibility around each one — whoever defines a problem, has it — and then do one of several things. You may decide to handle each problem separately: "This session we will talk about ways of using time-outs with Billy, and next week maybe we can talk about that holiday depression that you're worried about"; "Let's work on deciding what to do about Mary's school behavior, and then we can work on some of those marital issues."

You can also show the family how two or more problems are connected: "Susan, you don't like Jesse going out with the guys so much, and Jesse, you feel that Susan's always involved with the kids and doesn't want to spend time with you alone. Maybe one problem dovetails into the other"; "John, you're worried about Billy setting fires, and Billy, you're mad at your dad for ignoring you; I wonder if the fires are a way to let your dad know that you're mad and get him to pay attention." This connecting of one problem to another is the beginning map of the family's patterns. Doing this helps the family members see how their behaviors are interrelated, how one problem is actually an attempted solution to another. By describing the connection, the issue changes; the focus shifts from arguing over who has the problem to finding ways of breaking the pattern.

Finally, you can replace all the separate problems with one new problem, finding new problems is what assessment is all about. Tommy, for example, is referred by the school for truancy and comes to the first session with his parents. It's quickly apparent that the father is depressed and mother reports that she has been suffering with chronic back pain for the past six months. While on the surface you can look at these as separate problems, it is no coincidence, perhaps, that they have all erupted since the sudden death of Tommy's six-year-old sister last year. In this light it's useful to explore how the family, individually and as a whole, has coped with the loss. The separate problems may turn out to be all reactions to grief, which then becomes the focus of treatment.

Similarly, Theresa is referred for breaking probation and staying out on the street. The mother also complains that 12-year-old Eddy is fighting all the time with his younger brother, Jimmy. All these separate problems are linked, you believe, to the parents' lack of structure and limit setting within the home, and this, in turn, stems from the parents' ongoing struggle over the way the children should be handled at all. Again, the separate problems are boiled down to a different primary one, namely, the couple's relationship and difficulty working together. This becomes the focus of the therapeutic contract.

Giving the family a new problem frees them to find new solutions to replace the old, worn-out ones. The only tricky part for you as the therapist is that you need to make sure that you connect the new problem to the one that the family defines. Everyone needs to agree that there really is a link between the grief and Tommy's truancy, Dad's depression, and Mom's back pain, or between the marriage, Teresa's behavior, and Eddy's fighting. Sometimes this can be a hard sell, and you may have to work on the problems separately until you can gather more evidence to convince them that the connection really exists.

Developing a therapeutic contract often starts with negotiation over the problem; before you start negotiating be clear about who and what is the problem.

2. Look for What's Missing

There is a Sherlock Holmes story about a horse that's stolen from a barn one night. One of the clues that Holmes uses to solve the case is the owners' report that they *didn't* hear the dog bark that night. It is the absence of barking that catches Holmes's attention and seems to him so peculiar. Whoever came that night, he reasons, was no stranger; the dog didn't bark because he knew the person well.

Like Holmes, you too need to be able to recognize not only what the family presents, but what they don't—to look also for what's not happening, what's not being said, what's missing in the picture the family creates of themselves in front of you. These are the holes in the fabric of the family—the father who doesn't come to the appointment, the good things that Billy can do, the past, silence, the time the mother was in jail, anger, sadness, the oldest brother's ongoing depression, laughter, the grandmother's reaching out toward her granddaughter—all the things different members of the family can't do, avoid, or aren't aware of.

To see what's not there is to see where the family needs to move. This is the uncharted territory where the family's anxiety and healing lie. By moving toward these areas—asking the parents what Billy does well, inquiring about the mother's jail sentence, asking the father what he does when he feels angry, acting playful and comical with the younger children—you are helping the family members move against their own grain, move beyond the boundaries of the patterns, move toward their anxiety and the beginnings of change.

Seeing in the first session what's missing in the room and moving toward it, combined with recognizing who has and what is the problem, starts the assessment process. Ask the mother to get up and move next to her husband and see what happens. Ask about the other children, instead of just hearing about Angie. Talk about what's happening right now in the room, instead of everyone going on and on about what happened last Friday, and see how everyone responds. Talk about the good things in the week, rather than just the bad, and see if the others can follow behind you.

Movement into these holes is also the starting point for setting goals and tasks: "Mrs. Jones, it seems you've gotten good at seeing all the things the Mary does wrong. I'd like you to try and pay attention to the times she is doing something right," "Tom, you're always so quiet, and I bet Ann thinks you just don't care. Can you tell Ann what you're thinking about what she said?" "It seems you all have never talked about your father's death. Maybe we can all talk about it, even if just for a few minutes." "Helen, you are always in charge of putting Tommy in bed. How about you let John do it this week." By pushing the client to do what's not done, away from the comfortable and into the difficult, the process of change is started. Fine-tuning can come later.

When you feel overwhelmed in a session, look for what's missing right there in the room (what are we not talking about, what emotions are being avoided, what secret is lying somewhere in the corner of the family's past) or focus once again on the holes already mapped out (the mother's anger, the father's sadness, the child's inability say what he or she feels).

How do you learn to see and hear what is missing, rather than only what is present? By training your eyes, ears, and mind. As you listen to an audiotape, listen for the opposite, for what is not mentioned. As you watch a videotape, notice what the individuals and the family as a whole are not doing. Like Sherlock Holmes, ask yourself what would you expect to see or hear that you're not. With practice, what's presented will become an automatic springboard for zeroing in on what's missing.

3. Block the Dysfunctional Patterns

As mentioned earlier, patterns are the heart of family therapy, the way of organizing what you see, the complement to what you don't see. If in what's missing is where the family's anxiety lies, it's in the patterns that the ways of containing the anxiety are found.

The fact that the patterns are contained in what the family presents doesn't necessarily mean they're easy to see. The family doesn't usually think and talk in terms of patterns; they talk in terms of separate, isolated events: Eric fights all the time, my husband is always yelling at me. If they do link events, they're usually individual, chronological sequences— Johnny starts to complain, then he wails, then he starts kicking, then he falls down on the floor—rather than the horizontal, interactional ones that you are concerned with. It's your job to find these.

There are two basic ways of doing this. One is to ask "What happens next?" questions that help the client to describe them to you: "So after Johnny starts to complain, what do you generally do? And then he wails, and what do you do then?" This begins to map out for both the client and you the ping-pong moves, the connection between the behavior of one and the behavior of the other. Generally, the pattern runs until there is a shift in emotion—Johnny finally is slapped, he stops yelling and starts to cry—setting off a new pattern such as when Mother comforts him or he goes to his room until dinner.

The other way of detecting patterns is to see them in the room in the process. Mom tells Susan to sit up straight, Susan slumps even more, Dad tells Susan to listen to her mother, Susan snaps at her father, Mom shrugs and looks away, Susan sits up a bit, then slumps again, and it's over. This may be repeated with different content—the mother asking Susan to tell what happened yesterday, Susan saying there's nothing to tell, the father scolding Susan, and so on, with a change in volume—but it all stays the same.

Once you figure out what the pattern is the next step is easy: *Block the dysfunctional pattern.* Many newcomers to family therapy go into a panic because they worry that they need to have a healthy pattern already on deck to replace the dysfuctional one. But this is putting too much pressure on yourself. As you continue to observe and understand the family and begin to develop a positive vision of how they can be, new patterns will become clear; you don't need to be able to create them on the spot.

The bigger goal is simply to break the patterns by stopping them. This moves the family away from the comfortable and into their anxiety and toward change. Although their first reaction is likely to be to ignore you, or to slide back into the safe zone within two seconds, if you persist, continue to cut them off at the pass, the anxiety of the moment will push them to do something different, will push the family to find for themselves new, different ways of relating. This places them in the position of creating their own change, and allows you once again to simply fine-tune it.

4. Track the Process

Content versus process—the water versus the flow of water, what the sentence says and the fact that the sentence is a sentence, the complaints about the weekend and the act of complaining—refers to the two sides of the whole of what happens in the room. The clinician, like a movie director, pans in and out, back and forth—a close-up on the mom, a long shot that takes in the activity of the whole group, zeroing in on Karen's sadness, finding out just what the doctor did say, talking about last week, looking ahead to next week, talking about right now. You shift back and forth between the content (the words, the facts, the point of the story) and the process (who and how someone is talking, the fact that it is a story rather than question or lecture, the fact that it is directed to you rather than Andy sitting in the corner).

Different clinical theories place different emphases upon content. Cognitive theory, for example, starts with content and always returns to it: What exactly does John say to himself when he feels depressed, how can we substitute better content, better words, to replace his debilitating and disaster-causing ones? Language is the focus, not the how but the what, the words that lock and bind and limit our reality, that structure the messages which create our emotions and spark our actions.

Content seems especially important in the beginning of therapy— describe the problem, catalogue the history of past treatment, find out what the psychological report says; it's how the client talks and thinks about problems, it's the currency that builds rapport, it enables us to put together the pieces of the puzzle as the client and others see it. But content also rides upon the process, becoming a verbal Geiger counter, ticking away with intensity as the client moves toward anxiety, when the words spoken are new words, when they plow through to new emotional ground or slowly hack through to some new insight. Content is most valuable when it can acknowledge or, better yet, merge with the process itself: "I don't know what to say right now because I'm worried that you're going to get mad; tell me what you're thinking." This merging is the basis of self-awareness and self-reflection, the key to honesty and living in the present.

But all too often this merging of content and process never happens; they remain separate worlds. The content's ticking slows and eventually slacks off to a silence; the words lose their vitality and become sluggish, overweight verbiage whose only purpose is to sit on anxiety and flatten it, or fill up as much space as possible to keep it away. Rather than saying that you feel awkward or frightened and don't really know what to say, you talk about the weather, the ball game; you say what you think they want to hear. Even when the content seems on the surface to be more alive and honest, it's often incomplete because the words and emotion attached to the words never really match—Frank talks about being angry but has a smile on his face and talks with a glib tone of voice—or the emotions are never really acknowledged at all. Even though the words form a message, the real message that lies beneath is ignored.

A good therapist is always turning up the corners of the content, of course, to peek underneath and catch the mismatch of word and intent, to separate medium from the message. And it is the medium, the process, the content in motion, that is usually the most important in family therapy because it's in the motion, in the systems' interaction, that the problem is created and sustained.

Process—not only what the client says, but why and how the client is saying that right at that moment—becomes the raw material of patterns; patterns represent process cut into anxiety-binding shapes. When the content seems overwhelming or without meaning, it is the process, like the patterns and holes and problems, that you can return to and center upon.

To recognize process is to realize what's happening while it's happening: The father is distracting, the daughter is looking hurt but sounding angry, the mother is trying to pull rank by bringing up the past. It enables you to step back and take the long shot, see and change the patterns as they are unfolding, "catch" yourself and pull yourself out of the swirl, and consciously put on the brakes. Even though most of us, including the families we see, are good at recognizing the process in others, the skill becomes lost in close relationships where the patterns and process are so powerful.

By focusing on the process in the room, the family becomes aware again that there is a process. By your example they learn to separate process from content, see that the water and the flow of the water are different yet intimately connected, that the changing of one will change the other. Shifting the focus to the process not only helps the family to see the patterns as they are played out right there before them, but helps them experience what it is like to step back and out of them at the same time. Once this has been demonstrated and experienced, the family members can begin to learn to do the same on their own.

As with patterns, it's your job as the therapist to take the risk, and it is a risk, to shift the focus to the process when content no longer represents what's occurring. This is usually done with questions ("John, you're talking about the good times of the past, but looking mighty sad. How are you feeling right here, right now?") or statements ("Mary, I'm trying right now to offer a suggestion and I feel like you're ignoring me"). The client, be it one individual or the entire family, has to shift, is forced to stop and think about what just happened and is happening right then, and has the opportunity to move from meaningless content to meaningful content that incorporates the underlying emotions.

Often, however, as with initial stopping of patterns, the client's first reaction to your intervention is to resist you in order to reduce his or her anxiety—"I *was* listening," Mary mumbles back, both denying the reality in the present and avoiding the confrontation. But if you stick with the process—"Did you just feel like I was scolding you?"—and help the client to stay focused on what's happening in the present and cut him or her off from slipping back into the same content, the client not only plows new emotional ground within the relationship with you, he or she begins both to discriminate content from process and to learn to move between them.

As one of the basics, tracking the process allows you to keep a handle on what's always going on simply by asking what's going on. It allows you to immediately see the impact of your interventions—the story changes or stops, the anger shifts to sadness. By moving back and forth between content and process, both you and the client avoid creating and lapsing into your own stale patterns of behavior, which can bind anxiety and blunt the change-making process. But most of all, by tracking the process both you and the client can learn to tackle problems and derailments, such as hurt feelings or a misunderstood comment (those sources of resistance and resentment in the therapeutic and family relationships), right there and then, directly and immediately, as they unfold. The therapy stays on course, and the family sees how to confront problems quickly and effectively.

5. Experience before Explanation

The focus on process, patterns, and what's missing tells us that the more you can do right there in the room the better; by paying attention to these things you can see before you both the creation of the problem and its solution. The focus on who and what is the problem tells us that the more you can link what you do in the room with what goes on in the family's life and concerns outside the room, the better still; therapy doesn't merely become more talk about a problem, but is seen by the family as a viable, active means of changing it. What helps the clinician tie these two foci together is the skillful use of experience and explanation.

The world of therapy (and often the world of our lives) seems to be always divided, like socks in a drawer, into assorted pairs—content–process, past–present, individual–family, emotion–behavior, aggressor–victim, internal–external, anger–depression. While they seem at first glance to be dichotomies, at second glance it's easy to see that they aren't dichotomies at all, but actually different sides of the same coin, all related to each other like some large extended family that the clinician is constantly trying to reconcile and integrate.

And here's another set of twins: *experience,* the close cousin of process, who runs through the room intent on what happens, and *explanation,* the close cousin of content, who smoothes and soothes, who makes sense out of what experience has just done and connects it to the family's problem and needs.

Just like with content and process, the clinician moves back and forth between these two twins. A good balance is important. Let experience run too wild, too long, and the family feels overwhelmed, shaky, fragmented, frightened; everything is in shambles and their anxiety goes through the roof; more often than not they run away and don't come back. Too much of explanation and the family goes to sleep; like its cousin content on a bad day, explanation bores the family to death; the words wash over them, leaving them unchanged.

Explanation's strength is its calming presence, immensely valuable when lowering anxiety is exactly what you want. This is what the doctor does when she tells the frightened little boy that she is going to give him a shot in his arm and it's going to sting for a minute, or describes to the obsessing patient exactly what will happen in surgery tomorrow, and what it will be like after surgery while he's there in the hospital. This is what you do in the first session, when you talk to the family about what therapy can or cannot do regarding the problem, or what the format will be for the session.

The psychodynamic approaches have spent a great amount of attention on beefing up explanation's power and ability to mobilize change. In the psychodynamic vocabulary, these explanations are renamed "interpretations," and like the puny David facing Goliath, their lack of the kinetic power of experience is made up for by impeccable timing. Properly timed interpretations are in the psychodynamic process an art form. When hurled at just the right moment, these explanations strike the client right between the eyes, crystallizing all that the client has been moving toward in awareness. They shine a light on the vague shadows that the client has been slowly groping through; suddenly the shadows dissolve into something clear and hard. The client has more than an explanation, he or she has an "insight," an "Aha" experience that then can spill over into emotions and behaviors. Good interpretations are explanations that become transformed into experience.

The down side to this process is the length of time that it takes for it all to kick in. Because of the less directive role of the therapist, he or she has to wait until Goliath approaches and is within range, that is, until the slow building up of unconscious processes within the client begins to take hold. As a result, the therapy, even with frequent sessions, takes a minimum of many months, more often years.

The family therapist cuts this process short by taking a directive role and by using experience's energy within the process. Rather than waiting, he or she marches forward into the fray and begins to put a stop to patterns and to push the family to see what's missing. These raise anxiety and open up the possibility of change.

All this leads us to the fifth basic concept: Experience before explanation. If the primary goal is to get the family moving, to ride on the motivation that brought them into the office, they need, to paraphrase Fritz Perls, an experience, not an explanation. Bring the problem alive, get them to try something different, talk about what they don't want to talk about, have them taste something new—then mop up with explanation. What you're then doing is exactly what the psychodynamic therapist has been waiting to do for months, providing an explanation that crystallizes and shapes the anxiety that you have just generated. If explanation walks into the room with his bucket and mop too soon, while everything is still orderly and set, he stands around and everyone wonders why he's there.

By marching ahead with experience, you're not only breaking up the patterns, but desensitizing the family to the experience of change, to risk taking, to approaching anxiety; rather than always retreating from new situations, or, out of fear, always seeing in the new another example of the old, they're growing and adapting. We call the benefits of this experience and change increased self-esteem, risk taking, courage.

And, of course, you, as the clinician, are once again the best person to model this courage, to push yourself, armed with your theory and philosophy, into the holes that you see the family cautiously walk around, or that you sense by feeling the edges of your own anxiety. Doing this may sound daunting, but it doesn't need to be. Here are some examples of experience before explanation:

This mother is angry. For the last six months her 11-year-old son has been driving her crazy—getting into fights at school, earning failing grades, arguing with her all the time. She can't understand it, but she thinks the problem is the new kid in his class that he has been hanging around with. Had anything happened six months ago? you ask. No, she says, then hesitates. Well, she says, matter of factly, his grandmother, my mother, died back during the summer, but she had been ill for a long time, and we all knew it was coming. Tell me about your mother, you say. And she begins to describe her, and as she does her eyes become teary. And do you miss her? you ask quietly. The wall begins to break, and she begins to sob quietly for many minutes. Do you think your son feels the same way you do? She replies, I don't know, I guess, but we never talk about it. I wonder, you say, if all this sadness is connected to the way he has been acting, and you have been feeling.

At the urging of the school teacher, Jim brings in his eight-year-old daughter, Jenny, who has lately become moody and withdrawn. He is not so much concerned about why, but rather, what he should do about it. Her parents have been divorced for several years, and they continue to have a good relationship, Jim assures you, and Jenny has handled it well. Jim has been steadily and recently dating a woman named Cathy. He swears that Jenny likes Cathy, though Jenny says little to anyone, including you. You ask her to draw a picture of her family, and with some prodding she does. You show it to the father. There, clearly labeled in her eight-year-old scrawl, is a picture of her mother and father holding hands and smiling, with a smiling Jenny standing right in the middle of them.

It's the classic marital argument. Susan starts to make a suggestion, Tom feels criticized and snaps back, they both start escalating by using sarcasm, making faces, yelling, and bringing up old wounds and stories of the past. You tell them both to stop, and ask Susan to turn her chair toward you and tell you clearly what her suggestion is, why she is making it, and how she thinks it may help Tom. You ask Tom to keep quiet until she is finished.

Again we see the other basic concepts coming into play—clarifying the problem, moving toward what's missing, blocking patterns, focusing on process. But what each example also shows is the creating of experience in order to set the stage for explanation. You may have guessed the moment that the mother mentioned the death of her mother that the grief may be trickling beneath the boy's acting out. You could have cut to the chase and explained this to the mother, who might have nodded her head, but emotionally disagreed and discounted what you were saying simply because of the anxiety it created.

But gently leading the mother into her grief experientially connects behavior and the underlying emotion—the telling of the story of her son and her mother flow together—and her anger is quickly transformed before her and your eyes into the sadness it is. Once she is emotionally aware of the grief and can identify it resting within her son as well, your linking them together and redefining the problem in new terms to her now makes perfect sense.

The same is true with the father and daughter. The father wanted to know what to do, and you could have quickly given him a list of behavioral things to try at home. What's missing, however, is the content of the daughter's silence, and his own reluctance to look underneath the changes in his family and the impact of his new relationship. The daughter says to him through her picture what from you he might easily dismiss.

Finally, it's easy to see how the couple's verbal and nonverbal behavior is fueling old patterns of destruction. Rather than giving a mini-lecture on their poor communication (and possibly replicating the criticizing process), you break the patterns, give Susan a chance to talk and Tom to listen without all the nonverbal and verbal triggers, and provide a positive interaction right there in the room that you can then map out for them so that they can replicate it at home. And even if the change didn't work— even if Tom continues to dismiss what Susan says—you can see where and how it didn't work, and try something else.

Working within the experience helps the clients begin to see what you see, and emotionally readies them for new ideas and perceptions that the explanations provide. If you are moving too quickly and their anxiety is rising too high, thereby creating resistance (e.g., not paying attention, distracting, outright refusing to try what you suggest), you can use explanation as a brake to lower the anxiety, the same way the doctor does when explaining the injection to the little boy: "Susan, I want you to look at me rather than Tom so that you can say what you think without getting distracted by his nonverbal behavior"; "Jim, the reason I asked Jenny to draw a picture is that it's usually easier for kids to say how they feel through play rather than trying to talk directly about it"; "Mrs. Jones, I'm asking about your mother because I'm wondering how much the loss of his grandmother may be bothering your son, even though he doesn't talk about it. Often children's sadness comes out as behavior problems." Statements like these put a frame around the experience and make it just enough less threatening that you can continue to go forward.

There's always the temptation, especially when you feel overwhelmed, to use explanations like a blanket to smother the fire of anxiety (yours and the family's) before it gets out of control. But the better way to look at anxiety is to see anxiety as a tightrope that you and the family walk across together. Explanations are like the balancing pole that you hold in your hands and gently shift from side to side in order to stay upright and moving along the rope. With practice, your skill in using the balancing pole increases, and explanations become more and more part of the experience itself.

6. Be Proactive

Good novelists talk about creating the fictive dream, wherein the reader is drawn into the writer's world and emotionally becomes part of the story. The goal and challenge for the writer is to provide at just the right times in the right amounts enough description, dialogue, action, and strong characters to sustain the dream state, to keep the reader from becoming distracted by or more conscious of the writing and the reading of a book than the story within it.

As therapist you essentially want to do the same thing—pull the family into the therapy process and experience, focus on what's missing and on the process and patterns in a way that keeps them engaged, rather than bored (which makes them put down the therapy) or too threatened (which makes them slam it shut and run away). You start with the bringing together of visions, the family's in the form of their expectations and the perception of the problem, and yours, which is gathered from your unique impressions. The therapy begins with the melding of both visions into one.

As I've been saying all along, this requires that you take the lead, that you be the author, that you take a proactive rather than reactive stance. Families expect this, especially those who come to community agencies. They look to you to provide direction, answers, advice. They want their money's worth and expect you to work hard, like them, to earn it; a more passive role on your part only fuels their doubts about your competence, commitment, or strength to take on the family. More importantly, unlike individual work, where the simple presence of the therapist is enough to raise anxiety and push the client out of old patterns, the sheer greater numbers of people in the family can turn therapist passivity into therapist nonpresence; without your active interaction the family quickly falls into its well-worn dysfunctional patterns and re-creates the same experience they have at home. They just as quickly decide that therapy is essentially a waste of time and money.

Being proactive means sharing your vision as soon as possible, setting goals for each session, and not getting lost in content the way the family does, by stepping back and looking at the process. Once again, it doesn't mean being foolhardy, irresponsible, or dangerous, but it does mean being brave enough to try something different, being flexible and pragmatic enough to stimulate change rather than retreating from change by being too rigid and too much of a purist. When you feel stuck, try something else, even if it is to talk about being stuck. Rather than absorbing their helplessness, show the family through your behavior the value and workings of commitment and perseverance in the face of problems. Keep trying, keep moving within the session.

7. Be Honest

If being proactive keeps you moving, honesty keeps you moving in the right direction. Honesty is the essential ingredient of leadership. It's also the most basic of the basics, the true mantra that you return to when you fear that things have drifted off course and you're not sure what is going on or what to do: telling the family that you are confused, that you don't understand, that they and you need to try a different approach, that (gulp!) you made a mistake. This isn't saying that you use the family for supervision, but it is saying that you're not afraid to acknowledge the process, to be authentic rather than filling yourself up with false bravado. If you are taking the responsibility for leading the way, take the responsibility as well to say when you're not sure where you're going and that it's time to regroup and check the map.

This is hard for those new to family therapy because of the pressure and the expectation they place on themselves to have all the answers, to know it all and guide the family straight ahead. This is further fueled by some of the briefer therapies with their "miracle" questions and quick in-and-out approach, the strategic and hypnotherapeutic approaches with their magical aura—the new therapist is left feeling intimidated and incompetent.

But remember that the beauty of family therapy is that you don't have to work so hard, that by changing the process and patterns you are solving the problem. If you have a question and don't have the answer, don't panic. Throw it back to the family and ask them to figure it out with you. If you feel stuck, ask if they feel the same, see if anyone has any ideas. Family therapy has the potential to become good group therapy; your job is to guide the process and keep everyone on task.

This kind of honesty sounds easy, but isn't. We become afraid that the family will not only think we're incompetent, but absolutely know it, and run away, that if we say what we think, they'll get angry, they'll get even more depressed, they won't be able to handle it. In truth it's all a projection—we're afraid we're incompetent, that *we* won't be able to handle it. Rather than being honest, we much prefer to maintain our image and cover our tracks.

We're back to values, principles, and assumptions. My principles tell me that it is better to show integrity, to match my words and actions and emotions; that my honesty encourages others to be honest as well; that supporting greater integrity and honesty is, when you think about it, what therapy really is all about.

There you have it, the seven basics of family therapy, the core skills that can keep you on track and sane. Match them not only against your own conception of family therapy, but against your own personality and values. In the next three chapters we'll explore how these basics are applied to the beginning, middle, and end stages of family therapy.

LOOKING WITHIN

1. It's easier to develop skills when you're not under performance pressure. Increase your sensitivity to what's missing, the patterns, and process by watching it in others outside the clinical sessions. Sit back and watch what emerges over the next couple of staff meetings. Look at the nonverbal behavior of people at the tables around you in a restaurant. See how quickly you can begin to hear and see the holes, how quickly you can tell when a pattern is being repeated it, or what the verbal or nonverbal triggers are that set it off.

2. Another exercise in courage building. Try being honest outside the clinical room. Not big honesty in the form of confession, but small honesty in the form of staying attuned to your own inner process as you interact with someone, matching your words and inner feelings, taking the risk of talking about what is happening within the process. Undoubtedly you do this well already with certain people in your life (your daughter, your spouse, your best friend); try doing it with someone where it is less comfortable (a stranger, your supervisor, one of your parents). Be sure to pat yourself on the back for the effort regardless of how you think it turns out.

THREE

In the Beginning:
Great Expectations

Meeting someone new is always so awkward. The family coming for therapy has not only the normal social anxieties ("Will I be liked?" "What impression will I make?" "Will the kids misbehave and embarrass us?"), but new ones as well, especially if therapy is new to them ("Will I have to talk about my abortion?" "Is Meg going to bring up that one time I got drunk and slapped her?" "Will this guy ask stupid questions about things I don't remember when I was a kid?" "Will they blame me for what everything?" "Will it be boring?" "Will everyone gang up on me?")

From your side, things may not be much better—not only has your day started out with your car breaking down in the rain, in the middle of the interstate (definitely not a good omen), but the director has just come around *again,* not too subtly reminding everyone how income is down and that, by the way, your performance evaluation is coming up next month.

Then there's this family—the most popular private therapist in town has referred them, and you're breaking into a cold sweat thinking about how your budding reputation is on the line. To make matters worse, the mother told you over the phone that the daughter has recently been showing symptoms of what sounds like encopresis, something you haven't done any work with and, frankly, don't know a whole lot about; and the mother's already got an attitude, telling you that she hopes you're better than the last clown they saw.

The pressure is on from all sides—the family, the workplace, yourself—to do something to "hook" the family so that they will stay in therapy long enough to have changes begin to take hold, and to keep your head above water and be effective. This is no small task when you're having trouble just keeping track of the names of everyone in the room.

Yes, the beginning stage of therapy, those first few sessions when impressions are made, expectations are clarified, a treatment plan is developed, and the family and therapist discover whether therapy can help at all, is probably the most difficult. Even the most seasoned clinician feels the flutter of anxiety when a new family first walks into the office. Success in the opening stage depends upon establishing rapport, gathering all the information you're going to need to make it to the middle stage, and maintaining the family's motivation to come. And that requires more than just small talk about last week's football game and a three-generation genogram.

Good beginnings are a balance of listening and talking, assessment and intervention, content and process. It's a time for forming hypotheses, but even more a time for fostering hope. By the time those butterflies have subsided on both sides of the room, both you and the family need to begin to share a vision of what can be, and experience the feeling that this therapy might actually work.

Once again, this is easier said than done. Before talking about all the things you need to do, it might be helpful to first talk about all the things you don't want to do. This is often a good way of starting any case, knowing what you specifically want to avoid doing with this particular family. This knowledge can not only reduce a large amount of the clutter and the overwhelming feeling that there's too much to do, but it can increase the odds of accomplishing what you do want to do.

DEAD ENDS, DETOURS, AND OTHER DANGERS

Allen and Terry Adamson come in with their two sons, Daniel, age 12, and Brian, 10. The boys are constantly at each other's throats, says Dad, and to cap it all off Daniel was recently caught breaking into a neighbor's house with a couple of his friends. Both parents agree that the boys haven't gotten along since Brian was old enough to crawl, but things have been especially difficult the last six months. They had tried therapy one time before, a few months back, but only went once. All the therapist did was ask a bunch of questions, and didn't give them any advice. They thought it was a waste of time.

Here you have your presenting problem. Your mind may already be racing, formulating, based upon your theory, possible hypotheses and various avenues of questions to pursue. But before you go running ahead, stop for a minute and think about what would be good for you *not* to do. Here are some suggestions:

Don't wait to begin treatment. It may seem logical to think in terms of doing a thorough assessment first and then starting treatment, and in theory it's easy to make a case for this way of proceeding. But in the real world of managed care and brief therapy, assessments that go on beyond the first session are a luxury that insurance companies and agencies will no longer tolerate.

Most families won't either. At the agency where I once worked, a questionnaire was handed out to all new clients at their first appointment, asking them about their expectations of counseling. When asked how many times they thought they would need to come, most (over 60%) thought they would need to come two or three times; a sizable minority (over 30%) thought they would need to come only once. These clients imagined sitting down, telling the therapist their problem, the therapist giving them a diagnosis and some advice, and they're done.

The Adamsons aren't unusual. By the end of the first hour they're expecting something — an idea of what is causing their problems, suggestions to try out something at home, a clear sense of where therapy is going — and that it's going to help. To walk out feeling that they have simply answered a long list of questions, most of which seemed to have little connection to the problem, or have covered the exact same ground that they did with the other therapist — details of the break-in, questions about their parenting style, even questions about their marriage — and not much else, leaves them wondering why they bothered to come at all. They expect more for their time and effort.

Treatment doesn't come after assessment but runs alongside of it. Treatment, in fact, becomes part of the assessment. By making a homework assignment, for example, you not only give the family a way to work on the problem, but you give yourself a way of finding out what works (or doesn't work) with this particular family and a way of double checking your hypothesis. By asking the mother to say something positive to her daughter, rather than constantly criticizing, you are able to see how willing she is to follow your suggestions, how hard it is for her to actually do it, and if switching from nagging to praise actually helps.

If your assessment does need to take a certain amount of time (e.g., you want to do psychological testing on one of the children), clearly describe the time frame for the family so that they know when to expect some feedback and will avoid becoming impatient.

Don't continue to replicate dysfunctional patterns. While it's important to get a clear idea of the interactional patterns in the family, either by description or better observation, it's equally important to interrupt dysfunctional interactions, especially those tied to the presenting problem. If unproductive patterns of relationship are replicated too long in the session, the family is going to feel like therapy isn't any different from what they do at home.

What does this suggestion mean for the Adamsons? Obviously, if the boys are fighting too much at home, you don't want them to continue to fight for too long in the office, nor do you want the parents to repeat over and over again their ineffective way of handling it, such as continually scolding the boys but not stopping them. Similarly, if a wife complains to you that her husband is always running her life, you don't want him to go on too long about how wrong she is or how she needs to figure out why she's so sensitive. This is only more of the same process, and your silence not only may give the wife the impression that you are siding with her husband, but also may quietly reinforce the process by letting it continue.

Your silence, in fact, is never neutral. While you may be thinking that you are taking time to observe, or are doing your best to avoid taking sides, the net effect is that you are reinforcing the process in the room. If that process is destructive—if the couple is "fighting dirty" by bringing up the past, if the parents are ganging up on or dismissing the family scapegoat, if someone is threatening physical harm to another—your silence will be taken by the family as a sanction, and the destructive process will escalate. Your tacit acceptance of unhealthy interactions will not only make it harder for you to eventually interrupt them, but also will have damaged your credibility with some family members.

Even before the session begins, think about ways the presenting problem could come alive and be acted out on some level. Once you see how the destructive patterns unfold, be prepared to stop them.

Be careful whom you leave out. If you only talk to the parents and get their view of the problem, the boys may write you off as another adult who's going to get on their case. If you join with the parents in scolding Daniel about the break-in, he'll dismiss you as being no different from them. Similarly, if you allow Mrs. Adamson to go on and on about anger at her husband or her sadness about her dead father, the others present in the room, even if they are concerned about her, will feel left out, ignored. It will be harder to pull them in later.

Making certain no one is excluded from the process is an important step in building rapport with each individual in the room. Being overlooked leaves him or her with a distorted impression of both you and your role, and creates an additional obstacle that you'll have to overcome.

Don't overcontrol the flow of the conversation. One of the difficulties in the first few sessions is creating a balance not only between assessment and treatment, content and process, the most dominant person in the family and the others present, but between your leading and following. It's important for you as the therapist to take charge, to lead the family in the direction you need them to go, in order to gather the information you need to confirm your hypothesis, as well as to avoid the replication of dysfuctional patterns that they will so easily fall into.

But the danger to be avoided is the one of taking too much control, directing the process so closely that you are always initiating everything and the family learns to wait passively for you to do so. As the therapist you need to always exert leadership and control, but of the broad outlines of the process; you are more a facilitator and less a bossy or preachy teacher. What you would want to avoid is creating the expectation that you will always have the answers, ask the questions, or make yourself the center of attention.

Rather than seeing yourself as driving the car that is the family, you are more the driving instructor in the passenger seat. Ideally, you want to help the family stay on the road, letting them know when they are swerving too far to the left or right, coaching them as they go along—pick up speed here, slow down there, look ahead and anticipate the dangers that may come up—even occasionally using your own brake when you see the real possibility of a collision, but not grabbing the steering wheel out of their hands and driving them yourself. Although in the beginning you have to instruct more—setting down rules, clarifying expectations, showing them what buttons to push, what controls to use—once everything is underway and rolling, once they get more experience in running the process and knowing themselves, you can begin to sit back. Your list of questions gets shorter, the sermonettes more rare. Your task shifts more and more toward telling them when to take the next turn in order to get them off the well-worn path and toward their anxiety, change, and growth.

All this is a long way of saying that you want the therapy in those first few sessions as quickly as possible to realistically represent the therapy process as it will be. You want to give the family a taste of what therapy's like beyond the gathering of histories and the filling out of forms. If you are too active, bombarding the family with question after question, if you feel responsible for coming up with ideas about what to talk about, if you and the family feel that you are always the one to initiate and figure out the answers, rather than helping the family figure the out for themselves, you'll quickly feel overwhelmed and eventually run out of steam, and the family, not knowing anything else, will conclude that therapy simply doesn't work anymore.

Learning to use your leadership and power effectively takes time. If you are new to the field, the inclination is to overregulate by taking extended histories, limiting the dialogue by asking the never-ending questions, channeling all the communication through you. Often what drives this is fear—fear of losing control, fear that chaos will break out, fear that if the reins are held too loosely the process will stampede and gallop off and over a cliff.

For others the fear is the family's disapproval of them. Rather than clarifying expectations and negotiating goals, these therapists feel pressure to deliver exactly what the family seems to want in order to be accepted. When they can't or when the family changes their mind and expects yet something else, they feel like a failure or resentful toward the family's calling of the shots.

Learning to take a looser grip on the reins, seeing the therapy as a developing partnership, begins with a basic trust in the family and in yourself—a trust that the family can not only learn, but can take responsibility for their lives; a trust that in the worst-case scenario your courage and honesty will in themselves be enough to manage whatever may come up. The next step is in taking the risk, stopping your own pattern of control—stopping the questions, letting the family members talk—and discovering what happens to yourself as well as them when you do. Once you find out that your worst fears don't come true—the family doesn't hate you, the marital explosion isn't all that explosive, the stomping-out teenager comes back next week—you become less afraid, freer to experiment with your power and skills, more confident and flexible in what you do; not surprisingly, the family begins to learn to do the same.

In looking over this list of things to avoid it's easy to see that what you're avoiding is getting off on the wrong foot—the family's, by replicating the problem, taking sides, or by being too passive; or your own, by taking too much responsibility and control. This is what the beginning stage is all about—getting a good start that creates it's own therapeutic momentum. If you can avoid these four dangers, you're halfway there. The other half is knowing what to move toward.

BUILDING RAPPORT

You can ask all the smart questions in the world, but it won't matter if Allen and Terry think that you don't understand how they feel or that you're basically a jerk. Rapport is the matter of building the relationship, conveying competence and trust, being sensitive to the family's needs and fears, taking the family gently and firmly by the hand as you lead them in and out of their anxiety. Without rapport, without an emotional connection to you, your clients will be too frightened and will refuse to move.

So how do you build rapport? You show courtesy, addressing everyone by name, inviting them to sit down, apologizing if you were a few minutes late. You respect the family's culture—from the way they speak to the clothes they wear to the habits that make up their daily routines. You listen to what each person says, give each a chance to speak, and show that you're listening by making eye contact. You show that you know how they feel by acknowledging the emotions underlying their statements—"Allen, it must be really frustrating for you"; "Terry, you sound really worried about Daniel"; "Daniel, I bet you feel like your folks are always on your back." You can mirror the body posture of the person talking, or use the skills of neurolinguistic programming and talk the language of each person's perceptual system—"Allen, how do you *see* the problem?"; "Terry, how do you *feel* about what Brian just said?"; "Daniel, how do you *handle* it when your Dad blows up at you?"

Most of all you go back to the basics. You determine who has and what is the problem—Terry's worried about Brian, Allen's mad at Daniel, Daniel is upset about school. You carefully track the process by blocking the dysfunctional patterns, educating and explaining to reduce anxiety and increase awareness, raising anxiety by asking questions about what's missing, moving into areas even though it may seem impolite or painful to do so ("What 'things' are we talking about?" "What hurt you most about the divorce?"; "What are you saying your mother didn't like to talk about?"), not breaking off the interaction the moment two people start getting angry at each other and not letting others break in either. You ask Allen and Terry to talk in front of you about how to handle Daniel and point out how easily they disagree, or you uncover Allen's unexpected sadness as he talks about the last blowup with the boys. You initiate action so they learn that therapy is an active process, involving more than just answering questions and getting advice. You begin to create that vision of what can be by asking the family to imagine it with you. You be as honest as you can be.

Again it's not the precision that's important—the right answer—but the effort and the willingness to help the family find the right answer. If you can do even some of these things within the first session, the emotional connection, the rapport, will be there.

GATHERING INFORMATION

Throughout the course of family therapy there are basically two different foci and functions that you will shift back and forth between (1) time spent during sessions primarily for your benefit, time finding out about something you need to know (Bobby's school history, why the parents got divorced, the grandmother's problems with depression), information you need in order to come up with your own ideas about the problem; and (2) time spent specifically helping the family, time focusing on a specific goal that you want the family to accomplish (the father listening to his son instead of criticizing, the oldest daughter staying out of the fights between the parents). Most of what you do will be of the latter type; most of the information gathering is obviously in this beginning stage.

Figuring out what you need to know and finding it out can seem overwhelming. Simply put, there are two types of information you need: information about content, and information about process. Under each of these is the need for generic information, information that you would gather from any family you saw, and specific information, what your theory leads you to explore that would help you confirm your initial hypothesis about the cause of the problem.

We'll be talking more about specific theories in the second section. For now, let's just look at the generic content and process information that you should find out about.

Content information

What is the presenting problem? Who has the problem? Who is most concerned about the problem?

What is the family's theory, or theories, about the problem?

What has the family tried so far to solve the problem?

What are the family's expectations of therapy?

What is the larger context and history of the problem? Who else may be involved? What themes seem to constantly reappear?

Process information

How well do the family members communicate with each other (don't talk, have trouble expressing how they feel, interrupt and don't listen, etc.)?

What are the family members' reactions to you as the therapist (intimidated, highly sensitive, seductive, skeptical, dependent, passive, angry, aggressive)?

How anxious are the various family members? How resistant?

What is the emotional range of the various family members? What emotion is each person most comfortable expressing?

What's missing?

What patterns do you see?

The reason for listing many of these is obvious (e.g., presenting problem, the family's anxiety); others have been discussed already (e.g., noticing what is missing, tracking the patterns). Some, however, are new and require some explanation:

Theories about the presenting problem. One of the first families I ever saw was a poor family living on the father's disability benefits and food stamps. The son, age eight, was having major disciplinary problems at school, and I went to see the family in their home. As I walked through the door into the living room I could see the father in the corner sitting in his wheelchair. He was barking orders to his wife, who looked tired and depressed, but was doing her best to fetch whatever it was her husband wanted. The eight-year-old would periodically slam open the back door, the father would yell at him, the son would ignore him, grab something from the kitchen and slam back out. In the back bedroom was the 11-year-old son, who, it turned out, rarely came out of his room.

I explained to the father why I was there, and asked him about the problems his son was having. "You know what his problem is," the father said, squinting and holding his index finger up in the air, "he's allergic to cow's milk. You see, when he was a baby he couldn't drink regular cow's milk, and we had to feed him that soy milk. It's that soy milk that messed up his head."

Every family has a theory about the cause of the problem they face, even when they say at first that they don't know; it's part of our natural inclination to create some explanation rather than live with uncertainty. While it was obvious to me that this family had numerous problems for numerous possible reasons, the father's explanation for his son's behavior already determined the solution, namely, that there was none, that his son was irreparably damaged (like him, perhaps) by a common childhood event. Needless to say, the father was not optimistic about my ability to help his son learn to behave, and he saw my questions about his disability and his family as irrelevant and nosy.

Finding out in the first session the family's theory or theories for the problem is important not because they are correct, but because they tell you where the family believes solutions lie. The gap between their theory (milk allergy) and your own (family dynamics) lets you know how much you will need to educate, how much you will need to experientially connect the problem to the patterns within the family, how much you will need to explain why you are curious about the personalities and behavior of others in the family.

What has the family tried to solve the problem? You're seeking two kinds of information here. The obvious one is finding out what has or hasn't worked (e.g., spanking, ignoring the problem). Not everything has to be complex and convoluted; oftentimes the first and best line of approach is plain old problem solving—giving the family some basic information (e.g., behavior modification, child development, treatment approaches to enuresis) and discussing with them the options.

But the other reason for the question is to find out just how problem solving is done within a particular family. Who decides, who carries out the solution, what happens when someone disagrees, where does a reasonable idea break down? Tracking these process questions up front lets you know what problems you need to solve before you can solve the presenting one.

Expectations of therapy. Because *he* has the problem, the parents expect to drop their 11-year-old son off at the front door and pick him up at the end the hour; the husband imagines that you will have an intimate "girl talk" with his wife and help her to be less nervous about sex; the mother thinks you can hypnotize her daughter so she will be less obsessed about her boyfriend; the family expects that by the end of the first session you will write a letter to the school principal recommending the daughter be readmitted to school.

Families naturally have expectations about therapy, some realistic, others not. Establishing rapport involves giving the family what they expect, or at least explaining why you can't or won't. It's easy just to ask about this straightforwardly: How did you hope coming here would help? What do you think counseling will be like?

Themes. Themes can range from finding out that you can only depend on yourself, families are meant to stay together no matter what, you may try hard but never quite make it, or if you try hard enough you do make it, to the concluding sentence in a long paragraph of complaints—"No matter what I do, nobody in this family seems to appreciate it"; "Every time I get close to someone they leave"; "Men are just interested in themselves and can't be depended on."

These are the larger patterns that make up our lives as individuals and as families, the current that always runs beneath our everyday living, the morale of the story that is us. They're shaped from the messages we received from our parents about life, from what we saw modeled in their own lives, from the backward glance we take when looking at our own experiences. Together they become our private philosophy and list of truisms, our own variations of Murphy's Law, the expectation and, by the expectation, often the self-fulfilling prophecy of what life brings to each of the individuals in the family and the family as a whole.

Some themes are easy to hear by listening closely to the family's story—the way relationship after relationship always end the same, the way goals are always or never reached, the way kids always seem to go awry. They can be found in a genogram, guided fantasy, or projective testing, as the same images and outcomes are repeated over and over again. Others emerge only slowly, as the family begins to shed its anxiety and secrets. However they are gathered, they are as powerful as summaries of the individual's or family's life, their sense of destiny.

By stating or restating these themes to the family, the family is able to connect or separate this particular problem from the larger landscape of their lives. They can begin to listen for the theme's variations, and see how it's replicated and changed. When the theme can be expressed as an image — always making it to the dock as the boat pulls out, always reaching out your hand and having others turn away, always standing together back to back so that no one can sneak up and get you all from behind — the image can linger and come to express for the family or the individual the replication of the problem or the long-term goal to strive for.

Patterns of communication. Good communication is, of course, the elementary process that binds both good family life and good therapy. Often cleaning up the communication (letting everyone speak, blocking interruptions, making "I" statements, talking about feelings rather than facts, etc.) is all that's needed to help the family become unstuck and begin to solve their problems on their own more effectively. In the first session facilitating communication is often a priority.

Reaction to the therapist. The reaction of the different family members to you tells you what you need to do to establish rapport. If Dad is angry and silent, you goal is to calm him down and get him talking. If Mom seems intimidated and too sensitive, your job is to get her to relax and help her see more of your humanity.

Their reaction also tells you about your power. If the parents, for example, are extremely attentive to what you say, if they endow you with a great deal of knowledge or magic ability to fix their child, this tells you that you not only need to be careful about what you say, or decide if and how their stance is part of the problem, but determine whether you can use their reaction and expectation in some way to help you create change more quickly. Are they more likely, for example, to try using a behavioral chart at home? Would they be more receptive to your reframing the problem as the child's attempt to help their marital relationship?

Similarly, if your power is perceived as minimal, if you are quickly dismissed by the key people in the family, you will need to find ways to increase your power — take the time to improve the rapport between you and the members of the family, let them know about your qualifications and background, demonstrate your expertise by providing helpful information about the problem, or clarify your authority (e.g., your ability to write a recommendation letter to the court or the mandate to notify social services). Make sure they're behind you before you lead them into new challenges and changes.

Emotional range. Healthy individuals are able to express a wide range of emotions—anger, sadness, excitement—as these feelings arise from within. All too often, however, emotions are shaped and limited through acculturation (men aren't supposed to cry, woman aren't supposed to get angry); often suppressed or distorted through drugs or alcohol; acted out (e.g., spending too much money, cutting off relationships, getting into physical fights); or, as frequently develops within a family, delegated out to various family members—for example, Dad only gets mad, Mom always cries, Billy is disruptive in class or Tommy gets depressed.

These individual emotions become each person's own comfortable emotion, the only direct outlet for his or her emotional energy, while the other emotions are experienced vicariously through the other family members—Mom's easy tears express vicariously for Dad his own inexpressible deep sadness, or Billy's open hostility toward his father also allows Mom to vicariously express her own rage toward Dad as well. The need for the indirect emotional outlets is often strong, and even when the consequences are negative—Billy and his father have an awful relationship—the person needing the outlet reinforces them in some way. This readily locks the family members into unhealthy patterns.

Simply asking who feels what or observing the process will tell you what's missing in each person's emotional life, in what ways the emotional range of each individual needs to expand. Your next step may then be to shut down the vicarious outlet (stop Billy and Dad from fighting) in order to enable the other to begin to experience his or her emotions directly.

Needless to say, it's important that you give the family room to do this, room to wade into these new emotions, to discover and experiment with the fragile and anxiety-provoking feelings. This requires you to be comfortable enough with your own anxiety as they engage in this process, to resist your own inclination to dampen the process rather than risk its becoming too chaotic, to avoid offering the quick solutions, not as a way of fixing the problem, but more for the purpose of cutting off the growing anxiety in both you and them. This requires, once again, that you demonstrate the simple courage to move against your own grain, take the risk to see what new can emerge.

Much of the information about these questions will come from simple observation and listening; what is left, you can ask about directly. Taken all together they form a foundation for developing and confirming your own initial hypothesis and setting treatment goals.

FOUR

Great Beginnings II

THE FIRST-SESSION FLOW

There's no blueprint that will tell you how to handle a first session — what happens will depend upon the people, the problem, and your own style. But there are objectives to aim for and a way of thinking about the first session that can make it more manageable. A good first session is like a movement of a symphony or a well-written essay: There's an opening, the statement of the theme or problem, variations and development, a return to the opening theme, and closure, with each part connected to the one before. To make this all easier to follow, it may help to move through stages of the session sequentially.

1. The Preview

This is the information you get prior to the initial session. It may be the notes from the intake staff phone contact with one of the family members about the problem and its history, demographic information compiled on a form, or your own conversation with a member of the family. Whatever the source, this information is generally minimal, often blaming, but usually enough to get your wheels turning and give you ideas for developing an initial hypothesis.

Suppose, for example, you received the intake sheet for the Adamsons. "Boys fighting a lot; Daniel recently caught breaking into a house. Parents self-referred." Even with this minimum of information you can begin to mentally map out areas for exploration — the ways the parents discipline the children, any precipitating factors, whether the courts are involved, the way anger is handled within the family, and so on.

You can also decide whom you want to see at that first session. While some family therapy purists may tell you to bring in everyone, including the family dog, there is no need to overwhelm yourself. Bring in as many people as your anxiety and skill will allow you to handle and as necessary to enable you to gather the information you need. Once you're warmed up and have a better idea what's going on, invite the family dog and anyone else who's left or important.

2. The Opening

Armed with these preliminary ideas and your knowledge of what to avoid, you're ready to see the family. You meet them in the waiting room, lead them to your office, make sure everyone has a seat. A brief introduction — how formal or descriptive — depends on your own style, the need to match the style and culture of the family, your own sense of how much formality or information will help or hurt rapport. But whatever you say, by talking first you're helping the family to hear and get used to your voice, allowing them to settle down and get oriented before they have to talk.

Shift to small talk: "Allen, where do you work?" "Terry, what's it like to teach third grade?" "Brian, do you play soccer?" "Daniel, do you like the new gym teacher at your school?" This can be one question per person, or a brief chat with each one. This is the connecting, part of building rapport, part of assessing the anxiety of each person, their ability and willingness to talk, their ability to talk spontaneously and stray beyond your question, their attitude toward you. There's a fine line here, of course, between establishing rapport, calming everyone down, and procrastinating in order to avoid your own anxiety and having them feel like you are wasting their time. Once everyone seems settled, move on.

3. Tell Me Why You're Here

Time to go to work. "Did you all talk about coming here today?" Usually they haven't, and one or all of the children will shake their heads or shrug. Turning to the parents you ask, "Why are you here?" Notice who speaks up, whether the parents are in agreement or contradict each other. If they have discussed this at home, ask if someone can summarize what was said. What you want is a clear definition of the problem and an understanding by everyone of why they are there.

This defining of the problem and the therapy is the start of a larger discussion of problems in the family — "What do you think about what your Mom just said?" "Allen, do you feel as worried about this as your wife?" Don't let any one person do all the talking; check in with everyone about their view of what's going on. Daniel, for example, may tell about his version of the break-in, or the boys may start to argue right there in the room, demonstrating the problem the parents are describing. Watch what the parents do, but don't let it go on and on; remember, you don't want to replicate the problem too long.

If everyone talks in vague and general terms ("He gets in trouble"; "The boys just don't mind"), get the speaker to be more specific ("How does Brian get in trouble?" "What do they do when you ask the boys to do something?"). Specificity not only gives you and everyone else a better picture of behaviors involved, but helps to draw out the emotions that are masked by murky language.

The process goal is to get everyone talking more openly about things that are difficult. Be careful of setting up a pattern of asking questions and everyone giving one word answers or waiting for you to ask the next one. You want to encourage interaction as long as it isn't destructive. You may need to pull in the silent ones or gently restrain the domineering ones. This gives everyone a sense that you are in charge and able to control what is happening so that it is safe enough to speak.

After you understand the presenting problems, the next shift is to the family's theory. "So, Allen and Terry, why do you think the boys have been fighting so much?" or "Why do you think Daniel broke into house with the other boys?" Again, listen for agreement or dissension between the parents, listen to what the boys have to say, see how useful their theories are in approaching the problem — for example, "Daniel is just an angry boy [implied: like his father] who always starts the fight and gets into trouble" (scapegoat theory, with Daniel needing to be fixed), versus "We think the boys act up when there's tension between us" (interactive theory with willingness to deal with marital relationship). From the theory comes what the family members have done to try and solve the problem — used time-outs, ignored, yelled, tried to work on the marital relationship, and so on. Look for consistency, agreement, what works, who enacts and enforces.

Use your questions to track where the solution breaks down ("What do you do when he won't go to his room?") and to get a clear sense of the pattern ("I yell; he refuses; I call Allen; he pushes Brian into the room; Brian runs out; we give up") and why it takes shape. If it seems appropriate at the conclusion of this, ask how they specifically see therapy helping to do something different.

4. Explore

Once you have mapped out the ground around the presenting problem, it's time to go exploring. If you imagine the presenting problem to be like a large stone or wall sitting in the middle of field, what you're doing during this stage is walking around the field, exploring all the surrounding areas. Now you want to gather the information you need to build or confirm your hypothesis based upon your theory. For example, you may ask Allen and Terry about how they go about making decisions in general, or about their own childhoods and upbringing; you may ask everyone about the death of the grandfather a year ago.

And while you listen to their answers you're studying the process — the family's ability to communicate, the ability of the couple to give and take, when and with whom the children take sides, the ease with which various emotions are displayed or described. As you raise questions about a broader range of topics beyond the presenting problem (e.g., the past, death, sex, anger), you're expanding the boundaries of therapy beyond the family's initial expectations. Even if some of the questions or topics may seem irrelevant to them at this time, everyone at least knows that the subject is open to future discussion. What's more, you and they begin to realize that their lives are more complicated than the fraction they talk about, or maybe even think about.

What you're looking for is where the energy, and with it the motivation, most readily goes. You're seeking pockets of emotion, places where the family secrets and treasures are buried, discovering as it happens just how well the family can follow your lead, how much they try and stay on their own more comfortable path and resist yours. You want to continue to build rapport, you want to continue to move toward their anxiety. You want to create the balance between questions and comments, between your talking and their talking, and, if you feel like you are getting stuck or pulling teeth, you want to talk about the process and talk about getting stuck or pulling teeth.

5. Create an Experience

In the best of all possible first sessions, you would like to create out of your exploration an opportunity for the family to experience their process in a dramatically different way. It's actually not too difficult to do if you avoid replicating the problem and process; block, interrupt, or disrupt the dysfunctional patterns; and explore outside the comfortable range of the presenting problem.

One of the simplest ways of creating such an experience comes from the tapping of new emotions. Basically, you want to ask questions that give voice to the emotions that you suspect lie below the surface, that show the other side of a person, and track them until they are revealed. For example, you may ask Daniel if he misses his grandfather, ask him what he remembers most about him, ask what they said to each other the last time they met; the content itself is less important than its ability to stir the emotions connected to his grief.

Similarly, you may gently ask Terry, who always seems to be yelling at Daniel, to describe how she felt when Daniel was born, or encourage her to talk about her hopes for his future, or how she felt when her mother used to scold her—questions seeking to help Terry express that softer side of herself. When this type of probing is successful it creates some of the most powerful of experiences because they seem to catch everyone by surprise, bringing to the surface new emotions, ones that are rarely expressed within the family.

You can also create an experience through *enactments,* which encourage the family members to do something risky, something that goes against their emotional and behavioral grain—asking Dad to talk to Brian about school, having the couple discuss for the first time between themselves how they felt when the police called, having the boys plan then and there a way of sharing the Nintendo. Their response not only tells you about their ability to try something new, but unlocks new emotions as the behaviors holding them are broken.

Finally, you can create experience through interpretation and insight: talking to Dad, for example, about his own childhood, and making the connection that his reaction to Daniel's behavior is exactly what he just said he hated in his own father; describing to the couple the patterns of their own arguments and how they so well mimic those of the boys, or how the boys are fighting over the same basic issues that they themselves are afraid to fight about; helping Brian acknowledge that his misbehavior doesn't really help him get his Dad's attention, in fact, only makes matters worse. The insight becomes an insight not because of the accuracy of its content, but, rather, because of the emotional impact it has on the listener.

Creating an experience, however it is achieved, gives the family a fuller sense of what therapy is like, that it can be more than the talking they have already done at home. It increases intimacy and rapport, enhances your credibility, and gives you a sense of what possibly works with this particular family.

6. Go Back to the Problem

But you can't simply stir up emotions and leave them. For some clients, this will only make them fearful of the therapy process and of you as the therapist; others will feel anxious simply because they don't know where this is all leading. Once again, explanation follows experience. You have to ground the experience by linking it and the exploration back to their initial concern. Now that you have explored the area in the field around the stone, you have to return back to it.

This is where you lay out your hypothesis for the family: "I know you both think that the housebreaking has something to do with the boys Daniel was playing with, but, Daniel, it seems like you are still pretty sad about your grandfather; I wonder if those feelings are connected to the hard time you have been having lately." Or, "Terry, it seems like it's easy for you to get angry, and the boys have been doing a pretty good job of keeping you stirred up, but I also can see that underneath this anger is a lot of worry and concern and caring that the boys rarely get to see." Or, "Allen, it seems like you have been doing your best over the years not to be like your father, not to be abusive toward your children the way he was with you, but it seems that even though you are able to ignore the boys for a long period of time, it only makes matters worse, and eventually you blow up, confirming the fear that you were trying to avoid."

What you are doing is giving the family a new theory to replace the old one, showing them the problems that are undermining their ability to solve the presenting problem. This gives the family a new perspective, and with that a new energy and a new way of tackling the problem— Daniel isn't a bad kid, but a kid who is unable to express his grief; Allen isn't screwing up, he's struggling to overcome the modeling he received from his own father; Terry isn't a mean witch, but someone who has developed a tough side and is having difficulty letting others know how she really feels or what she needs.

Having said that, you need to know whether your idea flies, especially with those who hold the most power in the family. Ask each one for his or her reaction. Look for those who tacitly agree, but show little enthusiasm; it's important that the agreement be wholehearted. Unless Allen makes the connection among the boys, himself and his own father; unless Terry can agree that her more comfortable anger is blocking her expression of concern and distorting her relationship with her sons; unless both of them and Daniel see the link between the grief and the acting out; you have no foundation on which to build a therapeutic contract. But if you have laid the groundwork, if the rapport is there and the experience has been strong enough without frightening the family, they will agree with your point of view.

7. Set Goals, Describe Your Plan

This is the logical next step. If this is really the problem, then what do we do about it? Tell them, "I'd like to spend some time with you by yourself next time, Daniel, if you and your parents don't mind, to talk some more about how you've been feeling"; or, "Maybe it would be good if you both could try and switch roles; maybe you, Allen, could take over the disciplining so that Terry can have a chance to get out of being the bad guy. Why don't you both come by yourselves next time and we can talk about it."

This doesn't mean that you need to have everything all worked out in 50 minutes. If you still are in the dark about some of the information, if you need to spend more time getting to know one of the family members better, just say so. Say what you know, and say what you need to know: "I'm wondering how much this is all connected to the recent loss of your grandfather. Could we talk about this some more next week?" "I know I've been talking a lot to your parents today; would you boys be willing to talk to me by yourselves next time?" "I think I can help you with setting up clearer rules at home, but I'd like to do some psychological testing first." Being clear and specific about both what you need and how you are going to get it reduces the family's anxiety and gives them a sense of movement and direction.

8. Homework and Closure

Homework is valuable for several reasons. It lets the family know that therapy isn't just talking about things for an hour in a room, but working and making changes in their daily lives as well. It helps keep the momentum created in the session going. Most importantly, it gives you a way of seeing how motivated the family is both to follow your direction and make changes at home; it shows you what works and doesn't work, and where, in specific ways the change process breaks down. All this becomes the starting point for beginning the next session.

You might ask Terry, for example, to track those times when she begins to feel angry by sitting down for a minute and asking herself what she's worried about. You could ask Allen to ask his father what his father remembers about Allen's childhood or about his father's own childhood. You could challenge the boys to see if they can discover other, more positive ways (rather than fighting) to snag their parent's attention during the week, and see what works the best.

The homework needn't be elaborate: It can be as simple as the parents contacting the school and getting a copy of the test results, a parent listing problem times during the week, asking a mother and daughter to have a five-minute discussion on what was good during the day, or asking the father not to stomp out of the house when he starts to get mad. All it needs to be is something that helps the family link the session process with their real lives, and this initial session with the next.

Closing the session—shifting briefly back to small talk, perhaps, shaking hands once again, thanking them for coming, walking them out— serves as a ritual that provides a symmetry to the session, and helps to ease the transition back to the outside world.

Once again, all these suggestions are not a blueprint for what you have to do, but a way of describing the overall session structure, flow, and balance. If you keep this in mind together with the basics, the session will move in the direction you want it to go.

THE SECOND SESSION

They come back. The first session butterflies are gone, and everyone feels more settled. But the family more than likely is not yet taking any major responsibility for the process; you need to have specific goals and start things off.

What do you need to do in this session? First of all, you probably want to finish up what's left over from the last. Is there someone in the family whom you need to meet—the grandmother, the older brother who was working last time, the father who was out of town on a business trip? Is there someone whom you need to get to know better, someone who didn't quite connect with you—the little sister who spent the last session playing with the blocks in the corner; the father who nodded his head and said the right things, but seemed to be only half listening and involved; the I.P., who, in spite of your efforts, may still have felt beat up on by everyone else and who needs to see that you can be an advocate for him or her as well? Is there additional information that you need—background on the mother's depression, history about the father's past addiction, a clearer picture of just what the parents do when the kids give them a hard time, a better sense of just how much the little girl is affected by all the fighting.

It's in this second session that you may wish to pull the family apart (or bring them all together if you decided to only see part of the group before)—seeing one of the parents individually if you felt he or she was holding back for some reason last time, doing play therapy with one of the children to build rapport and to get a better idea of his or her world, talking to the siblings without the parents to see how they act differently. These are all ways of creating intimacy, defining goals and establishing contracts with various family members, narrowing problems, or determining where the energy and motivation most lie.

If you decide to split up the family, however, it's important that no one feels left out or paranoid about what's going on behind his or her back. Tell the parents why you want to see the boys by themselves so that they don't imagine that you're going to be pumping them to reveal the family's secrets. If you see one child, spend at least a few minutes with the others, so that they don't feel excluded and so that you don't reinforce the notion that only that child has problems. If you see an adult alone, balance it out either by then seeing the other, or by seeing the couple and having the individual explain what you both discussed.

If you see family members individually, don't be fooled into thinking that what you think you may say to one "in confidence" isn't likely to get repeated to the others. Telling a wife that it seems that her husband has trouble with intimacy, or telling a brother that his sister probably is jealous of him is often a surefire way to have these other people find out what you think and for it to be used against you and them.

In addition to finishing up you want to find out more about what works. This is where you ask about the homework, either in your small groups or all together. Simply by asking, you're giving the family the message that you take homework seriously and that you expect them to do it. If they didn't do the homework, you need to dig beneath the lame excuse (e.g., "We were just so busy") and find out why: Did they not understand, were they too anxious about doing it, or does it reflect something about their attitude toward you, the therapy, or your assessment of the problem?

Pinning this down tells you where the resistance may lie and the ways you may have created it. You may discover that you were moving too fast, asking them to do more than they could emotionally handle, or you didn't do a good enough job in selling your theory, leaving one of the key people unconvinced and uncooperative. Or perhaps the family's response only replicated the way they respond to other problems, challenges, or pressure from the outside, namely, by ignoring them.

If they did the homework, you want to know what they thought about it. Sometimes the family will do exactly what you ask, the assignment will accomplish exactly what you behaviorally hoped it would, but the results seem to have little emotional impact on the family. Sure, Dad spent more time with Brian, and they had a good time, but Dad says it wasn't much different than the times he'd done it before and seems unimpressed. Dad probably doesn't see the connection of the assignment to the problem or the theory or has not aligned with you. If the assignment was tried but didn't work, that is, the family wasn't able to carry it out (Mom still got mad, Brian still was fighting), you want to track where it broke down so you can help the family fine-tune it or rethink your hypothesis.

It's also a good idea at this session to ask the family what they thought about the last session. Not only may you find out what someone didn't like or what made them uncomfortable ("I felt you were taking Allen's side," "I was surprised how hard it was talking to the Brian about his schoolwork"), you may also find out what may be most effective with each of them simply by what they tell you they remember about the session ("What you said about my father really got me thinking," "Having a chance to hear what Terry really thought was helpful," "Feeling that it wasn't all my fault helped me be less critical of myself and them"). Finding out whether interpretation, delving into the past, building self-esteem, facilitating communication, or something else had the largest impact is important in knowing just what to do more of.

Finally, you want to use this session to help the family further understand how the therapy sessions are related to each other, the presenting problem, and the overall treatment. How they do this is primarily by following your lead. If you ask, for example, how their week was, or what problems came up, they quickly assume that the therapy will include monitoring on a week-by-week process. If, on the other hand, you take a less directive role and ask the couple or family what they want to talk about, or continue to explore their past, the family will begin to think that this is what the meetings will be like.

Because they look to you to set the pace, it's important that you know what pace you want to set and that you be deliberate in what you're doing. Think about the way you want to use the session process, not only so that it will be most helpful to the family and fit your therapeutic style, but also so the family can begin to learn to do the same. Once again, the best route to take is one of creating balance between initiating and responding, the individual and the group, assessment and treatment. If you continue to keep tight control over the process or continue to ask lots of questions, the family will easily begin to fall into the pattern of waiting for you to ask the next question or pick the next topic, and become too anxious and resistant if you then suddenly want to shift gears.

Of course, it helps to back up your actions with clear communication—"I know I've been asking a lot of questions during these two sessions. Next time I won't be; I'd like you to think about what we need to talk about and bring it up." If you need to continue some one-time assessment activities for a few more sessions (you want to do psychological testing for the next two weeks), let the family know, and explain how the next phase will be different so they can begin to think ahead.

By the end of this second session you should feel more certain about your hypothesis, feel more connected to everyone in the family, have gathered the missing information that you needed or know what is left to get, and have an idea of what works. You want to know that things are on track and, more importantly, that the family feels the same way.

THIRD-SESSION SHIFT, OR HOW DID I LOSE THEM?

Generally, by the third session things have settled down; your assessment is complete or nearly complete, rapport is high and the family feels comfortable with you, expectations are clear, and the treatment process is turning the corner toward the start of the middle phase. But not always. Sometimes the third session seems to slide out from underneath you—the family gets ornery, maybe even quits, or everyone, including you, suddenly seems to run out of steam. This can catch you off guard, and it's easy to blame yourself for doing something you're not aware of doing. Don't. Here's some of what might be going on beneath the third-session shift:

• Some families come in for therapy in crisis and are crisis-oriented. They may take a couple of sessions to calm down, but once they do they've gotten what they wanted and are ready to leave. They don't see the need to continue and simply drop out. If they do, they are often exhausted by expending all their energy on the crisis and may have difficulty working on the underlying issues, or doing the preventive work that can keep the next crisis from brewing altogether.

If you suspect the family is this way, you may decide to educate them about crisis reactions and the possible recurrence of the problem, offer them an appointment to come back for a checkup in a few weeks or months (to encourage a preventive, proactive stance rather than a reactive one), or briefly work to help them see the connection between underlying issues and surface behavior. But if they are ready to go, let them do so with your support. Unless you have clear clinical reservations— for example, the son still seems extremely depressed and potentially suicidal—let them leave feeling good about themselves, rather than with the message of guilt from you that you think they're failing to follow through. If they feel supported in leaving, they will feel supported in coming back.

• Similarly, some families take two or more sessions just to ventilate and get things off their chests. Once they're emptied, anxiety sets in about the process (what happens now), or they look up and realize that you're in the room with them and panic over what they think you think, and what you might do. One way to handle this is to anticipate it—talk about the process, give voice to their feelings, map out the logical next step.

• After a couple of sessions countertransference and transference begin to settle in. The parents decide that you are not as all-knowing as they originally thought, you begin to feel that the family is not as motivated and honest as you initially believed. They close up or drop out, you start acting more pushy. Anticipating these changes and talking to your supervisor will help keep you from overreacting. Talking about this with the family ("It feels like we were going strong for a few weeks, but now we're slowing down"), educating and normalizing the process ("Most families in counseling feel most enthusiastic the first few weeks, then they begin to feel that they are not making as much progress as they thought"), helping them sort through their feelings ("Terry, you seem annoyed about what I've been suggesting") can keep these emotions from replicating the family process and undermining the therapy.

• If you see only a portion of the family the first time or two (e.g., the mother or father isn't able to come), they may feel left out of the process, or resist coming in and sabotage it for everyone else, causing them all to drop out. In couple therapy this often takes the form of the wife coming in first, then her telling her husband that she saw a marital therapist, who now wants to see him with her. Out of his anxiety he promises to make all the changes in the world and convinces the wife to discontinue. Seeing everyone together as soon as possible, even doing telephone outreach to the missing person, or predicting this process for those attending and helping them respond to the other can prevent this.

• Sometimes when parents come in around child problems, they are fine while the child is being discussed or while you are evaluating the child, but panic when you shift to larger issues or the marriage. The key here is connecting the large issues to the child, and monitoring the parent's anxiety. If you move too quickly or push to hard for them to focus on what's too threatening, they will drop out.

• Families who are mandated by the courts or another agency to come for therapy may show up for the first couple of sessions, long enough for you to say that you saw them, or for them to say that they came, then drop out basically because they don't want to be there. Contacting the referring agency right away and deciding with them how they want things to be handled if the family doesn't continue to come can help clarify your role, and provide a united front to the family.

Except for mandated cases, the driving force behind all these third-session shifts is anxiety generated by the transition from the presenting, surface, out-there, crisis orientation to the underlying process, depth, in-here focus—all of which happens within these first few sessions. The key to walking that fine line between too much and too little anxiety lies in avoiding radical shifts. Maintain openness and honesty, focus on the process and make it as representative as possible of the way therapy will be; move quickly enough for the client to feel that something is happening, but not too quickly if the family feels pushed into something they don't agree with.

But, as was said in the first chapter, there's still much that will be beyond your control: There are expectations the family simply won't reveal, and there are other pressures on the family's life that makes them decide that therapy with you or therapy at all is no longer needed. There's no need to beat yourself over the head; you can only do what you are capable of doing.

The challenges of the beginning are the challenges that come with starting any joint enterprise, those of finding or creating compatibility of personality and perspective, reaching an understanding and agreement about the nature of the relationship, about the way time together will be spent, and how it all will work. It's a time when the rhythm of the therapy hasn't taken over, and you are forced to rely more on your own personal strengths. But if you can succeed in accomplishing the goals you set out for these initial sessions, most of the hard part is over. You're ready to move on to the next stage.

LOOKING WITHIN

These exercises are designed to help you increase your awareness of the issues surrounding beginnings and to increase your observation skills by practicing them outside of therapy. Go ahead, try them over the next week.

1. Think again about your own theory, values, and personal level of anxiety. What are your greatest strengths? Whom do you feel it is most important to see in the initial session? Whom would you not want or feel comfortable seeing (e.g., small children, extended family)? What would help you most in reducing your own anxiety? See if you can develop in advance rules of thumb for first sessions that would work best for you and the families you work with.

2. *Rapport.* We all vary in our natural sociability and outgoingness. If this initial connecting with families is awkward for you, try improving your skills in less pressured situations—meeting someone at a party, talking to the person next to you on a bus or standing in line. Increase your risk taking and comfort in connecting with a wider range of people.

3. What's your comfortable emotional range? What feelings are difficult for you to express directly? What emotions are you particularly sensitive to in others? How does this affect your clinical work? While you can't make yourself feel, you can begin to see how others in your life may serve as vicarious outlets for you, expressing what is difficult for you to express. You can also slow down and ask yourself what emotion may be lying beneath your comfortable one. What else may you be feeling when you are so angry, sad, jealous, tired?

See if you can increase your ability to define the comfortable emotion of others.

4. *Themes.* Hearing themes is a matter of floating along the top of a conversation, avoiding diving down and getting stuck in the details of the content, making yourself listen for metaphoric connections, repeated phrases and images, recurring patterns. It takes practice to develop this skill. Practice listening for themes in your nonclinical conversations with friends, neighbors, family. You'll know if you are on target simply by restating the theme back to the person and seeing if it resonates for him or her.

5. Think of something that someone in your family—nuclear or family of origin—does that particularly bothers you. Write it down and describe it fully. Then consider in what ways at least two other people in the family are—or even might be—involved in provoking or maintaining this problem. For example, your father may drive recklessly partly because your mother is timid or is always telling him to slow down. Your spouse may seem to always overreact to one of your children because you seem to him or her to underreact to or side with that child. See how these new perceptions affect your feelings.

FIVE

The Middle Stage:
Are We There Yet?

Once you've made it past the beginning stage, you come to the broad, flat prairie land of the middle. There's a sigh of relief, not only for making it through the challenges of the beginning, but, as you look out ahead, for the regularity, the cooperation, and the familiarity that the middle stage seems to promise. This, after all, is where the bulk of the treatment will take place, where the vision created and the goals of change agreed upon in those first few weeks are forged into something solid and permanent.

But as the relief starts to wane and the work begins in earnest, the ground, you discover, turns out to be not as flat as it at first seemed; there are still plenty of ruts and bumps ahead. For every good session or week there's one that isn't quite as good; skills that you laboriously help the family to learn—communication, parenting, assertiveness—have to be constantly retaught or fine-tuned; just when you think all the crises are behind you, one flares up without any apparent warning.

All this makes for the famous "working through" of the middle stage. The work of working through is the grind, the feeling that you are not so much digging down deeper into the layers of the family structure and individual personalities, but more digging a hole, filling it back up, and digging it out again. Even though the family is able make a great deal of progress in those first few weeks, it all turns out to be so easily derailed. For three weeks in a row everyone in the family listens better to each other and avoids those destructive verbal eruptions, but then Uncle Harry shows up for a short visit and the tension causes everything to collapse back into chaos. Mom is doing a good job of sticking to her rules, but then she has a hard day at work, the kids double-team her when Dad isn't home, and she caves in. Dad may be better able to handle his temper with the children, but continues to easily flare up around his wife. New skills haven't been integrated and the endurance necessary to sustain change on an everyday level still hasn't been developed. The gains are fragile, and it doesn't take much for it all to fall apart.

GETTING STUCK

While two steps forward and one step back is probably the most common pattern seen throughout the middle stage of therapy, there are other variations. Sometimes a family will initially make progress and then not only lose ground but be back to zero within a matter of weeks.

Teresa, for example, a single parent, comes in with her two adolescent children, Lavone, age 15, and Kenisha, age 13. The presenting problems are Kenisha refusing to go to school and Lavone staying out late. In the first couple of sessions Teresa is able to revise her initial theory that they were bad kids made worse by their friends, and she works hard at implementing the structural-behavioral changes that you suggest—having a meeting with the school and Kenisha to discuss Kenisha's complaints and develop a plan for her return, and taking a stronger stand at home about the necessity of her attending school regularly; as well as setting clear limits with Lavone, and contacting the juvenile court for disciplinary backup.

It works. Kenisha goes to school for three solid weeks, and after a stern talk with the court officer Lavone gives up testing his mother's new resolve and is staying home at night. But then just as quickly everything unravels—Kenisha stays home a couple of days because she says she's sick, and it's the beginning of the end. Her excuses become thinner and thinner, and Teresa seems to lose her ability to get Kenisha to school. Lavone at the same time activates the other front and stays out later and later, with no consequences by Teresa. Within a month everything seems back to where it started.

What's going on here? Certainly some of this is predictable. Most families make some progress and feel great about it. But then there's some slipup, such as Kenisha's missing of a day of school, and they fear that the gains were illusory. What they don't fully appreciate is that progress was made because they did learn to do something different. They have to learn that setbacks are inevitable simply because they are inexperienced and haven't yet learned to integrate the new skills. They have to learn that they must not give up or forget what they learned. Even after they slide back, the same skills that helped them before will help them again.

Teresa needs ongoing support to help her keep the principles of maintaining structure and hierarchy clear in her mind and stay on track; she needs to fine-tune and anticipate dealing with the kids' specific behaviors, such as what to say and do when Kenisha says she doesn't want to go to school, or when Lavone comes home three hours after curfew.

But also eroding Teresa's ability to maintain change may be the presence of other problems — Teresa's low-grade but chronic depression, her poor health, or her demanding elderly mother — that weren't apparent during the initial assessment, one or all of which may sap her time and energy and make it difficult for her to keep on task. Other people, who originally seemed to be at the far outskirts of the family, may now appear to be more involved and undermining of the family's efforts. Teresa's boyfriend, it turns out, is in the home more often than not, and his rising jealousy over all the attention the children suddenly seem to be getting causes him to urge Teresa not to be so hard on the kids or to stand up for them when she tries to impose the new rules.

Other times there is not so much the backsliding or the erosion by other problems and family members, but a case of revolving scapegoats; just when the presenting problem is well on its way to being resolved, a new problem with another family member flares up. Kenisha, for example, isn't going to school, but Lavone is doing well. Within a couple of weeks Kenisha's back on track, but suddenly Lavone is talking back and slipping out at night to meet his friends on the corner.

What all of these variations represent is the family's dependency on the patterns to maintain the emotions and roles within the family. In spite of her attempts to become firmer and more consistent, Teresa still frets or yells or spends all her time consumed by the children, and gives the boyfriend cause to remain on the outskirts; even though Kenisha seems to be better she's merely switching emotional places with Lavone and taking a turn at being the "good child" for a while. The anxiety of creating more fundamental change in both parenting and the mother–boyfriend relationship continually pushes the family back toward variations on the familiar.

So does the sense of loss. What change implies is not only the learning of new skills and roles, but often the emotional and psychological giving up of what the members of the family have for so long thought of as "life." Teresa, who has, for as long as she can remember, not only worried about her children, but put them first, now must take a different stance and begin to think more about herself and her relationship with her boyfriend. In doing so she not only needs to develop deeper levels of intimacy and self-knowledge, but let go of some of what she considered her motherhood. It's a change that creates, a least for a while, a hole in her identity, one that she will need to grieve before she can fill. It's this kind of grief that runs like an undertow beneath the changes up above and contributes to that sluggish, slowing down, plateau-like feeling of the middle stage.

ANTIDOTES TO STUCKNESS

So what do you do with all this slipping, sliding, and sticking? There are a number of remedies, the choice of which depends partially upon the problem, partially upon your own preference. Here are some ideas to consider:

Grind it out. This is the modus operandi of the middle stage. Though it can be boring or exasperating, this plodding over the same ground again and again, your working to keep everyone committed and on track can also turn out to be extremely valuable for the family. This is especially true for those crisis-oriented families who never developed the skills of consistency and follow-through, who quickly grow impatient or become distracted; it's your perseverance that ultimately seeps into their thinking. Your goal is to keep everyone from giving up or going off, to help them cognitively separate out the urge to slip back from the anxiety of change itself, and help them see how each one of them copes with the stress of change in a different way.

As the family becomes more skilled and aware of their own process, they can be seen less often. If Teresa is pretty much holding her own, having her check in with you every other week or so may be fine. Shifting to such a monitoring role is not only an endorsement of her growing capability, but a way for you to avoid session dread.

Mix it up. Grinding it out, however, doesn't have to be deadly. The middle stage is a good time to reinforce the skills and concepts by changing formats and introducing experiential work on an irregular basis (doing it on a regular basis only flattens its potential impact). Bring in additional family members, for example, Teresa's boyfriend; see siblings together or individually; do some guided imagery; have family members take turns making live "sculptures" or poses of the family relationships as they see them. This not only helps avoid the therapeutic ruts and keeps the family interested and engaged, but helps ferret out additional problems that may undermine progress.

Separate/clarify problems. As other problems begin to poke their heads above ground, you have to decide how they fit into the larger patterns. Sometimes it's clear that the presenting problem is only a smoke-screen, a more comfortable way for the client to enter the system and determine just how helpful or sensitive you really are; although Teresa, for example, may initially come in about Kenisha, by the second session it becomes clear that it is her relationship with her boyfriend or mother that is bothering her the most. In cases like these the presenting problem seems fairly minor, or is quickly resolved or dismissed by the family, and as the clinician it's easy to move to where the client's energy and anxiety lead you.

But sometimes it's you, not the client, who needs to do the leading. Even though Teresa is quick to dismiss her depression as just the way she has always been, it becomes apparent to you that this is what has been making it difficult for her to implement the disciplinary suggestions you have made; unless her depression is relieved, she'll not have the energy to make the needed changes in her parenting. Similarly, you may feel that her relationship with her boyfriend holds the key to her acting more effectively as a parent. Your job not only becomes one of helping her see that not only are the two problems related, but that the second is actually more important. How you decide to link and prioritize this array of problems rests upon your theory and its notion of causality.

Finally there are times when you need to decide whether a new problem is really a new problem; a variation of the old, such as revolving scapegoats; or a distraction. Just as families outside of therapy will return to comfortable problems when their anxiety gets too high, so will they do the same in therapy. As you begin to help Teresa look more closely at her relationship with her boyfriend, new crises may arise at school with Kenisha or at home with Lavone that zap attention away. If you've done a good assessment and know what the family's comfortable problems are, you won't be led astray, and can help the family stay focused.

Normalize, label, diversify. Predicting to the family the backslides, the shift in scapegoats, the eruption of crises, the feelings of anxiety and ambivalence, the sabotage by others in the family, does more than make you look smart. It gives the family a sense of control as they, too, learn just what the process of change entails, and helps you all keep from becoming discouraged.

Labeling the process has a similar effect in increasing control. For example, labeling for Teresa the school issues as her comfortable problem, the area where much of her attention and emotions so readily goes, helps her and the rest of the family do the same. The labeling, the naming, helps the family gain some distance and perspective when the problem and the emotions arise. The family can begin to see it as you see it, as part of the larger pattern, and can decide how much of a priority it really is.

Finally, helping the family diversify their emotional outlets and expand their emotional range by interrupting the well-worn patterns and pushing them to the edge of their anxiety—helping Teresa confront her boyfriend, helping Kenisha talk to her teachers about problems, rather than cutting class—is the best way to ensure that they have more emotional space to grow toward. Unless they each can develop greater emotional flexibility it becomes all too easy to remain dependent and caged within the roles and patterns that they know.

Approach the loss. How you handle the underlying loss, the extent to which you allow it to emerge or be recognized partially depends upon your theory and focus. If, for example, you are doing brief, solution-based treatment, these emotions will most likely remain untouched. If your focus is primarily upon behavioral patterns, you may decide, rather than defining the grief, to simply continue pulling the family along against its undertow until they finally move beyond its grasp, and the new behaviors, and the emotions they bring, take hold.

It also depends upon your personality and your own emotional willingness to approach these feelings. If loss is a difficult issue for you, if you are in the middle of coping with changes within your personal life, it may be easy for you to minimize its impact or deliberately decide to avoid the subject. Such an emotional stance can become even stronger and seem more valid when coupled with a clinical theory that can support it.

A simple, honest approach, of course, would be to talk about loss directly. To ask the family what they sense they're losing or fear they may lose helps them to see that moving forward always involves leaving something else behind; it helps them realize that our expectations of life, even when life is difficult, readily come to match whatever we have grown used to.

This kind of talk not only keeps the family, as well as yourself, from being discouraged by the sudden stall in progress, but opens the door to the larger subject of grief within the family's experience. It's not uncommon to have long-forgotten and unexpressed emotions of past losses suddenly stirred. As these emotions rise to the surface and are finally expressed, these past losses begin to heal, and the family's emotional range has another opportunity to grow.

Be brave. We're back once again to courage, for this is the most basic antidote to all this stuckness and backsliding—tracking the family's emotional pulse by staying close to their and your own anxiety even as distractions arise or new skills gradually become ever more comfortable, and taking the risk of honesty when the ambivalence and grief begins to seep out beneath the behavioral changes, challenging both you and them to resist the temptations of lapsing back into the old familiar patterns. It is your willingness to continue to move ahead that helps the family to do the same.

Keep in mind, however, that even with the courage, you can't change the basic landscape. The plodding through new problems, the reassessment and reclassification and reeducation will remain part of this middle stage. The going, in spite of your best efforts, may still seem slow and stretch on longer than you at first thought.

HIDDEN SABOTAGE

The family's slipping, sliding, and backtracking are manageable because they are expected and obvious to you as an outsider to the system. The greater danger of the middle stage occurs when these same dynamics go underground, when you and family become emotionally intertwined, and you become part of the system, or when you put up your own roadblocks to just how far the family can go. Here's a quick breakdown of some of the possibilities:

Immersion in the system. In the room with you are Bill and Helen and their three children. The presenting problem is eight-year-old Joey's tendency to play with matches (he was caught trying to light the living room curtains on fire one day), but it is really just one of many crises that keep the family in turmoil. You've already decided that Bill needs to take a more active role in parenting, that Helen is overwhelmed and depressed, that communication between the parents is lousy, that 10-year-old Patricia is parentified and barely keeping her head above water, and that four-year-old Tom is likely to follow in his brother's path. You've decided that your initial goals are to pull Bill back into the family process and facilitate communication and problem solving among everyone.

But as soon as you ask how their week was, a verbal free-for-all erupts. Each of the kids simultaneously starts telling his or her version of the story of how a hole got knocked in the wall of the kids' room. Helen suspects that Joey did it on purpose; Bill pipes up but is quickly drowned out. You try to separate and make sense of the stories, having everyone take a turn and finish what they want to say, but before this incident is resolved, Helen is off on another, which leads the kids to yet another. The best you can accomplish is to keep everyone from talking at once.

This kind of immersion into the family process, becoming swept up and away, is fairly common, especially among beginning therapists. Rather than leading the process, you, the clinician, are limping behind, or are quickly caught in the swirl of family interactions. Either because of your lack of skills or courage, the family finds themselves doing in your office what they generally do at home, and you are left feeling overrun, overwhelmed, exhausted, fragmented, confused, and eventually just as crisis-oriented as they are.

Sometimes, however, rather than becoming emotionally washed away, you wind up filling in one of the gaps in the family roles. You may, for example, join with Helen and actually stand in for the inactive Bill, scolding Joey, backing up Helen's rules, putting the lid on Tom. Or you may identify with one of the children, and find yourself encouraging Joey to vent his anger right there and then in the room. If there has been a loss recently within the family, for example, the death of grandparent or a divorce and the leaving of the father, you may, with the family's silent blessing, step right into the empty shoes. Once locked into the role, you no longer have to struggle as an outsider, and the family no longer has to figure out what to do with you. Pull up a chair, grab a plate, have some dinner, join in. The process remains the same; all that's changed is that there's another seat at the table.

This, of course, is the lure on both sides, namely, the quick and easy reduction of anxiety all around. From among the choices that the family offers, you find a role that fits your psychological makeup. Even though you may feel like you're working, not much work is really going on; even though the family knows they're in therapy, it all feels strangely familiar. You're no longer pulling against the family's grain, and the family is no longer threatened by questions or comments that make them feel uncomfortable.

This kind of unconscious seduction is, of course, very different from the conscious, deliberate taking of sides, for example, specifically backing up Helen as a way of modeling such behavior for Bill, or verbalizing the anger that Patricia may be feeling but not saying. Here you are flexible, rather than entrenched; you're able and ready to pull back or move to another role as the need arises.

Parallel process. Helen yells at Joey, Joey fights with Tom, Tom kicks the dog. The dog bites Tom, Tom hits Joey, Joey steals Patricia's hair brush, Patricia runs to Mom. Off to counseling steps Mom, who now turns to you, the clinician. The emotional buck gets passed up and down the line, as the patterns of action and reaction are played out over and over again. Just as it is easy for you to get caught up in the swirl of emotions and roles, it's easy to step into line and pass the buck yourself, generally to your supervisor.

Parallel process is a variation of immersion, an unconscious process by which the clinician continues the process rather than stopping it. When the clinician walks into supervision all emotionally wrought, overwhelmed, and complaining, it's up to the supervisor to do the stopping, and push the process back down the line. He or she does this by stepping back from the process, helping the clinician to see just what is going on, modeling and empowering the clinician to do the same with the parent.

But sometimes, unfortunately, the wave rolls over the family from above. If, for example, the supervisor is under a lot of pressure by the agency head, or the clinician, new to the job, is under probation and feels enormous performance pressure from the supervisor, it doesn't take much for all this anxiety to work its way down and get dumped on the family. Rather than the clinician remaining cool and collected, he or she is displacing onto the family everything he or she feels; suddenly the clinician is breathing down the parents' necks, telling them how they need to shape up and get their act together. It's easy then for the parents to pass this all down to the children, who then may take it out on each other, the dog, the cat, or the kids sitting next to them in class.

Needless to say, all this can easily get the family off track, and worsen their woes. Rather than therapy being a safe place to try new behaviors, it becomes instead a forum for the clinician's or agency's own emotional chaos. Making it all the worse is the clinician's inability to see the impact he or she is having. Few families have the courage to tell the clinician to keep his projections to him- or herself, or the self-confidence to really believe that what's happening isn't their fault. If not corrected by the clinician, they'll eventually drop out, convinced once and for all that they are hopeless or that therapy ain't worth a damn.

Countertransference. Immersion and parallel process certainly reflect countertransference issues in that something within the clinician's own personality is hooked and pulled into family system without his or her awareness. But there is another, more generalized form of countertransference in which the clinician is not so much ensnared by a particular family's dynamics, but instead brings to the family a whole host of unconscious land mines that result in his or her avoiding or inappropriately reacting to what the family offers. In effect, the clinician is creating his or her own roadblocks that limit the family's therapeutic progress.

If, for example, you are easily intimidated by men such as Bill who have high-power jobs, are older than you, or seem controlling, you may find rationalizations to exclude him from the therapy: "It's too bad that he has to work so late, but rather than cancel, the rest of us can go ahead and meet without him." If he is there you may simply ignore him (thereby also replicating the family process and providing a double whammy), join with Helen and gang up against him, use her to vicariously express your own anger or fear, or silence Helen and act ingratiating toward him as a way of winning his favor.

Similarly, you may have difficulty dealing with problems of sexual abuse, or verbal abuse, or depression, stemming not from lack of skill, but from a deeper set of personal reactions; the topic is then never brought up or is minimized even when it's clear to an outsider that it's important. Or you find yourself always reaching the same emotional boundary lines in the course of the therapy. With the help of innumerable rationalizations (the mother needs to see someone individually, the family isn't ready to deal with Dad's addiction, they aren't working, they need time to consolidate the gains that they have made), relationships are cut off just when the client becomes too dependent, too provocative, too angry — anything that touches off your own emotional bottom line — and in defense you quit.

Again it's anxiety and the blind spot to the anxiety that are the drivers here, that make for such widespread, across-the-board patterns of avoidance, under- or overreaction, or vicarious expression of emotion by others. It's anxiety that distorts what the clinician sees and hears, that turns a rationale into a rationalization that limits or undermines the family's progress.

Collusion. Finally, there is a form of sabotage that arises out of the therapy culture that you and the family create. Rather than becoming immersed in the ongoing system or filling in already established roles, you and the family create your own roles and patterns around the therapy process, all of which are just empty shells, lacking vitality, valuable only for the predictability they offer.

Each session, for example, may follow the same format, propelled by the same questions or comments — "How was your week?"; "Let's pick up where we left off last time." Then Dad complains, Mom discounts him, you mediate and give advice which is never fully followed. Or the mother comes in complaining about one of the children, but this is only a learned warm-up for her talking about her ex-husband or for your simply asking questions about her past. The content is less important than the spending of time together and enjoying the feelings of intimacy.

Collusion is in place when the therapy has fallen into a rut which everyone silently agrees not to change. There's the appearance of movement, but little is actually changing; form has superseded function. Everyone is comfortable rather than challenged. The emotions generated within the session (the mother's feelings of closeness and intimacy, the father's feelings of resentment toward his wife, the clinician's feeling of power or indispensability) become the new comfortable emotions that fuel and maintain the therapy's roles and patterns. The therapy rolls along, sometimes for years, with its primary value being only that of stability.

Again, it's not stability that's bad in itself; it often, in fact, can be a legitimate goal, especially in chaotic families. It becomes dysfunctional when it's serving the needs of the clinician — namely, those of binding anxiety and avoiding the confrontation and risk taking the family needs in order to change — when it is supported by rationalizations rather than realistic family needs. As with the other forms of sabotage, collusion, if unchecked, undermines the therapeutic process.

COUNTERING SABOTAGE

Ideally, all of this should never go unchecked, and usually it doesn't. One of the primary lines of defense is good supervision. Because the supervisor is further removed from the family system, he or she is able to see the patterns that the clinician may be blind to, can detect the parallel process rolling his or her way by the clinician's presentation of the case, knows the clinician well enough to recognize the similar distorted reactions that show up across the clinician's caseload.

And even if the supervisor doesn't have it all worked out, but sus-pects that the clinician is more entangled than he or she intended and senses that the clinician is rationalizing his or her behavior but isn't certain, by simply raising the issue ("I wonder if you are stepping in for this mother who is so passive"; "I wonder if the way you feel now as you are talking is very much the way the father felt"; "I wonder if you are afraid to con-front this grandmother"; "I notice you have a hard time dealing with adoles-cents who act like this"), the statement or question itself becomes a crowbar for prying up what is lying underground. What was hidden is now out in the open; the unconscious is made conscious and loses its power.

You, as the clinician, can also do your own prying. This kind of self-supervision requires that you step back and look at the process of the ses-sions, if not when you are in it, at least in quiet, later. It requires that you know enough about the family to be able to anticipate the holes and traps and roles that can ensnare you. It requires that you know enough about yourself and your own weaknesses and sensitivities that you can see the larger patterns that emerge in your clinical work, the cutoffs and avoidances and attractions, the overresponsibility, the need for clients to express what you cannot. If you have this kind of awareness, then you will be able to emotionally separate the rationale from the rationaliza-tion, to tell whose needs you are most trying to meet.

The family can help with this process as well. By automatically reevaluating the therapeutic contract at regular intervals, they (and you) can have the opportunity to say aloud whether everything is on course, rather than their being forced to drop out due to confusion or resentment. If there has been an imbalance in the family sessions, if one member has been ignored or felt ganged up on, or if new goals need to be set, here is the chance for it all to get out in the open. These, of course, are the times that you need to be most sensitive, most open to the nonverbal as well as verbal communication of everyone in the room. If you are only willing to hear what you want to hear, you'll always get what you want, unfortunately at a cost to the family.

But the simple solution is always the most reliable. If sabotage is driven by the avoidance of anxiety, it is the presence of anxiety, your ability once again to stay at the edge of change, in the process, in the room, in your self that is the best antidote. It's when the process gets too easy, too com-fortable, or too predictable for too long that you know something may be going off track, that the family's needs may be compromised, that you have lost your power as an outside agent to affect change. Even if you're not sure at that moment what is the right thing to do, by returning to the basics of honesty and courage, you're recentering yourself and the process on the right path. The experience of doing this, of slowing down and defining and taking self-responsibility, will itself lead you and the fam-ily to where you need to be.

FIRST AID FOR THE AWFUL SESSION

Apart from the bigger problems and patterns of sabotage and induction into the family system are those occasional awful sessions that every therapist has. These have less to do with the family's dynamics and more to do with the simple fact that you're having a bad day. Maybe you were awake most of the night before because your kid was sick and throwing up every 15 minutes; or perhaps you had a blow-up with your spouse about the dog peeing on the carpet *again,* just as you're walking out the door to go to work; or your mother called last night to say that, oh, by the way, she felt a lump in her breast, and though it's probably nothing, she's scheduling the earliest possible appointment she can with her doctor, but don't you concern yourself with it at all.

So you walk into work feeling groggy or irritable or worried, and actually the last thing you want to do is to listen to more people and their problems. But you do, and Henry makes that same smirk every time his wife Betty talks about the trouble Freddie gave her that week, and you feel like clobbering the guy. Of course you don't, but you do come down on him pretty hard, and, of course, all he does is deny feeling anything special, and you wind up even more frustrated. Or maybe Denise starts with her whiny pleas to the boys to stop arguing, but you're so tired that you just let it go until, before you know it, the boys are running out the door and down the hallway. She falls apart and starts crying, but you can't spend much time helping her because you're trying to find out which direction the kids went.

These kind of sessions undoubtedly are hard to shake off. They leave you feeling angry and guilty and worried. You kick yourself for being so mean or lazy, for getting into this stupid kind of work, for getting a dog, for getting married, for that matter. You're mad at this family for doing the same thing over and over again in spite of your best efforts for the last six sessions to try and get them to do something different. You're worried they'll never come back, you hope to God they never do.

Slow down. It's not the end of the world. First of all, give yourself a break. Sure, you could have done a better job, but you did the best you could at the time. Mistakes are called mistakes rather than tragedies because you can correct them. So take a couple of deep breaths and figure out what you need to do next.

Did the session leave you so concerned about the impact on the family that you need to do something before the next appointment? Is Henry apt to be steaming mad and take it out on Betty or the kids all week? Will he decide not to come back? Is Denise feeling so wrecked that she's likely to collapse all together and lose all the ground she's made? Will she get depressed and start having suicidal thoughts again?

If you feel that someone in the family will act out or emotionally go into a tailspin, or if you just don't know what might happen and that makes you too uncomfortable, do something. Call up the family later in the day to see how they're doing, what they're thinking, to apologize to Henry, to reassure Denise. You don't need to spend an hour on the phone—you can talk more about what happened at the next session—but do some crisis intervention. If you can't reach them, leave a message on the answering machine asking them to call you or to simply say that you realize that it was a tough session and you're just checking in, or write them a brief note and mail it. Don't obsess or feel helpless—do something.

If you feel that yes, they'll be back and it's not urgent to talk to them, wait until the next session. Start the session cleaning up the last one: "Before we get started on whatever you wanted to cover, I'd like to talk a bit about what happened last week." Then talk—apologize if you feel an apology is in order, talk about your feelings in the process ("I felt frustrated when . . . "), talk about yourself ("I realize I didn't say much last week. I was preoccupied because . . . "). Then ask the family to give their impressions of the session: Denise says she felt overwhelmed; Henry didn't understand why you kept asking the same thing over and over again, and, frankly, it was bugging the hell out of him. Or, often following the family's established pattern, they may say nothing about it—"It was a little confusing," says Denise, "but okay." "No," says Henry, "I don't remember anything being wrong." Only later, after their trust and assertiveness increase, may they say something about it.

Regardless of what you do or don't say, you're modeling a way to admit and repair mistakes, showing them how to take responsibility, how to communicate clearly when communication has broken down. This can be a powerful experience for families who always sweep things under the rug or have such terrible blowups that the only way they know to contain them is to completely close topics off. Once again, approaching your anxiety and dealing with the therapeutic derailment by looking at it squarely with honesty, clarity, and empathy are the most and the best you can do.

With all the movement in the practice of therapy brought on by managed care and the press of brief work in recent years, the traditional image of the middle stage seems to be changing; it is less the long, flat stretch that it used to be and more a way station between the beginning and termination. But even if the stages of therapy are more compressed, the challenge to appreciate the integrity of each stage remains.

To say to yourself or to a family that we have reached the middle of the therapy, that this is a plateau and not the end, that repetition and relearning are the nature of this time is to define and map the contours of the change process itself. It's shaped by your theory and, at a deeper level, by your own values and beliefs about your role, the purpose of therapy, and the developmental process. How you think about the flow of the therapy process, in this stage and the others, will affect what you, and the family, will come to expect and eventually discover.

LOOKING WITHIN

Just as the exercises of the last chapter focused on skills and issues related to the beginning stage of treatment, these exercises focus on those of the middle stage. Once again, take the risk and give them a try.

1. Think about a couple of ongoing or past cases. When do you stop with a case, how do you decide when to stick with it? How much do you believe change is occurring even when it is not evident? When does stalling out become resistance and when is it a time for incubation? How do you know when you are taking too much responsibility for change within the family?

2. *Countertransference*. Think again about the kind of clients that are most difficult for you to work with. How do you respond to these clients? What role do you usually take? How does this role limit your therapeutic flexibility? Does it offer any therapeutic advantages? Would it be helpful to explore your reactions with your supervisor or discuss them with a therapist?

3. What kind of problems are emotionally the most difficult for you? How do you respond to them? What is your emotional bottom line? What kind of rationalizations are you susceptible to? How do handle loss, in yourself, in others? Again, are these indicators of unresolved issues from your past that need your attention? Who do you feel comfortable talking to about them?

4. Increase your awareness of parallel process by noticing it in settings outside of clinical work. Notice in a store, for example, how a child will complain to the mother, and the mother will then turn and complain to the father; or at work the way the director's urgency over some matter will trickle down through the supervisor to the staff; or even at home when your spouse lectures or your child whines to you and you pass it along and do the same to someone else. Practice stopping the process.

SIX

Endings: Parting Is Such Sweet Sorrow

To terminate or not to terminate? Where to draw the line? When to say enough is enough?

When they stop bringing in problems? When the I.P. is no longer the I.P.? But what about the trouble the couple continues to have if they try to talk to each other for more than five minutes? What about the mother's occasional claim that the father drinks too much? Should you try and tackle that even though everything else seems to be going along okay? And what about the growing dependency that you sense the family has on you? How do you get them to see that they can really manage things on their own, without your cutting things off and having them back to ground zero in a week? No doubt about it, good endings, just like good beginnings and middles, require that special kind of clinical sensitivity.

Yeah, right. Half the families never make it beyond three sessions; before you ever get a chance to think about, let alone say out loud, any of your termination speech, they're long gone. They decide the fee is too high, or that the insurance won't cover your treatment after all, or that Medicaid won't reimburse, or that managed care has a five-session cap. Or the only one who ever makes it in is the mother, and she decides after a few weeks that she isn't going to give a damn if no one else in the family will. Or, to everyone's surprise, Sally's dad decided that she could come out and spend the whole summer with him, and she left town last Friday. Or after two sessions everyone in the family decides they're better — Bobby did go to school for a half-day last Monday and only had one fight, and besides, Dad's going to be out on a long truck haul and won't be back for three weeks; we'll give you a call when he gets back. So much for those penetrating, moving moments of human connection and contact. Reality, it seems, wins out over profundity every time.

But it's not always that way. There are times when endings do come in a planned way, when the word termination is actually spoken aloud and discussed, when the good ending not only brings a psychological closure to a good therapy, but completes a healing deep within. Even if the formal endings rarely come with the hug or pat on the shoulder in the doorway or the long slow walk down the office corridor for the last time, endings really are important enough that they should be part of your beginning, part of your assessment, part of your vision, and ideally, of the family's vision as well.

Endings should rarely be a surprise to you. Just as your own theory tells you about the beginning and middle stages, your own theory becomes the starting point for defining the endings as well. If, for example, you are doing brief therapy, or have a 10-session cap on treatment, the ending will be fairly clear. If you see your role as long-term consultant, giving families a boost up to get over the latest developmental hurdle, and then pulling back, waiting in the wings until the next cycle arises, you can share this vision with the family from the onset and map a course together. If therapy in your mind and values is a process of peeling away layers, going ever deeper into the family or individual's psyche, then what others might call an ending may for you only be a plateau of the middle. Whatever your theory may be, it establishes the parameters of the work.

As you begin to assess a particular family, these parameters will be fine-tuned even more. If a family is the kind that lives from one crisis to the next, you will probably be able to predict in advance that they'll be ready to leave when the current crisis is over. If they dropped out of past therapy when the therapy turned a corner toward the marital relationship, this again will be a time of anxiety and retreat, and you will need to decide in advance how you will handle it. If the family has a pattern of avoiding grief by finding reasons to get angry and prematurely breaking off relationships, you can anticipate this shift with you and be prepared to try and cut them off at the pass.

Neither should any of this be a surprise to the family. In good therapy the expected length of treatment should all be out in the open, all part of the therapeutic contract. If you work under a session limit because of your or the agency's approach, it's important to let the family know at the first session. This time limit will push them not only to work harder, but also help them sort through and narrow their focus to the most pressing problems. If, on the other hand, you only do long-term work (e.g., a year or more) clarifying this and the rationale for it (your belief in the need to resolve underlying past issues) will enable them to understand the process, pace, and focus, or to decide that this isn't what they want at all, and thereby avoid both of you becoming frustrated.

If your work is somewhere in the middle, varying from a few sessions to a few months depending upon the nature of the problem and the family, you may decide to say merely that, or simply tell the family how often the contract will be reviewed (e.g., taking a few minutes every five sessions or so to see if everything is on target). However you decide to handle the therapeutic time frame, let the family know what it is.

It's also valuable to talk to the family about termination as part and parcel of their other family patterns. If the parents in the Wilson family, for example, tend to cut off relationships when they don't get their way (pulling their child out of private school when their son isn't given the classes they think he should have, not talking to relatives who don't take their side in a dispute over a will), it would be opportune to point out in advance your concern that they may want to drop out of therapy if at some point you, too, don't seem to go along with what they want you to do. Similarly, in the Harris family, George, the father, may tend to pull away from everyone and retreat to his workshop whenever conflict arises at home. Highlighting this pattern and expressing your fear that he will stop coming to therapy if the sessions seem too volatile makes his cutoff more transparent and less likely to happen.

By labeling for the family the ways they may be tempted to use premature endings to help them cope with difficult, but potentially rewarding, opportunities for growth, their retreat, if and when it comes, loses some of its seductive and automatic quality. By your discussing their pattern of termination well in advance, your confrontating them about the process becomes less of a personal attack and more of a challenge.

Mapping these time frames and patterns isn't any guarantee, however, that it all will turn out the way you think it should. With some families there seems to be a running struggle over who pulls the plug and when. Even though Mary, for example, is no longer hanging out with that 20-year-old biker, you think it would be good for the parents to iron out some unresolved divorce issues if they are to keep the same problems from coming up with the younger children; they, however, are ready to quit. Even though Bill and Helen are talking and making decisions better, Bill's underlying depression, you feel, still keeps the relationship from becoming more intimate, yet both of them feel that all is fine.

How much of this is client resistance to treatment, therapist resistance to ending, or a power struggle over who runs the show depends again upon your theory, your view of the problem and the scope of therapy. Your task, and the limits of your power, lie in making the family aware of your perspective, the clinical options you see, the rationale, and the possible consequences of each option. The contract, in order to remain viable, continually needs to be clarified and renegotiated, with the endpoints clear.

QUITTING TIME

No matter how and where you envision the end, and how open the family is to discussing it, there are plenty of signs to tell you when a family is ready to quit. One of the best, of course, is that everything is better. The presenting problem is resolved, as are the underlying reasons for it. There is a noticeable relaxation, even boredom in the sessions—that edgy overreaction and crisis mentality have dissipated, conversations fall to small talk, clients start forgetting some of their appointments or find reasons to spread them out, and you find yourself wondering what you should do next. The sense of purpose and direction seem unclear.

What you do next is say what you have been thinking and feeling—that things are better and have been steady for awhile, and that you're wondering what they want to do. Generally at this point the family members start nodding their heads and give a sigh of relief because they finally have permission to say what they have been also thinking for the past month. Once you broach the subject of termination they're ready to make a beeline for the door.

If you put this discussion off too long, however, if you don't say what you both are thinking, some families will just drop out. Even though they're doing better, they don't necessarily have the courage to tell you they want to leave—they're not sure how you would react, they have too many unclear mixed feelings about it themselves. Rather than plow through all this, it's easier for them to simply stop coming. In fact, if you were never to follow up, many families would never contact you at all again. The longer the time, the greater the awkwardness and anxiety. Three years later you'll meet them in the checkout line at Food Giant, and if they don't look away or head for a different aisle, they'll casually mention how well everyone is doing.

Obviously, however, not all families leave because they're all better. Some are a little better or not much better at all, but problems on the job, financial pressures, or illness take over and push therapy to the bottom of their "To Do" list. Again, while this often can be a replication of a family's crisis mentality and difficulty with setting priorities, it also can be a realistic response to the events in their life. The loss of a job, a serious illness, the sudden death of a parent—all life transitions that may possibly benefit from the therapy support—are so overwhelming and emotionally demanding that they monopolize the family's energy and resources and make other obligations, like therapy, feel like additional burdens. While some families will describe all this to you in the last session, others may only leave several garbled messages with the receptionist saying they will call back and never do, or they will begin to miss appointments and eventually drop out of sight.

Finally, there are those who are ready to end because things as they see it aren't better, or may be even worse than when they first started — Vinny was having some trouble going to school, but now Andrea is talking about how depressed she is and the parents are fighting like never before. They may be angry at you for stirring up trouble, or feel invaded by your seemingly constant prodding. Or they have already spent 500 dollars and you're still asking questions and giving them no advice. A few might be angry enough to tell you how they feel, but most will just call up and cancel because of car trouble. They never call back.

Sometimes you have to agree with them. The therapy hasn't been going well, and you were hoping to pull it out in that next session when Grandma and Grandpa show up and talk about their own marital woes, or after you got the results of the psychological testing on Vinny. Other times the problem is one of expectations or timing. Somehow their vision of the process and your own were never clarified or reconciled. They expected you to see Vinny by himself and fix his head in two sessions, and here you are bringing in everybody and asking a lot of stupid questions about their childhoods or how they feel after a fight. Or perhaps you spent three sessions doing an assessment, and on the fourth you're turning up the heat on Mom and pushing her to make decisions when she's never done that before. Their anxiety goes through the roof, they don't understand the rationale for it all, and they decide to leave their trauma making to home.

It's hard not to feel angry with yourself if a family pulls out after a bad session; it's even harder when you thought things were going fine. The therapy may have been more important to you than to them, or in spite of gains they still felt that they weren't getting what they wanted. Feeling rejected as a clinician is no small thing, especially if your self-confidence is shaky or if a lot of your own identity is caught up in your work and how well you do it.

It's unrealistic to expect there to be a balance in the therapeutic relationship always. There will be some families that you like more than others, or even whom you like more than they seem to like you, and their leaving stirs up all those little-kid feelings of being bad, wanting a second chance, making things right. There's the urge to call them up, see what's wrong, have a chance to explain what you did, what you meant, to encourage them to come back.

At first glance these thoughts and fantasies may not seem to you like bad ideas, and on some level they aren't, but they're amplified by your own countertransference feelings of loss. It's best to sort this all out with your supervisor first, to separate out your sense of rejection and loss from the family's clinical needs. If this seems to be happening frequently, if it becomes clear that your need for the family is compromising your ability to do your work effectively, some therapy for yourself may be in order.

So what do you do if they drop out? Mail them another appointment card, call them up, track them down and bang on their door, leave them alone? How you respond depends upon your own individual style and relationship with the family. Some therapists like to call and some families don't mind this at all; the connection by human voice, the ability to talk and listen becomes not only a good way of reaching out to the family, but, if need be, reaching a more personal closure. Other families feel this is invasive; your calling feels to them like you're checking up on them, tracking them down, putting them on the spot; it only encourages them to make up all kinds of transparent excuses and promises that they'll come in next time. It's an individual decision. Only you know how a particular family would respond to your calling, only you know how comfortable you would feel doing so.

The middle ground between calling and waiting for them to call is to write a letter after the family has missed appointments or seems to have dropped out. While writing lacks the intimacy of voice contact, it can still be an intimate form of communication that avoids the feeling of invasion or being put on the spot. The client can read the letter at his or her leisure, or reread it if anything is unclear. The note can be simple and matter of fact—"Sorry you couldn't make our last appointment; give me a call so we can schedule another"—or more descriptive and therapeutic—"I've wondered if you feel that the therapy hasn't been helping as much as you hoped it would. Perhaps it would be worthwhile for us to talk about this, to help me understand better what you're needing, and for me to better explain what I'm thinking."

It's important on your part to say as much and as sensitively as possible what you think the client might be feeling and thinking and what you would like to do. In effect, you are providing in written form your half of the dialogue that would ideally happen if the client came in to the office. Give the client a few weeks to respond. If you haven't heard, follow up with whatever your normal procedure is (e.g., simply close the case, send a letter telling the family that you are closing their case, and the like).

FIFTY WAYS TO LEAVE YOUR FAMILY

Of course, there are times when you're the one who wants to terminate. You feel like they're not getting anywhere or your supervisor tells you the waiting list is three miles long and you need to get rid of some old, longtime cases to make room for the new. Perhaps they never really follow through with your suggestions, or the people have rubbed you the wrong way since you first met them in the waiting room, or the couple is going to court over a custody battle and you can not only see a subpoena and ugly battle with you in the middle coming down the pike, but the sheer waste of hours of your time spent waiting in a courtroom.

And so you literally jump for joy when it snows or they call up to cancel because of a dead battery; you put off returning their phone calls, or call back, let the phone ring once and hang up; you find yourself sending follow-up letters with the wrong zip code, or you seem a little bit too enthusiastic when they suggest having the school psychologist work with Susie at school instead of spending the money to see you. Short of paying them not to come back, or quitting your job and leaving town, you'll do just about anything not have to go on.

Countertransference raises its head. It demands some thinking and reflection on your part, alone and with your supervisor, especially if this is part of a larger pattern for you. What you do with it depends on your theory. You may decide that you need to work it out in your own therapy while you continue to see the family, and that with enough supervisory support you can work through it with them; you may think it's simply a matter of personality clash (you can't like all the people all the time); or you may feel that it interferes with your ability to work with them, and that you need to pull out.

Whatever you decide, it's best to be honest with the family. If you decide to terminate, this can be particularly awkward. How do you tell a family that you don't want to see them anymore? While it's tempting to take the cowardly approaches listed above and attempt to drive them away with your neglect, or worse perhaps, rationalize to you and them that they really don't need to come anymore, it's dishonest and destructive. Instead, you need to use all your good communication skills (the "I" statements; talking about yourself, not them; talking about feelings, rather than facts)—you take responsibility, you say that the problem is yours (if you believe it is), you say that it's affecting your ability to help them and you have some other options for them; in short, you just honestly tell them. And then you listen, and make sure that they don't blame themselves or misunderstand and think that they need to try harder, and offer to talk some more about it if necessary.

Sometimes, of course, you really do need to leave, not just the family but the work—you're quitting your job, you've been fired (no, not really), it's the end of your internship, you're going back to school to study 13th-century English literature or septic tank repair, you're moving to Oklahoma. These are easier to explain, but often only a bit less awkward. The family feels abandoned, and all their little-kid feelings of being bad or old memories of grief are stirred up. You need to give the family as much notice as possible, help the family members sort through these feelings, give them permission to get angry at you for pulling out, or angry at you for having the flexibility to do with your life what they feel they cannot. When handled well, these kinds of leavings can be invaluable experiences for mending old wounds.

Finally, there are times you need to leave the family, or, rather, have the family leave you, for clinical reasons rather than personal ones. After a few sessions you realize that the problem is more complex than you thought—the 14-year-old is bulimic or the mother shows signs of multiple personality—and you lack the skills or the backup to handle it on your own.

Or perhaps you see that it is clinically better to farm out part or all of the treatment for now. The father needs inpatient drug treatment before any progress can be made in family therapy; the mother needs social services in order to get environmentally stable before any therapy can be effective; the son is becoming psychotic and needs hospitalization for evaluation, medication, and stabilization; the family is too chaotic to effectively use or even get into outpatient services, so they need home-based work for a few months in order to settle down and then transfer back in. Your role changes from a family therapist to a referral source, from seeing everyone to seeing only the remaining few.

As with the other forms of ending, transfers, too, can stir up old childhood feelings of abandonment. When one person is farmed out—the father will be in inpatient treatment but the family will continue to meet—it not only unbalances the family process and creates a loss for those continuing, but the person leaving feels like the child sent off to foster care. If the focus simply shifts—if, for example, after seeing the entire family a few times you decide you need to do play therapy with four-year-old Mary—not only is the notion of the I.P. more ingrained, but the other children may particularly feel excluded and abandoned.

Again, the approach to all this is one of honesty, of open discussion, of your speaking about and raising questions about all the normal feelings that come with such change. The family needs to know the why, the how, as clearly as possible. The more they have invested in the process and the relationship, the more important it all is.

If an actual transfer is to be made, to another therapist, to a hospital, or the like, it's valuable to go personally to ease the transition. This "turning over" eases the change for the family, gives you a chance to describe in front of the family member your summary of the work and the problem, or gives the client the opportunity to sort through his or her feelings and describe your relationship and work together to the new clinician. This process not only provides some closure, but helps the new person be aware of and sensitive to the loss issues that may arise as he or she begins.

GOOD ENDINGS

Regardless of the circumstances, what you are always shooting for are good terminations. They are like any other good death—they leave enough time and space around them for everything that needs to get done and said to actually get done and said. Their basic elements include everything you've read about in all those textbooks: Give the family notice; set an ending date; explore the feelings about the leaving; expect testing, crises, and everything to seem to fall apart, or, better yet, predict the crises for them so they realize that it is all part of the ending process; and review all the skills learned and progress made. Help the family see that their own feelings of loss and abandonment don't take away from their ability to go it on their own.

There are two basic ending formats that most clinicians use. One is the "do it and leave"—setting a date several weeks or months in the future, meeting at the same regular pace (weekly, biweekly), and sticking with it no matter what. Usually the date is negotiated with the family and may be built around another convenient marker, such as a summer vacation or the start of the school year. The other is the "fade away," the spacing out of sessions over a longer period of time—weekly, then monthly for a couple of months, then again in three months, then in six months if it is needed.

What you choose depends upon your own preference and the needs of the family. The "do it and leave" format has a counting-down effect that's more clear and definitive for the family, but can raise anxiety, which in turn promotes crises as the count gets shorter. The "fade away" format reduces some of the anxiety by giving the family an opportunity to see for themselves that they can really handle things on their own. But it also gives the impression that the ending is less defined, making it easier for them to push it away, to pretend that it's never going to happen. It also may stretch things out so long that other developmental life events may pop up ("Would you believe it, Jane just got pregnant!"), fueling the need to continue monitoring, or to crank treatment back up. Oftentimes the family can be given a choice, and the clinician only needs to enforce it.

Of course, enforcement can sometimes seem difficult when the termination crises start to mount. The best approach is a matter-of-fact one, reassuring the family that they know what to do, helping them think through the problem if necessary, intervening in as minimal a way as possible, interpreting the crisis in light of the upcoming termination. Generally, if things are handled in this way the first couple of times, the crises will rapidly diminish.

This doesn't mean that you may not have doubts—maybe they need more time, more support; maybe I'm throwing them out the door and they're not ready. Maybe you're right, but maybe it's your own separation anxiety, your own loss, your own sense of inflated importance. Talk it over with your supervisor, a colleague whose opinion you trust. Take the time to separate out your reactions from theirs.

It's often good to have some form of a closing ritual. This is especially true for families with whom you have worked intensely—home-based cases, cases you've seen for a long period of time—or where there are young children who are not fully understanding the ending process. Drawing a picture all together, doing a formalized recitation of the changes each has made, sharing a meal (this is easy and usually quite appropriate with home-based work), doing a closing experiential exercise (a guided fantasy about the future or about giving each other symbolic gifts), all have a way of bringing together and acknowledging the mixture of emotions that endings entail.

As you have done all along, you once again set the pace, model the way to do it. You're the one who needs to talk about the mixed feelings that both you and they have. You're the one who keeps everyone and everything on task so that distractions don't derail this part of the process any more than any of the others. You're the one who with honesty and caring shows the family how people can leave and continue with their lives.

The door is always left open, not for continued crises, but for another round of work, for problem solving, or for a quick consultation as the family moves through new stages of development and old issues once again raise their head. Some families, of course, never return; others make the out-of-the-blue phone call on some Thursday afternoon asking the out-of-the-blue question, sometimes seeking useful information, sometimes just seeing if you're still there; some come back a year or two or five later for a few sessions or a few months. And once again you start, hoping to pick up where you both left off, but not surprisingly finding out that you both have changed. A new beginning with new expectations.

Again, the reality of practice makes these good endings rarer than they should be, but when they are good they are invaluable for what they offer: the sense of groundedness, completion, and definitiveness. At that last session there's that wonderful sigh and sense that something important has happened here.

We have finished our trilogy of the beginning, middle, and ends, having tried to cover all the basic parameters of family therapy practice. We're now ready to look at family therapy with specific cases over the course of the developmental cycle.

LOOKING WITHIN

1. Take a few moments and think back over endings in your own life, those clearly marked—the graduation from high school or college, your marriage or divorce, the death of a parent—or those numerous unmarked ones—the way you and your childhood best friend just drifted away, the gradual ending to your relationship with an old boyfriend or girlfriend, the way your father one day called you up for your advice.

Try to remember how you felt, the feelings that led you to the ending, the way you handled those emotions, how free you felt showing them to others, how you behaviorally coped in the days and months that followed. See if any of those patterns affect your expectations of termination with clients, or affect your own emotional bottom lines in your work.

2. As you did with middles, take the time to think about your notion of termination, your role, your stopping point according to your theory. Are there times when termination has more met your needs than those of the family? How can you increase your awareness of these countertransference reactions when they come up in your work?

3. How do you personally handle rejection? For what types of families or under what circumstances would clients' leaving be particularly hurtful? Imagine talking to one such family, saying how, why, you felt the way you did. What personal issues, if any, does this stir up for you?

4. Take the time to think once again about your own needs in doing family therapy, your own issues of loss and separation that may affect your practice, your own ways of avoiding families you do not like.

5. What kind of cases and problems would you automatically consider transferring out because you feel your skills and knowledge are limited? How could you increase those skills?

6. Develop termination rituals that reflect your own personality.

SEVEN

Billy's Got a Problem:
Kids in the Family

Billy sits quietly, scanning the toys on the shelf, his arm tucked under the arm of his grandmother, as she describes why they've come to see you. Billy has been with her now for about two months, says Ms. Williams, and she is having a hard time getting him to do what she asks. She always feels like he's pushing her; she thrusts out her big hand to emphasize how she feels. More often than not he'll throw a fit if he doesn't get his own way and, she admits somewhat sheepishly, she sometimes gives in just to settle him down. But settling down isn't what he does too often; he's always doing something. In fact, the only time he's quiet is when he's sitting in front of the TV or sleeping. He's doing well in school, though. No problems there; he likes it, has friends, and seems smart. The grandmother turns her head and smiles at Billy. She looks exhausted.

It's hard for you to imagine so much energy coming from such a little boy. Although he's seven years old, Billy looks five; he's so short and skinny. His eyes are clear and bright, but he avoids eye contact with you. He's seems a little bored, a little scared.

Billy came to his grandmother's home following a three-month stay in a foster home. He had been living with his mother and her boyfriend and his three-year-old half brother until one night the boyfriend beat the brother to death. Although Billy was home at the time, it's unclear how much he saw. His mother told him that his brother had choked to death on a toy. The boyfriend was arrested and convicted of murder and is now serving 15 years in prison. Although she was there when it happened, Billy's mother was not charged. Billy, however, was removed from the home. The mother continues to live in the same town she had been, some 200 miles away, and hasn't seen Billy for five months. Ms. Williams is angry at Billy's mother and his father, her son Edward, for ignoring Billy. She's worried about the effects of the death on him, worried about his reluctance to talk about it.

Living with the grandmother are her husband, Ray, who, like her, is in his late 50s, and her middle son, John, who is in his late 20s, recently divorced and the father of a three-year-old son whom he rarely sees. Grandmother's youngest son, Ben, is stationed in Thailand in the Air Force. In addition to caring for all these men she also looks after her own elderly parents and runs errands for them daily. No wonder she looks exhausted.

The start of each new case is like standing at the edge of a dense forest. More often than not, all we see before us is the faint markings of a path going into the trees. As we take the first steps into the wood, gather our impressions and begin to organize them around the client's personality and motivation, our theory, personality, priorities, and interests, we discover that the forest is actually crisscrossed with numerous paths. While we usually assume that there is only one path that takes us where we want to go, we see that there are, in fact, several.

Together with the family we make choices, trusting our intuitions or values, following the most pressing needs, closing off one treatment option, trying another, coming back to the first, trying still a third. While our knowledge and experience can give us some idea of what we may expect, it's only by actually working with the family over time, seeing the consequences of our choices, setting and resetting our priorities based upon environmental and psychological changes that we can actually know how close we are to coming out on the other side.

In this chapter we will be following the story of Billy as it actually unfolded in the course of his therapy with me. As we reach decision points along the way, we'll stop to consider some of the options that were available. As we do, consider how you might decide to proceed in a similar situation.

Start by taking a couple of minutes to develop your own impressions so far. If you were seeing this family, what, according to your own theory, would you want to know? What is your tentative hypothesis about the cause of Billy's misbehavior, his tantrums, his high activity, and the ways this family may need to change? What's missing in the process, in the family system? Where would you focus first? How would you like to make contact with Billy? How do you envision the course of therapy?

Okay, time's up. Here's a short list of brainstorm ideas:

Presenting problem. Billy's testing limits at home, and his grandmother is having difficulty managing his behavior. She's also concerned about Billy's reaction to his loss and trauma.

Possible family concerns. It's unclear so far why Ms. Williams has difficulty setting limits with Billy—does she lack the parenting skills and knowledge or does she struggle with her own feelings of anxiety or guilt?

What about her high level of stress and possible depression? Can her husband, Ray, and her son John provide support, help with parenting, be more involved with Billy?

And what about Billy's role in the family structure—is he a scapegoat, a vicarious expression of anger for other members of the family? What is the marital relationship like? How has John coped with his own sense of loss surrounding his divorce and his son, and what impact has that had on the family?

Possible concerns for Billy. Obviously he's struggling with grief: the loss of mother, father, brother. He may feel guilty about his brother's death, the boyfriend's imprisonment, feel responsible for his parent's abandoning of him. He may be suffering not only from posttraumatic stress from his brother's death, but other violence toward mother and him that we, as yet, don't know about. Is he identifying with the aggressive boyfriend or does his behavior reflect normal testing of limits in a home with new rules and structure? Is he clearly depressed, or does he have attention deficit disorder?

Strengths. Billy's grandmother clearly cares and seems committed to him. The home environment, although stressful, overall seems stable. Ms. Williams is willing to seek professional help. Billy, in spite of all the trauma and change, is doing well; he's not severely depressed, destructive, or oppositional. He can make friends, does well in the school structure, and must be fairly bright.

Therapeutic options. Options include family therapy with grandmother, grandfather, Billy, and John to improve communication, define clear rules and roles, reduce stress, strengthen the hierarchy, explore loss, develop support and nurturance for each of them. What about including Billy's mother and father in the family therapy to focus on loss, roles, support, coparenting? Working with Ms. Williams on parenting skills alone or together with her husband in order to help them manage Billy?

Perhaps supportive individual therapy with Ms. Williams would help her to reduce her stress and to be better able to act with Billy more consistently. Psychological testing for Billy could be considered; it may serve as a quick way of assessing his personality and coping skills and isolating underlying emotional conflicts. Individual play therapy with Billy will help him work through his past trauma and grief, provide ongoing support, help him learn better ways of coping with his emotions, provide him with a positive male role model to offset the negative ones he has seen. Maybe some combination of all of the above.

Therapeutic don'ts. Don't want to replicate in any way the abuse or abandonment. Don't want to overwhelm or abuse grandmother.

Therapeutic dangers. Feeling angry or frustrated with Billy or his grandmother. Feeling overwhelmed or wanting to quit case. Taking over-responsibility for the family.

These last two points need some explanation. Most families have a way of pulling us in either to make up for their unproductive ways, thereby stirring our own countertransference responses, or to replicate them, and, in the language of Minuchin and structural family therapy, inducting us into their system. Just as it's valuable to brainstorm all that we can do with a family, it's just as valuable to be consciously aware from the beginning of all that we shouldn't do and to remain alert to our becoming emotionally snarled within the system.

With Billy, for example (or any client, for that matter), we clearly know from the first session that we don't want to be aggressive, emotionally or physically, like the boyfriend was, nor do we want to abandon him as his parents did. Similarly, we want to be careful that we don't do anything to perpetuate his grandmother's feelings of being overwhelmed or abused by pushing her too hard, nor to replicate her behavior and be inconsistent or unstructured in our approach; this will only further confuse her and leave her more inconsistent than she already is. The presenting problems and symptoms become broad working metaphors that can tell what to avoid and where to be careful in our approach.

But knowing what to avoid is only part of helping the family. The other part is knowing the emotional dangers inherent in the specific family's dynamics. At the outset, for example, it might be easy for us to think of Billy's parents as heartless and be unable to imagine our doing anything remotely similar to what they did. But stepping back and looking at the case more realistically, we need to acknowledge that there may be something about Billy and these circumstances that might make us at some later point, too, feel frustrated and enraged; that there is the danger that the family dynamics may be replicated and that we, too, may feel like the boyfriend and want to clobber him; that we may get demanding or invasive or insensitive to endings or breaks in contact. We may find reasons to send him off for individual therapy, or decide that the case and family is simply unworkable.

Similarly, there is the danger that we may end up feeling like the grandmother, overwhelmed and willing to give in, or feeling that we have to do it all on our own, and become rescuing, overresponsible, and exhausted. If we aren't careful we may take on one of the other family roles — John's or the grandfather's ambivalence or passivity, perhaps.

By acknowledging the therapeutic dangers inherent in a particular case we are acknowledging the well-entrenched family and individual dynamics that pull at us like an undertow toward the replication of the family's problems, behavior, and emotions. Only by looking out for them, only by looking in and sensing when we are becoming emotionally en-snarled, can we step back and regroup.

Again, at this point, we don't know how much of this will come to pass, and we need to assess Billy and his grandmother more. But through our brainstorming we have defined both our therapeutic possibilities and our limits. We have a clearer view of the therapeutic space we can work within.

THE WORLD OF CHILDREN

Some clinicians feel awkward about including children in family therapy. Two cultures, two different worlds—those of the children and those of adults—both need to be explored and understood, yet doing family therapy with them is difficult. Parents feel they have to be careful about what they say around the children; children, especially if they are young, often feel intimidated by the office, the questions, and the seriousness of all the talk that they don't understand. Like Billy, many children sense that they are in an adult place and grow quiet unless welcomed in some way. How you bring together these different worlds once again depends upon your theory and style. Once again, there are many paths from which to choose.

Some clinicians prefer to see the parents alone first. This gives them a chance to gather background information about the problem, the child, the marriage without the child distracting or the parents feeling inhibit-ed. This adults-only meeting also binds the clinician to the parents more firmly, suggesting from the start a partnership among the adults. At the end of this session, the clinician can then decide whether to see the identi-fied child or the rest of the family, or perhaps even continue working with the parents themselves, either to focus on their relationship or to help them change their parenting style and become change agents themselves in the home.

The disadvantage of this format is the awkwardness of bringing in the children later. While this is generally not a problem with young chil-dren, and may even make it easier for them since they sense that the par-ents are comfortable with you, preteens or adolescents often feel mistrustful and worry that unfair things have been said about them behind their back (and often they have). While you can handle this straightforwardly and show your openness and sensitivity by simply asking them how they feel about missing the first appointment, you may have to work a little harder to gain their trust.

The classic family therapy approach, of course, is to see everybody in the family together for the first session. The therapeutic rationale is that you will be able to see all the interactional patterns and roles at one time, to shift the focus away from the I.P., to reinforce the notion that it is a family problem, a product of interaction rather than any one bad guy. Often a more pragmatic reason is simply to make coming to the appointment easier; child care is or can be difficult to arrange, particularly for single parents, and it's more efficient to drag everybody in at one time. Whatever the reason, whole family sessions can be both powerful and overwhelming. If you feel overloaded by too many people in the room at first, you can break it down into more manageable pieces or draft a cotherapist.

There are a couple of keys to feeling comfortable with a whole group. One is to keep in mind that you don't have to talk to the entire group all the time. You can talk to one person at a time, asking questions to gather the information that you need. If you allow everyone to have his or her say, and if each person feels that you understand, the family will calm down.

Second, ask them to talk to each other in productive ways that you direct—"Mary, try telling your sister what hurt your feelings, rather than calling her names"; "Dad, tell Susan how you feel right now"; "Tommy, tell your mother why you think her rule is unfair"—and just keep everyone else from butting in. Rather than being controlled by their impulse to argue with each other, the family members will quickly learn other ways of expressing these feelings; by discussing problems and emotions with each other right there in the session, they'll be doing more of the work, and you'll feel less stage fright and pressure to fix everything.

Finally, remember once again to be easy on yourself. Your first couple of whole family sessions will seem the most difficult. After that it will all be downhill and with continued practice will seem easier and easier. If you feel stuck, remember to go back to your basics. Above all, be honest.

The middle ground between adults-only sessions and whole family sessions is the format of Billy and his grandmother—the I.P. and one or both parents. Here you initially see those involved with the problem, and then sort out later who else to bring in or split up. The advantage of this format is that it is easier to manage, and although not all the interactional patterns are apparent, you're able to nail down those surrounding the parent–child interaction.

Whatever format you choose, even individual work with one parent, you are, of course, still doing family therapy if you're thinking systematically, that is, in terms of the interactional patterns that characterize family relationships. Calling yourself a family therapist isn't restricted to those who pile 15 people in a room at one time.

While any of these formats can help you place the child and problem in the context of the family, the problem usually remains, especially with young children, of how to more fully assess the child, how to enter his or her world when he or she may be overshadowed by the presence of parents or doesn't fully understand all the verbiage that's being tossed around. Some individual assessment is usually in order.

It's generally best to start your relationship with young children by seeing them together with their parents. Have the parents describe why they came, clarify your role with the child, and get enough background to know what you want to explore with the child individually. As you talk together with the parent and child, the child will come to feel more comfortable with you, will get used to the sound of your voice, and will learn from the parents that you are a safe person. Then when you ask the parent to leave, the child will be less anxious and feel more comfortable staying with you.

If, however, the child squawks at the idea of being alone with you or throws him- or herself around the mother's ankle as she makes for the door, don't force it; therapy needn't be a traumatic experience. Let the parents stay for awhile when you begin to play with the child.

WORKING WITH PLAY

If fitting children into the family therapy process seems hard for some clinicians, the notion of play can seem even harder. Some simply don't feel comfortable with play; they prefer words rather than crayons or blocks, the direct approach of problem solving rather than the symbolic world of puppet stories or fantastical worlds within sand trays. Others just don't feel comfortable around children as people and will choose either not to treat them at all, or to work through the parents. Still for others the problem with play therapy isn't one of discomfort, but skill and experience—they simply don't know enough about doing play therapy or aren't convinced of its effectiveness.

Just as it's important to be aware of your own theory and values regarding your approach to families, it's important to be clear about your own approach to children. How do you feel about play therapy? Do you see it as a tool for assessment, treatment, or both? Can play be a healing process in itself or is it more effective as a backdrop for talk therapy? When is it better to do individual play therapy than work with the parents or the child together with the parents? When is play therapy contraindicated? What do you personally like and dislike about doing it?

In order to feel comfortable with play therapy it's often helpful to think of it in relation to adult therapy. Play is for children what words are for adults, namely, a medium of expression. Because children lack the vocabulary of an adult, because their brains physically aren't developed enough to create the concepts and analogies that the adult mind can, words are only flimsily attached to thoughts and emotions. Play becomes the child's vocabulary and the entrance into his or her world. Just as the adult expresses him- or herself through fantasies ("If I would only win the lottery"), wishes ("I wish I didn't have to travel so far to work"), images ("I could see myself just wringing his neck"), the child does so through play. The family who lives in the dollhouse always fights, and here comes the policeman to tell them to stop; the lion puppet tries to eat the mouse puppet and the mouse runs and gets help from the zebra; the clay turns into a snake that slithers along around the outside of the bedroom and scares the little girl; the picture of the family leaves out the little brother, and the little boy is a tiny speck squashed between the two angry parents.

Here are the child's needs and conflicts expressed just as clearly, though more symbolically perhaps, as those of Emily who's having a running battle at her office with her boss. And so while Emily complains about the way her boss screwed her once again, five-year-old Jamie, sounding just like her mother, yells at the doll for not going to bed. By asking Jamie why she is so mad or by pretending that you're her little girl who wants to stay up just a little longer, you're working within her medium, just as you are by asking Emily why she feels like her boss is being so tough on her or what she thinks she can do about it.

What do you need to do play therapy? Not much. Crayons, paints, drawing paper, clay. Some blocks, a dollhouse, people figures to live in the house, some cars, trucks, an ambulance perhaps. Puppets, animal figures, toy soldiers, some Legos. Board games—for younger children, Uno, Candy Land, Chutes and Ladders; for older ones, checkers, Battleship, Risk, Sorry. Or check out the host of psychological games available on anger control, divorce, problem solving, and simple communication. Get a deck of cards, or hook up a mini-basketball net over your door and use a Nerf ball for the basketball. Most of what you need to get started can be found in discount stores or obtained from garage sales or friends whose kids have outgrown their toys. Set them out in your office where the children can see them and choose them.

Apart from the theory and techniques of play as a medium are the practical questions that you need to consider with each individual family. Will this family, for example, support the play therapy process; that is, do they see it as an appropriate way to help their child and spend their money? Is there any danger of the child's I.P. status being reinforced through individual focus? Are you and is the family willing to give you and the child the time you both may need to engage in what may be a slower process? Is the child motivated to do play therapy?

If you are a play therapy purist, if you see it as a self-sufficient form of treatment for children this last question may seem foolish. After all, there is no right way to play in play therapy, just as there is no right way to talk in adult therapy. Even if the child refuses to play or plays in a seem-

ingly closed and unproductive way (e.g., plays checkers for the whole session for 20 weeks), this in itself is part of the process; it tells you something about the child's ability to relate to adults or follow rules, approach
emotions or manage anger, compete against others or be assertive. It's
all grist for the mill, just as it is for adults who remain mostly silent or
only occasionally grunt.

All this is true, but beneath the question is the issue of the child's
expectations and use of the therapy process, the notion that some children, just as some adults, use one form of therapy more effectively than
another. Some children, for example (especially starting at age 10 or 11
on up), see any form of play as too babyish, and would much prefer to
talk, or at best use some structured play (e.g., board games, cards) as a
background activity, a way of containing their anxiety while they answer
questions or initiate conversation. Others do not want to play so much
as hear their parents talk and have their questions answered, or with your
support, get things off their chests and solve problems at home or school.
Still others are so reluctant or anxious about seeing you that the most effective and efficient course may be to work with the parents and effect
changes at home through them.

What you actually wind up doing with children then is, as with adults,
a blending of your medium and theirs, your needs and style with theirs,
a mix of the ideal and pragmatic, fine-tuned for each case. With one particular case you may decide to use play therapy only as an assessment tool
before moving into family therapy or parenting work. The play becomes
a way of gathering information about the child that can then be passed
on to the parents to help them view their child in a different light, or to
help you develop behavioral strategies that the parents can implement at
home. If, for example, it becomes clear through play that Bobby is worried about his parents divorcing, feels that he has to take care of his
depressed father, or feels guilty about his younger sister's cerebral palsy,
this information can help the parents be more supportive of Bobby or moti-
vate them to talk to him about what has happened.

In another case it may be clear to you that play therapy may be the
best not only for assessment but for treatment as well. Only through the
play process may the child be able to express many of the emotions that
cannot be talked about directly—Todd expresses his anger at his father by
drawing a picture of him and then scribbling over and over it with a black
crayon. Or what you do together doesn't really matter—playing rummy
this week, drawing pictures next week—only by playing together with you
may the therapeutic relationship become the support that allows the child
to talk about his or her fears and worries. As the child becomes less anxious, more open, you may decide to intersperse total family sessions, involve other siblings in the play process, or work concurrently with the
parents.

It's important to remember that the therapeutic contract is not only between you and the child, it's also between you and the parents. How you ultimately choose to work must reflect the parent's concerns and priorities as well. If, for example, they are particularly disturbed by the behavior of one of the children, spending a few sessions in the beginning in individual play therapy with that child, rather than pushing for family therapy, not only builds your own rapport with the child, but addresses the parents' immediate concerns, and gives you a stronger basis for recommending family therapy when you do; after all, you have "evaluated" the child, and have your own sense of what the child needs most. If, on the other hand, the family is in crisis, initial time may need to be spent in total family sessions, putting out the emotional fires at home before you can shift toward individual work with the child.

The bottom line here is that play therapy with children is another approach, another modality that you can flexibly integrate into your family therapy models and adapt to the needs of a particular child and family. How you do this will depend upon your own clinical and personal strengths and style and values.

BREAKING GROUND:
FIRST SESSIONS WITH THE CHILD

When a child is quiet in the first session or two with parents, it's especially important to make the effort to connect with him or her. Because Billy was this way when I saw him together with his grandmother, I decided to meet with him for a few sessions alone to build rapport, find out better what he was like, and discover how he would use play therapy. Surprisingly, Billy was eager to be seen alone.

After glancing around the room, Billy made a beeline for the Legos. He matter-of-factly told me that he wanted to build one of the models pictured in the instructions. He could read well for his age, and had good spatial perception and coordination, that is, he could figure out what he needed to do much better than I could. He quickly began to gather the pieces he needed and enlisted my help in finding some of them, all with an air of seriousness and intensity. When I tried to ask him about his coming to the agency, about living with his grandmother, or about his father, or his mother, he would ignore the question, say he didn't want to talk about it, or say he didn't know. He kept all of his focus on the Legos and all of his communication limited to directing my help. At the end of the session, Billy hadn't finished his model, and he asked me to save it for next time. He wanted to know when he would be coming back.

The next several individual sessions weren't greatly different. Billy still talked little, though when asked he mentioned without much enthusiasm that he saw his father over one weekend, and described in a few sentences his school and teacher. When asked to draw his family he said that he didn't draw people well, and when asked to draw anything else he said he didn't like to draw much. He did play Candy Land and tried to cheat when it appeared he was going to lose. When I said that he wasn't following the rules he seemed upset and reluctantly gave in. In the second game Billy made up new rules as he went along so that it always worked to his advantage. Again, his mood was fairly solemn, but he mentioned several times that he liked to come and wanted to know when he was coming back. It was clear that he was becoming attached to me.

Impressions? What seems most striking is Billy's need for control of the session—directing me, controlling the conversation, controlling the outcome of games. What don't we see? What's missing? Obviously no strong emotions, like anger; no discussion about his past or the trauma; no aspect of his inner world, his fantasies; none of his misbehavior that his grandmother is reporting in the home. Billy wasn't replicating his problems in the office. Why? A quick attachment to this new adult, an adult male?

All this isn't surprising. Many children who have been traumatized have learned to cope by controlling themselves and others. They're both protecting themselves from other inner and outer dangerous emotions, and on some level replicating the control they experienced from powerful adults. Billy has learned that it's more important (and safer) to be in control than to be who he is. The only place he shows his emotions is at home with his grandmother.

Was Billy a good candidate for play therapy? The answer lies in your orientation. From a psychodynamic, more nondirective perspective, it's a ridiculous question. If the client shows up and sits in the chair, you are working in therapy even if the working is both of you slogging through all the defenses and layers of resistance. Billy was clearly showing up; in fact, he enjoyed coming and liked me. At a minimum the relationship had the potential to give him an opportunity to be with a man who isn't abusing or rejecting, offsetting the male images he has within him.

The better question, which a more directive therapist may ask, is whether Billy was using the play therapy process effectively. The answer would probably be no. Compared to children who start re-creating their inner and outer worlds from the get-go, Billy was not using the play as a medium for portraying his emotions and conflicts—instead, he was only showing his defenses. On the other hand, while he may have been closed off to his inner life, he was not resistant to the therapy process itself. Some children clearly don't want to be in the room, not because they are anxious about the process, but more because their parents made them come and they want no part of it. They refuse to play or do so passive–aggres-sively because they're angry. Billy was not like this. He was playing out his life; it was just going to take awhile to reach the deeper layers of it.

What would you do? Would you see him in play therapy, maybe have someone else see him individually, or stick to family or parenting work? It might be a good idea to see his grandmother before making any decision.

THE REST OF THE STORY: ASSESSING THE GRANDMOTHER

Ms. Williams comes in alone; her husband, Ray, is driving all over the state delivering supplies for a hardware store. Although it's just 11 in the morning, she already has that dog-tired look. After she got Billy off to school, she needed to stop by her parents' house to take them to the grocery store for a few things. After lunch she's going back to help her mother clean the house.

Ms. Williams talks easily. Billy seems to have settled down some in the past couple of weeks, but he still gives her a fit at times, especially in the past few days that Ray has been away. Although John, her son, is usually home in the late afternoon, he does little with Billy and does even less when she's having a hard time with him. She's not sure how much longer John will be staying with them; he keeps talking about moving out. She knows she ought to be more consistent with Billy, but his tantrums wear her out, and she starts feeling sorry for him. She finds herself mak-ing bargains with him all the time — bribing him with TV, treats from the store, desserts — if he'll clean up his room, finish his homework, not pester her in the grocery store. Sometimes it works, sometimes it doesn't.

Ms. Williams can easily talk about Billy's mother — about how she didn't like her from the start, how Billy's mother dumped Billy's father, Ms. Williams's son, for that lowlife who killed his own child. But she sounds more sad than angry. She has mixed feelings about her own son — maybe he's just having a hard time right now, maybe he will eventually take custody of Billy; five minutes later she says he really doesn't show any interest in the boy, and she just ought to realize that Billy will stay with her.

It's clear, however, that she's overwhelmed. She is the caretaker of her immediate family and her family of origin. There's a history of depres-sion in the family, and even though she shows no vegetative signs, it's hard not to believe that she gets pretty depressed at times. She clearly seems committed to Billy and overall is doing fairly well, especially considering the fact that she is doing it all alone.

When asked what she wants, Ms. Williams says she needs help learning to be more consistent. She feels that it's good for Billy to see someone himself; she is still very worried about the effects of his brother's murder on him. She doubts that Ray, her husband, will ever be able to come in and questions whether it would make any difference, since he is away from home so much.

Once again, impressions? An overworked grandmother with a good heart. A soft touch who has a hard time setting limits for both Billy and herself. She's motivated to work on her parenting, and that's certainly needed. She supports individual therapy for Billy, and it already seems to have a somewhat positive effect. What to do about her husband, Ray? Try to bring him in? Is it realistic if he really is away so much? What about her son John? If he is really going to move out, would it be better to help Ms. Williams be able to handle Billy on her own? Can she learn to set limits in other areas of her life, such as with her parents, and reduce her stress?

We are at the first fork on the path. What to do? In situations like this it's helpful to look first at what the family is willing to do and weigh that against the possible results of pushing them to do something different. My reasoning at the time was as follows: This family's motivation is for play therapy and individual help with parenting. Sessions with Billy and his grandmother at this stage wouldn't seem promising—we could imagine it turning into complaints of the week, a lot of questions, silence from Billy, and to him only a milder form of verbal abuse. As he feels more secure and settled and begins to open up more, this format may become a possibility.

What about play therapy with Billy? In spite of Billy's control in the sessions, they seem, from his grandmother's report, to have a positive effect on his behavior at home. This may have to do with the process and therapeutic relationship, Ms. Williams's own decrease in anxiety now that someone is there to help her or help Billy deal with his past, or both. In the long run, of course, the play could ideally become a flexible medium for unlocking emotions, and the consistency of a positive relationship may counter the negativity and loss of the past men in Billy's life.

But there are downsides to just doing individual play therapy. Rather than bringing in the grandmother and other parental figures in Billy's life and helping them learn to relate better to him, there's the danger that I, as the individual play therapist, will, in effect, displace them, making what's already occurring worse. Even if I decide to take this on, I need to be clear and certain about my commitment, especially if the process and progress will be slow. If I become too impatient I'll wind up replicating the problem and become another abandoning man in Billy's life.

Working with Ms. Williams alone may help her set the structure Billy needs, reduce her anxiety, and increase her self-confidence. But is focusing on her practical or foolhardy? Can she continue to carry the load of the families alone? Does she have another choice? How much will seeing her alone only maintain a potentially dysfunctional system?

Of course, these are not the only possibilities to consider; your theory may suggest other approaches. You may feel it is important to dig deeper into the historical roots, either through a Bowenian approach and examination of the family patterns, or through psychodynamic therapy with Ms. Williams in order to explore her own depression, past losses, or over-responsibility. What about a play therapy group or a battery of psychological testing for Billy, a parents' support group for Ms. Williams, or a psychiatric evaluation for her depression? How about moving the therapy into the home? A home-based therapist could see Billy and his grandmother there, where the problems are occurring; give Ms. Williams hands-on demonstrations of parenting skills; and perhaps have greater success in pulling in Billy's uncle or grandfather. All of these are possibilities.

As it turned out, what was finally decided on was the combination of individual play therapy with Billy and parenting education and support for Ms. Williams — a decision reflecting my own skills, interest, and orientations; the availability of services (e.g., home-based services had a huge waiting list); and the family's motivation and immediate needs. This decision was presented to both Billy and Ms. Williams, and everyone seemed satisfied.

MAKING PROGRESS?

For the next few months I saw Billy individually each week in play therapy, and saw his grandmother, either in individual sessions or for a few minutes about every other week at the start of Billy's session, to discuss parenting problems. Billy continued to need to control the session and would resist my suggestions to interest him in drawing, paints, storytelling, sand tray, clay, talking games, and other more expressive mediums.

Just as it's important to give adults a clear sense of the range of topics and forms that therapy may take, so is it important when working with children to help them see the range of what play therapy offers, and to find the medium that best suits the individual child. Some children, for example, love drawing or painting, but hate dollhouses or board games. Others don't seem to care what the activity is. Many active children like to play outside, others seem attracted to the containment or regularity that the office session provides. It's up to you to introduce the choices and help the child discover the forms that allow him or her to best express his or her inner self.

Billy rejected all these less structured forms because they created too much anxiety. He was able, however, to gradually express violent themes through playing with cars and trucks (creating gigantic crashes), toy soldiers where battles always ended with his army defeating mine, and — surprisingly — with wrestling.

Billy was a big fan of professional wrestling, and knew a lot about the different characters, their strengths, weaknesses, and, most importantly, whether they were "good guys" or "bad guys." In a typical session he would move the furniture in the room to the corners, assign me to be a particular "bad" wrestler — The Black Knight, Sergeant Destruction, Lowthar the Crusher — while he would always be Hulk Hogan or this week's world champion. Rules were set up (e.g., where the ropes were, whether it was a tag team, how you were pinned, how long the match was) and clarified at each session. Although Billy only weighed about 60 pounds, it was here that he became most animated, most aggressive, and where he always had to win. And he did; I made sure of it.

What's going on here? Is this therapeutic? Doesn't this rough play only replicate the physical aggression he had already seen? Certainly, and that was the therapeutic rationale for doing it. Through the wrestling matches Billy was able to play out the anger that was being bottled up or dumped on his grandmother. He also was fighting with a big strong adult man, on some level not much different from the one who terrorized him. But now he had the opportunity to win. In his imagination he became powerful and able to overcome his enemies, rather than a helpless victim. But with the outlet also came boundaries; the rules of the play and my clear restrictions on his aggression (you can't punch) taught Billy the beginnings of self-expression and self-control. Finally, this play provided Billy with a way of making physical contact with a man who, in reality, was not aggressive, but more nurturing. While he was pretending to pin me to the mat, he was, in actuality, getting hugged back.

And actually this all helped. Billy settled down more and more at home and, with support from me, Ms. Williams was able to set clearer limits. She used time-outs and the taking away of privileges, along with verbal positive reinforcement to shape Billy's behavior at home. Within five months the presenting problem — Billy's testing of limits at home — had waned considerably.

But not all the time. Here and there were periods of a week or two where things would slip at home — the grandmother was less consistent with the rules, the structure began to collapse, Billy started pushing, and the grandmother gave in, setting off a self-feeding cycle. From the grandmother's point of view it was Billy who started the backsliding process. For some reason he had a hard day or week and began to test her. From where I stood, it was Ms. Williams who actually started the cycle. Some additional outside stress would stretch her psychological resources, and she was unable to maintain her consistent focus on Billy.

Within the five months several environmental disruptions and emotional crises had occurred — Ray was unemployed for several weeks before he found another job, John was having problems with his ex-wife and getting depressed, and Ms. Williams was worried about her father, who was having pain in his hip and needed to go to the doctor. As the stress increased and Ms. Williams became more worried, upset, and depressed, she let things go, opening the door for Billy to return to his old behaviors, and thereby further increasing her own stress. As the problems were resolved, for example, when Ray found a job, the structure returned.

What sense do you make of this dynamic? It depends on how you think about it. Do the new parenting skills collapse in the face of stress because they are still fragile and not well integrated? Although she seems generally to keep it at bay, does Ms. Williams's chronic depression grind her to a halt when the stress is high enough? Is Billy simply overly sensitive to changes in his environment and his grandmother, or is he falling back on the skills and responses he had to learn to survive when he was with his mother? Does he become defiant as a way of getting his grandmother's attention when she seems preoccupied and he starts to feel abandoned? Perhaps Billy is trying to save his grandmother, pull her out of her depression by his negative behavior, replicating perhaps what he did with his own mother? Is he needed as a problem at these times because he also provides an outlet for his grandmother's or the family's frustration and anger? Has he learned to sacrifice himself as the scapegoat?

All of these are possible ways of looking at the pattern, and they're important only in the way they help you proceed. Once again, consider the options and your own inclinations. Would you support Ms. Williams in staying on track with the parenting, perhaps interpret to her Billy's behavior and role in the family based upon his past experience? Would you advise her about how to solve the problems at home or to recognize the limits of her own responsibility, offer support or specific skills (e.g., teach relaxation exercises) to help relieve her anxiety, refer her for medication? Would you bring in Ray or John, or both, to get to the source of the stress, and use the crisis as an opportunity to get them involved in the family therapy process? Would you do something different with Billy perhaps, increasing the frequency of his sessions, or working to help him express his anxiety verbally rather than behaviorally?

All of these are workable. You could try one of these, several of them, or something altogether different, or decide that these changes are, for right now at least, merely a blip and do nothing different at all.

I decided to do something else. In situations like this it's often useful to go back and look at what's working and to find ways to support those processes. Overall, the current approach of doing play therapy with Billy and focusing on parent education and support with Ms. Williams was creating stability at home and improvement in Billy's behavior. It didn't work when the stress became too great for Billy's grandmother. If there was a way of reducing her overall level of stress, then crises, when they arose, would debilitate her less, and, I reasoned, she would be able to continue to maintain the structure that Billy needed. Pulling in Ray or John, or helping Ms. Williams find ways to reduce the responsibilities she had with her parents all theoretically have the same impact, but, practically speaking, weren't in her view or mine at the time good options. Trying to make such changes would be enormously difficult (so who would help the parents?) and would undoubtedly create even more stress, only compounding the problem.

And so I supported her in maintaining the behavioral structure as much as possible (the redoing and reinforcing that is part of the middle stage), and emotionally by simply listening to her. I also arranged respite care for Billy a few days a week after school and on alternate weekends, an idea that both Billy and his grandmother thought was great. He would spend time with another family, one that was part of the community respite program. This program arose out of the community need to help over-loaded parents of physically and mentally disadvantaged children, as well as families like Billy's, by giving them a break on a regular basis, from a few hours to a couple of days at a time.

As it turned out the respite family that was assigned to Billy had two boys around Billy's age. The family did a lot of activities (soccer, camping) that Billy didn't get to do at home, and the parents in the family were both supportive and good at limit setting, exactly what Billy needed. Ms. Williams appreciated the break, and Billy not only enjoyed the time there, but found that he could separate from his grandmother and she and he would be all right.

It helped. As the crises came and went, both Billy and his grandmother were able to step outside them a bit better. More importantly, Ms. Williams was better able to see the connection between her stress and Billy's reaction, and could even anticipate the start of the negative cycle; his behavior was seen less and less as arbitrary or instigating. All the pieces seemed to be coming together.

EIGHT

Billy: The Story Continues

IN THE MIDDLE OF THE MIDDLE

As we discussed in Chapter 5, the middles of treatment are a time of developing skills and reinforcing changes (in infinite variations, it seems) over and over again until they can be permanently integrated into the family's patterns. It also often becomes a time when the focus of treatment will shift—once the child problem is settled, the marital issues come to the surface, or there is now the time and trust in the therapeutic relationship to explore a parent's individual concerns (e.g., his or her own past history of abuse, depression, or problems with sex or drugs), or the scapegoated child settles down and a sibling begins to have problems—as the family's still active dysfunctional patterns push the pathology in a new direction. After a quick start, individual sessions with the child may seem to level off and show little movement, but crises may break out elsewhere in the family; or, as the parents become more organized and united in their parenting, individual sessions may become increasingly productive. If the child has become stronger and less symptomatic through individual work, it may be replaced by family sessions.

Billy slowly progressed during the months of this middle time. While he was still relatively emotionally and verbally closed to his past, he began to let go of some of his need to be in charge. In sessions he no longer needed to direct me. His trust allowed him to compromise; he was more sensitive to my feelings; his play themes became less violent. Wrestling, once so intense, became more of an occasional thing. At home, Ms. Williams was by and large able to maintain the structure that Billy needed, and with the help of regular respite, things generally went smoothly. But then everything became unsettled once again; the parents came back in the picture.

Although his mother hadn't seen Billy for two years and had no contact beyond a couple of letters, she now started writing, telling him that she wanted to come visit. Ms. Williams would come into sessions waving letters, wondering what to do, how to respond, to Billy, to his mother. She had fantasies of his mother taking Billy away, of her filling his head with something (she didn't know what) about the past, and causing him to regress back to where he started. Why couldn't she, the grandmother wondered aloud, just leave him alone?

Ms. Williams' reaction wasn't unusual. Any time an absent parent comes back into a child's life, it creates anxiety for both child and caretaker that can severely disrupt the system. For Ms. Williams the mother became a threat; even though the grandmother had legal custody, the mother was his mother, and could, it seemed, take him back if she wanted to. Making it all the worse, of course, was Billy's reaction. He idealized his mother and was excited about the prospect of seeing her again.

Ms. Williams realized she couldn't stop the visits without court action, but she decided that there needed to be some supervision, and so she drafted some additional relatives to be around when the mother came. I asked about Billy's mother coming to a session—this would not only provide a safe forum for meeting and talking, but would give me an opportunity to see this other important person in Billy's life up close—but no, she was planning on coming on a Sunday only for a few hours.

She didn't come—no phone call, no letter, nothing. Fortunately, the grandmother and I had discussed this possibility. Ms. Williams was both relieved and angry. Billy said little. Ms. Williams's temptation was to use this as a launching pad for showing Billy just what kind of person his mother was. But I tried to help her see that this was her agenda, her emotions, very separate from Billy's own grief and coming to terms with his mother and their relationship. I tried to talk to Billy about it, made interpretative comments about how he might feel, offered to help him write a letter to his Mom. In typical Billy style, he remained closed and quiet.

On the heels of this incident reentered Billy's father. Suddenly he, too, expressed an interest in increasing his visitation, and even talked to Ms. Williams about taking custody of Billy. The reason for all the renewed interest wasn't clear; Ms. Williams suspected that it had something to do with his stable relationship with his girlfriend. Because he was her own son, his appearance was less of a threat, but only slightly. She quickly made clear to her son that Billy (and she) could not handle any whimsical or quick changes. If he was serious about custody, he could prove it by visiting regularly, and everyone would see how things went over the course of a year.

Billy was less excited about his dad's visits. The parents had divorced when Billy was two years old, so his own memories of his father were nonexistent, and his experience with him since he had been with his grandmother had been disappointing and sporadic. Again I invited the father into a session, but he couldn't make it. The father saw Billy on weekends for about a month, but then started to find reasons not to come. Within two months he had stopped seeing Billy altogether.

Not only can in-and-out involvement be devastating for a child, it's often infuriating for you as a therapist. It's difficult not to identify with the child, be angry at the parent, and project your reactions onto the child. But while your own countertransference can give you a clue to how the child may be feeling, your focus is on helping the child sort through his or her own grief reaction.

For a few months Billy remained stable in spite of these rejections, but then stronger emotions began to surface. His mother wrote another letter, and Billy refused to look at it. When Ms. Williams pressed it on him, he tore it up. He started having tantrums again at home when he couldn't get his way with his grandmother, and often refused to go into time-out when he misbehaved. Finally, there was an incident at school where a child pushed him on the playground and he attacked the child with such ferocity that it took three teachers to pull him off. He kicked one of the teachers so hard that he cracked her leg bone.

But the deterioration didn't stop there. His classroom behavior became increasingly oppositional, culminating two weeks later in another outburst, in which he turned over all the desks in the room. Now not only was Ms. Williams in a panic, so was the school administration.

In individual sessions Billy said little, and behaved no differently. In a joint session with Billy and his grandmother, Ms. Williams repeated what Billy had told her, that the boy that Billy had the fight with reminded him of Tom, the mother's boyfriend. What actually came out of the session, with questions and prodding by both the grandmother and me as Billy sat on the floor near my chair, were Billy's memories of his brother's death, his hearing the commotion in his brother's room, his own fear about what was happening, the screams of alarm by the mother, the police, and, most of all, Tom's blaming him for his brother's death.

The memories and the emotions were finally breaking loose. Whether they were triggered by the reappearance and subsequent reabandonment by the parents, the lowering of his own defenses through therapy, just the passage of time, a combination of all these reasons, or none of the above is for you to speculate. But the net effect was that his emotions were coming to the surface and he needed support in verbalizing them and adequate channels for expressing them, as well as clear messages about what was real and what was not.

What was not true, of course, was Billy's imagined responsibility for his brother's death. As both his grandmother and I talked with Billy, it was clear that Tom's accusation had clearly stayed with him over the years, haunting him.

Drawing his feelings out was difficult but important. We could have simply stopped there and told Billy that Tom was wrong and that he wasn't to blame. But this kind of response often feels to a client like a too quick, flip dismissal of his or her strong emotions, and it has little absolving effect. We needed to give Billy the opportunity to say why *he felt* he was to blame, and by our questions and listening let him know that we understood how he felt.

Slowly he did, in half sentences and mumbles; he said how he felt that he should have somehow stopped Tom, that somehow he should have protected his brother. As he spoke both his grandmother and I listened and restated and sympathized with his feelings, and then reassured him as other adults who knew him and cared about him (in contrast to Tom, who didn't) that it truly wasn't his fault. This seemed to calm Billy. Still, Ms. Williams worried about having to say the right thing to Billy at home. I coached her instead on how to help Billy feel that it was all right to talk about all this, as he needed and wanted to.

But Billy didn't talk any more about this at home. Later that week he had another, seemingly unprovoked, outburst at school. The school principal arranged a meeting of all the people working with Billy.

COORDINATION WITH SCHOOLS

School behavior and performance are an important part of your assessment of a child or adolescent. The perspective of teachers, guidance counselors, and principals can help you gauge how widespread particular problem behaviors may be, how the child responds in a setting different from home. Billy, for example, traditionally did well at school, as well as at camp and the respite home, environments where the structure remained consistent. School, in fact, for Billy and many other children, often becomes a place of important regularity and emotional security.

But it is also possible for home and school to become emotional dumping grounds for each other. Some children are quiet and well mannered at school, but belligerent at home. The home may be a safer, more secure place for the child to be him- or herself, or a place where trials and traumas of school life (being teased or picked on by other children, feeling criticized or castigated by a teacher, feeling embarrassed or shy) get acted out.

Similarly, the child who is perfect at home may be a holy terror in the classroom. Sometimes this reflects the home's low expectations of behavior — the child can essentially do whatever he or she wants, and rebels under the rules and regulations of the classroom — but probably more often it's the case that home is not a safe place to show anger. The child copes by acting good at home, and expresses the underlying, angry emotions at school. A positive change at one site may or may not create positive changes at the other. The child whose behavior starts to come under control at home may start to act up at school in response. It's good to check both to see that the child is truly integrating the changes, and that the home and school are working together.

Oftentimes, of course, they aren't. While the school personnel are ideally concerned about the welfare of the whole child, in more pragmatic terms they're most concerned about the child as a learner. If the child is a good student, completes the work, and keeps his or her hands to him- or herself, underlying emotional issues can be easily ignored. When the child refuses or stops learning, bothers other children, or becomes a distraction in the class, as Billy did, the school sees a major problem, and at this point the child may be referred for counseling. It's the school that has a problem, one which the parents or child may or may not see.

It was the school that was now having a problem with Billy. The school teacher and administration were frightened by this 60-pound boy, by his rage, by his unpredictability. Unlike some other schools, they had no protocols for handling children like this, no organized response, such as time-out or restraints, to such behavioral or emotional outbursts. Instead, they reacted differently each time, and often, in their seeming panic, overreacted. One time, as Billy flung desks around the room, the teacher cleared all the other children out and watched through the window in the door until uniformed police finally arrived. With this response they had helped to re-create Billy's past.

In large, multidisciplinary meetings with school personnel, the therapist has several tasks, depending upon the particular child and circumstances. Sometimes his or her job is simply to be an advocate or support for the parent, who may have clear ideas of what he or she wants for his or her child, but who feels intimidated by all the heavyweight professionals sitting around a table. Other times the school wants input from the therapist about the counseling, insights the therapist may offer in formulating a plan for the child at school; the therapist is often in a unique position to serve as a bridge between home, school, and office, providing a unified point of view for managing the child. What the school personnel generally don't want is the therapist criticizing their efforts, or telling them, unless they ask, what they should do. Their goals and needs for the child may be very different than those of the therapist, and, like the therapist and the parent, they too feel they are doing the best they can.

So what could I say about Billy? Although I had talked to Billy's teacher several times in the year, I reviewed for everyone else (the principal, the guidance counselor, the school psychologist) the history of my work with Billy—how he had responded to play therapy over the course of almost a year, about his need for control, and the gradual easing up of these defenses, of the grandmother's work in providing a more structured environment at home, which Billy needed to feel safe. I also told them, with Ms. Williams adding details along the way, about Billy's recent experience with his parents, and the disclosure of his memories about both his brother and the abusing boyfriend. Finally, I said that I thought that Billy was actually getting better, that his recent behavior, though disruptive, was linked to anger and grief that he had kept such a tight hold on for years. Their coming more to the surface was part of his healing process.

This last point was hard for some of the school personnel to accept, but when heard in the light of Billy's history and with my interpretations, they were able to agree. Framing these changes as positive gave the school personnel a new perspective, as well as helped them be more sympathetic to Billy's situation. Hearing this summary helped the grandmother realize just how far Billy had come.

If you were working with a child who had been traumatized early in life, presented with minor behavior problems, expressed little about his experience in many months of therapy, and now began to have emotional outbursts and destructive behavior, would you think he was really making progress (things have to get worse before they get better approach) or would you think that he is really beginning to fall apart? According to your theory and perspective, what recommendation would you make to the school people? What would you feel the child needs most at this time?

With the new, aggressive behaviors we are at another fork on the path. Should Billy remain in the school, or will this potentially become an arena for negative reinforcement of destructive behavior, deteriorating social relationships, handicapped learning, and increased self-depreciation? Does he need a different school setting, one more structured or geared for children with emotional problems? Is such a placement premature, would it represent a falling into the trap anticipated at the start, namely, another abandoning and giving up on him as his parents have? Should I as the therapist do more—increase sessions, take a more directive approach, secure some sort of evaluation or consultation? Consider medication?

Difficult calls. The most immediate answer is, of course, that it depends. Depends upon what the school can tolerate and provide in the way of a positive response and services. Depends on how able Billy may be to verbalize, rather than act out, his anger and sadness. Depends on how long it takes for Billy to work through his grief and anger and become less explosive.

What was finally decided at the conference was that more emphasis would be put on prevention. The school administrators still didn't feel comfortable with any form of restraint, but they would more closely monitor his behavior over the course of the day. The teacher would check in with him and see how he was feeling, especially when he seemed irritable, would take time to help him talk about and solve his problems with other children. And because he was seeming to have more difficulty in the afternoon, they would give him supervised individual computer time, which he enjoyed, as a reward for good behavior and for a less stressful afternoon. Finally, the school psychologist would meet with Billy weekly for a half hour to further shore up problem solving and support within the school.

It seemed like a good plan, and everyone felt optimistic. It also all seemed to dovetail well with the home and therapy goals — developing consistent supportive but structured environments, helping Billy verbalize rather than act out his emotions — while I would continue to address the underlying grief and anger in play therapy. Billy's teacher and grandmother talked to him about the school changes, and the therapist reclarified them and tried to gauge Billy's reaction when he saw him at the next session. Billy seemed fine with it.

But the changes didn't hold. After a honeymoon period of a few weeks, Billy exploded one morning when the teacher wouldn't let him get up to sharpen his pencil. The school administration once again panicked, and this time suspended him. They refused to allow him back into school until further evaluation could be done. I made arrangements for Billy to spend two weeks on the children's ward of the local private hospital.

GOING TO THE BIG HOUSE

I thought the school's idea to get a thorough evaluation done was a good one. The old dynamics were beginning to be played out — the emotional explosions on both sides, the cutoffs, the potential abandonment. Two weeks would give everyone a break, a respite, a chance for regrouping and recharging. And some new information and recommendations might come out of the workup. Having someone with new eyes see a case is often invaluable.

Still it's hard not to see a sudden hospitalization in the middle of therapy as cause for disappointment. For some therapists it punctures not only their own unrealistically high expectations for themselves, but their own exaggerated sense of therapeutic self-sufficiency, their belief that they should be able to do it — fix the child and family — all on their own. But while hospitalizations can feel humbling, they can be useful.

As could be predicted, Billy did well in the hospital. Once again, the tight structure decreased his negative behavior, and group therapy with other children his age helped him to be more verbally open about his feelings overall. While he didn't talk much about his brother, father, or mother, he willingly participated in all the activities, kept a journal, and was able to make brief comments about his past to various staff.

Some changes did come out of Billy's stay in the hospital. The psychological testing confirmed that he was suffering from posttraumatic stress disorder and depression. The evaluators agreed that his recent explosive behavior was a result of a relaxation of his defenses through therapy and a relatively more stable home life; they suggested that the therapy continue as it was. Billy was placed on imipramine to relieve his depression and Clonadine to reduce his aggression. But it was the formal reporting of the findings by the hospital psychologist and psychiatrist to the family — grandmother, grandfather, and John — that had the most impact, especially upon both the men.

Consultations are often valuable not only for what they offer in terms of information, but also for who delivers it and how. In this case, the clout of the psychologist and psychiatrist in their white coats in a wood-paneled office carried authority that I as the therapist could never match. The evaluation, the testing, the medication sent a clear message to these men that Billy truly had serious problems and needed their help. (Of course, in a different setting with a different family this could backfire — the medication becomes proof that the child is the only one with the problem, and reinforces his or her role of scapegoat.) With my prompting, the psychologist and psychiatrist strongly encouraged the men of the family to become more involved and back up Ms. Williams as much as possible.

The confrontation had an effect. When Billy went home a few days later there was renewed energy in the family. John, in particular, not only supported his mother when she set limits with Billy, he started taking a more active interest in him, playing catch in the evening, helping Billy with his homework, stepping into a paternal role. Although the school administration kept their fingers crossed, they took Billy back in, knowing he was now on medication. His teacher reported that he seemed more calm, more steady in his mood, and better able to do his work.

Often there's a honeymoon effect after a hospital stay. With the respite, new information, or change in treatment, the fact that the child is discharged (and therefore medically certified as better), it's easy for everyone to have renewed optimism. The problem is, of course, that all this optimism can wear off in a matter of days and, now that the "hospital solution" has become a solution, it's tempting for parents to bounce the child right back if things start to slide back downhill.

Such transition problems become even more difficult when a child has been in the hospital for several weeks or months. Like the family of the navy father who goes off to sea for six months, the family with the hospitalized child learns to reshape itself around the hole created by the child's absence. The parents have forgotten just how time consuming the child really is, or how quickly tension and triangles can build, or another child has been able to slip in and take up a lot of Dad's attention that used to go to the hospitalized child. The child has to make a new slot for him- or herself, and, unfortunately, it easier for everyone to just let him or her fall back into the old one.

CALLING IN REINFORCEMENTS

Such falling back happened to Billy, but not for lack of trying. Crises once again began to brew — Ms. Williams's father fell down and hurt his leg, Ray was laid off again from his job at the hardware company, and John's five-year-old son came to stay for a few weeks while his mother was in the process of moving.

Everything fell apart. John was spending free time with his son, and Billy resented him and all the attention he was receiving. The grandfather was now around the house more, but the noise and commotion created by the additional grandson, as well as his own depression around his job loss, made him irritable and withdrawn. Ms. Williams, who had been doing so much better with the support she was receiving, once again became overwhelmed, anxious, and depressed, causing Billy to become highly sensitive to her moods and more demanding. Again his grandmother caved in and gave in; again the structure began to collapse.

The deterioration spilled over to school. Although there were no explosions, Billy began to act up. He talked back to his teacher, argued with other children, wasn't completing his work. The school went back to Plan A, with the weekly meetings with the psychologist and afternoon computer time. This seemed to take the edge off, and gave the school some sense of control. In therapy, Billy was able to talk about his jealousy and resentment of his cousin — a remarkable achievement for this silent child. I supported the grandmother and grandfather and worked with them to solve problems and stop the backslide, but neither one could really get mobilized. In order to avoid another hospitalization, I decided to call in reinforcements.

Home-based services were started to supplement the office-based therapy. A female therapist went out to the home twice a week for a couple of hours to help the grandmother and grandfather (when he was around) with hands-on ways of managing Billy in specific situations, primarily by coaching the grandmother and supporting her with limit setting and time-outs. She also met with John and tried to help him blend together his relationships with his son and Billy, as well as encouraging him to back up his mother. Finally, the home-based worker served as a support system, someone for Ms. Williams to talk to about the stresses and strains she was experiencing. Although the family was cool at first about having this stranger in their home, they warmed up to her quickly. In addition to all this, Billy's respite care with the other family was also increased.

But all this extra support and help wasn't enough. Even though Billy continued to use his individual sessions productively — both playing out and talking about his anger at the cousin, the abandonment by the uncle, his worries about his grandmother — and actually behaved well for a couple of days after a session, he couldn't stay that way. Neither could the rest of the family. Within a few hours after the home-based therapist left, Ms. Williams or the grandfather would undo everything the clinician tried to reinforce. Even when John's son returned home to his mother and some of the stress was reduced, the structure in the home remained weak.

Billy had another explosion at school, and it came seemingly out of the blue. He punched a boy and bloodied his nose, slipped out of the teacher's grip when she tried to stop him, kicked her, and then ran out of the school and hid in some bushes off the school property. The police were called, and they found him.

Billy was expelled. The most the school administration could offer for the three months left in the school year was home tutoring. Now that he was home all the time, his grandmother was frantic. Both Ray and John were working temporarily on full-time jobs, and she was stuck home with Billy all day long. He pushed at her, and she invariably gave in just to get some peace.

Another crossroads. Once again several therapeutic options open up. Should individual therapy for Billy, for Ms. Williams, or home-based services be increased? Send him back to the hospital, have his medication reevaluated? Maybe just wait it out? Again, it depends on how you see the problem. How much did the presence of the other grandson re-create and refuel Billy's own dormant feelings about his younger brother? (I tried to pursue this with him but got nowhere.) Is the chaos and abandonment, this time by the school, increasing Billy's anxiety and fears? How much of Billy's behavior is the product of the family dynamics, where Billy is so entrenched in his role, where the grandmother is so overwhelmed, and her potential supports so unavailable? How much history — of Ms. Williams's own childhood or that with her children — being replicated?

The difficult decision that was finally made came out of a discussion among all of us who were involved with Billy — me, the home-based therapist, the grandparents, the school principal and the special education coordinator, the school psychologist, and the respite care coordinator. The consensus was to place Billy in a treatment center for at least six months.

Here he could attend school in a setting that could appropriately respond to his behavior (small classes, token economy, use of time-outs and re-straints if needed). He would get individual and group counseling, and, ideally, have a chance to focus and work more intensively on his past trauma and loss, develop his social skills, and learn more effective ways of handling his emotions. The center was close enough that the family could visit as his earned privileges would allow, and the overall plan was to gradually increase visitation stays as time of discharge became closer.

The home-based therapist would also continue to come once a week to do family therapy. Both she and I felt that the family wasn't stable enough to maintain the structure Billy would need even after discharge because of environmental and emotional problems within the family. Ms. Williams's depression needed to be addressed, probably through medica-tion, perhaps also individual therapy or marital therapy; the men in the family needed to change their roles and become consistently involved in parenting if Billy was going to be able to grow up in their home. Finally, Billy was to continue to see me two times a month as a way of maintain-ing our relationship, keeping a check on his progress, and offsetting his sense of abandonment. Everyone was to meet with the facility staff on a regular basis.

The family and I felt both failure and relief with this decision. The initial goal of not abandoning Billy seemed betrayed—here the boy was to be sent away, replicating another loss, another desertion by the adults in his life. On the other hand, time was running out. The next year or two would, to my mind, be crucial in Billy's development. Unless he was able to grieve his losses, heal the trauma he experienced, and find healthi-er ways to express his emotions, his current behavioral patterns could so-lidify, increasing the risk that he could, like his mother's boyfriend, become dangerously violent. The grandparents, too, looked ahead with anxiety. Unless Billy could learn to manage his emotions and behavior or they could learn to better handle him, he would, as an adolescent, easily spin out of control.

And, of course, Billy had his own mixed feelings. It was explained to him by his grandparents and myself that the grandparents and the school were having trouble giving him what he needed. We all wanted him to be able to go to school, rather than stay at home (something he wanted very much), and this seemed the best way to do it. We reassured him that the move wasn't because he was bad or being punished. He liked the idea of going to school, and was excited about all the activities that the center provided. Knowing that he would be seeing and talking to everyone on a regular basis seemed to reduce much of his anxiety.

Although Billy had a difficult adjustment at first, within a couple of months he calmed down, and he quickly moved up their level system.

Although he did not talk much in individual therapy, he did open up in group; there were a couple of other children who had lost parents through death or divorce, and this helped him talk about his own feelings. When he came home on weekend visits, he seemed to the grandparents to be better behaved and more open. When he came to see me, we primarily spent the time catching up and playing games—more relationship maintenance than any therapeutic exploration.

The family procrastinated on seeing the home-based therapist, and this contributed to a five-month extension of Billy's stay at the center. Part of this procrastination came from the family's need to have a break from focusing on problems. Part was probably due to their difficulty understanding how talking about parenting would be helpful if Billy wasn't there to create problems. And a good part of this was their own anxiety about stirring the family pot and talking about family problems that weren't specifically tied to Billy.

Like most families who have focused their attention on the problems of one child, Billy's absence made them more acutely aware of what else was wrong in the family. Without the ability to use Billy as a familiar distraction, they became more aware of the tensions, the problems, and their first reaction was to ignore the whole thing.

But the home-based therapist persisted. Just as the family members needed to learn how to interact with each other without Billy being in the center of them all, they needed to learn how to interact and trust the home-based therapist without exclusively focusing on Billy and his problems. It took a lot of reassuring by the therapist, a lot of interpreting and normalizing of how they might be feeling, a lot of explaining over and over again the connection between Billy's long-term improvement (and coming home) and their ability to change the way the family operates.

It took Ms. Williams almost four months to go to the doctor and start on the Prozac that he had prescribed. It took more than five months before the couple consistently would meet for couple therapy. Family sessions with John were eventually included when the marital issues spilled over or when there was a need to talk about parenting issues.

Billy is now back in public school and doing well. He continues to check in with me once a month or so, and because of the skills he learned at the center and the fact that he's getting older, we talk more now and play less. He still has no contact with his parents, but more and more he is able to look at those relationships as a reflection of them and not himself. Although he's put much of his past behind him, losses (the death of his dog, his uncle moving away for a few months) spark his defiance and irritability, test his grandparents' ability to maintain their limits, and stir memories of his brother's death.

And while the present seems stable, the risks for the future are still there. His grandparents had trouble in adolescence with all their children, and while their awareness and parenting skills have increased, the danger of sliding back into those patterns remain. It's made all the worse by the simple fact that the grandparents are getting older. They may physically find it more and more difficult to keep up with a growing adolescent.

The normal ups and downs of adolescence are right around the corner for Billy. As is typical for teenagers who have been abandoned by their parents, Billy's feelings about his parents—anger at their neglect, curiosity about what they are like—will undoubtedly come to the surface. These feelings in turn will drag up the unresolved past all over again: his wondering what's wrong with him, his guilt over his brother's death, perhaps, his anger that things have turned out the way they have. Without emotional supports from the adults around him—his grandparents, me, his uncle—I could imagine him becoming depressed, acting up and potentially getting into trouble with the law, or being at risk for drug abuse. We can't live in the future, but, ideally, by anticipating these dangers, they may be prevented. That may be the most that we can do.

LOOKING BACK

Partially successful cases like this one are a familiar experience to anyone who has ever worked with troubled families. What this case has in common with many of them is the overwhelming impact of environment. For many of the families that are seen in clinic or agency settings, the difficulty lies not with motivation or ability to learn skills, but the multiple problems that seem to constantly badger the family—unemployment, poverty, illness—that keep the family in a crisis mode and make it difficult to maintain a positive momentum. Even with all the family work and residential treatment available, these environmental forces may still drag them down. Through therapy they, ideally, will acquire fewer internal distractions and greater family resources to help them weather these emotional storms better.

What this case also illustrates is that all clinical work doesn't turn out smoothly, that with the best of intentions and skills, treatment becomes derailed, new approaches have to be tried, and, often, a combination of services need to be included—good clinical work is pragmatic. It's also circular, with one path connecting to others. Therapy, for example, could have started with the family and moved toward individual work with Billy, or started with the marriage, if the couple would have permitted it, and then tied into Billy's concerns. The initial focus could have been on the school, helping the faculty to better accommodate his needs, or to carry their more structured approaches into the home. Regardless of where you start, you eventually will cross the other paths.

The story of Billy also illustrates the limitations of each of the systems and institutions: the family's reluctance to change its way of parenting; the school's own goals, needs, and inability to control Billy's behavior; scheduling limitations that prevented me from seeing Billy more often; the limited resources available for respite or home-based services; the financial limits of the local community pushing them to support more expensive residential treatment only after all the other options had been tried. The limits are neither good nor bad, but simply another practical factor in the decision-making process.

Finally, the story of Billy illustrates the resiliency of a child and family to survive trauma, and the inestimable effect that love and commitment can have. Without the family's ability to care for and see Billy for who he is and can be in the future, without some commitment on my part to stick with Billy and his family, rather than farm the family and their problems out along the way, it's easy to imagine Billy going from foster home to foster home, in and out of the hospital, increasingly locked in a downward cycle of negative behavior and self-fulfilling prophecies. Now his future, while still uncertain, is resting upon an increasingly larger base of past and present experiences that include people who only want the best that life can give him. In the life of a child, this often is the best we as adults can do.

LOOKING WITHIN

1. If you haven't done it already, write down your own assumptions about problems in children. What is the major source of the problems — within, without? What is the role of development, of family, of the past? Where do the solutions lie? What is your primary role as the therapist?

2. What type of problems with children would you have the most difficulty with — acting-out 10-year-olds, sexually abused children, hyperactive or aggressive children, children who have suffered a loss — not only in terms of your skill, but your own emotional response? How are you to handle such cases and emotions — avoid them by farming them out, becoming controlling, minimizing the problems, becoming overwhelmed and passive, overidentifying with the child?

3. If there was something from your childhood that you most regret, what would it be? What do you wish your parent or parents did more of for you? How do you wish your relationships with your siblings was different when you were a child? What aspect of this has had an impact on your work with children now? *How* has it had an impact?

4. What skills do you most need to develop in working with children — play therapy, art therapy, psychological testing, work with younger children or with older ones, integrating children in the family process? How could you learn those skills? *

---

*Take a look at the play therapy texts listed in the Suggested Readings for more information on theory and techniques.

NINE

"See How She Treats Me!": The Parent–Adolescent Struggle

"So, how was your week?"

Ms. Harris, a slight woman with gray-blond hair and drooping shoulders, takes a quick glance at her 15-year-old daughter, Ellen. Although Ellen is slumped in the corner of the couch, it's easy to see that she's several inches taller and about 20 pounds heavier than her mother. Her head is turned away, and she's staring absently at the lamp.

"Okay, I guess," says Ms. Harris. She sounds tentative and glances again at Ellen. Ellen, still looking at the lamp, just breathes heavily.

"Actually, we did fine until I tried to get Ellen to clean up her room."

"I *did* clean my room!" snaps Ellen, whirling around to face her accuser. "*You* just didn't think it was good enough!" She is glaring.

"You left all those clothes all over the floor, after I asked you nicely to pick them up." Ms. Harris sounds almost angry, but she's holding back, being careful.

"I said I was going to wear them, didn't I?"

"Yes, but—"

"And then *you* wouldn't let me talk on the phone!"

"I asked you if you could call back later because I was expecting a call from Louis." Ms. Harris sounds a bit firmer this time.

"I told you I was almost done!"

The mother turns to the therapist. "And do you know what she did? I asked her again nicely to hurry up, and then she had a fit, ripped the phone right out of the wall, and threw it down on the floor!" She seems mad, but suddenly her lower lip is pouting out, and then she collapses

119

into quiet tears. "I don't know why she needs to do things like that. I didn't raise her that way."

"Oh, you're pathetic!" sneers Ellen.

Welcome to the world of adolescence. Here, in Ellen, we see perhaps a larger version of what Billy potentially could become, and in some ways these families are similar. Just as Billy was dealing with the loss of his brother and parents, Ellen, Ms. Harris, and the two younger children, Marie, age 12, and Betsy, age 8, are all dealing with the death of Harry, their father, of a heart attack a year and a half ago. Since then the family has struggled financially, with Ms. Harris working two jobs, and emotionally, as each of them tries to fill the hole in the family, in their lives.

But it's Ellen who is the center of concern. She's the one who has gotten into fights at school, who's having rages, who tries to boss her younger sisters around and hits them when they don't do what she wants, who demands and challenges her mother, and who feels entitled. Ms. Harris, in many ways like Billy's grandmother, makes feeble efforts to assert control but, more often than not, caves in. Here at the third session it's clear that both Ms. Harris and Ellen have some major changes to make if both are to survive this adolescence.

MOVING UP

But there are also significant differences between Billy and Ellen simply because of the differences in age. As we move up the developmental ladder from children to adolescents, there are dramatic shifts in the therapy process. Here's a quick list of some of the obvious ones:

The stakes are higher. While an elementary school-age child like Billy may get suspended from school, or tear up his room when he is angry, teenagers like Ellen won't have much trouble taking drugs, shoplifting, getting pregnant, running away—that is, engaging is seriously dangerous activities that could have long-term consequences on their future.

Different parenting skills are needed. Ms. Williams, under the worst conditions, could, with a little bit of help, always pick Billy up and put him in his room for time-out. Ms. Harris can't do that with Ellen. Parents of teenagers must use other skills of persuasion, reasoning, and verbal enforcement.

Others outside the family have increasing influence. Younger children are most affected by their home and school environments, environments created by adults who are in charge. Ellen, however, is not only reacting to her mother, or even internally to the loss of her father, but, like other teens, to the wider circle of friends who pull her in various directions as she struggles to define for herself who she is. They are the other voices that she hears in counterpoint to those of her mother.

Parents often under- or overreact. Recognizing your waning influence upon your child, aware of the risks intertwined within their decisions, realizing that the time you have to affect your child's life is quickly running out all can have the effect of intensifying the parent's reaction. Some, in panic, overreact and overcontrol their children—threatening, demanding, pushing him or her to be more responsible, to stay away from trouble, or, better yet, to not grow up at all. Others, swinging too far the other way, feel that it is too late to turn things around, and allow their child to have full rein over them and their own decisions. Such parents have essentially given up.

But what drives these over- and underreactions are the parents' memories of their own adolescence—a distorted still life, perhaps, of what never was, more often the painful throb of some past mistakes, the ongoing regret over roads not taken, or the aching awareness that they and their parents failed in important ways. These memories are powerful and push parents to try to stop history from repeating itself with their own children.

Therapists' reactions can be more intense. It's not only the parents who are sensitive to the risks and dynamics of adolescence; so, too, are therapists. When an adolescent is referred for therapy by the court—the "one last chance" before being sent off to a correction center—it's the therapist, as well as the teenager, who's under the gun. When a therapist sees destructive family dynamics souring the child's life, but faces parents too overwhelmed or impotent to change them, when a therapist wants the best for the adolescent but feels stifled by bureaucracy or limited community resources, the therapist, too, can feel that time is running out. He or she starts to believe that it is necessary to work hard and fast in order to avert dire consequences, or decides, like the parents, like the community, that it isn't going to matter and stops trying.

The adolescent has more opportunity to fill a surrogate role. The elementary school-age child can, of course, learn to copy and fill roles in the family. If Billy had stayed with his mother, for example, we could easily imagine him eventually taking on more and more the boyfriend's control or violence, or stepping in to emotionally support her whenever she had trouble with her boyfriend.

But this filling in of roles becomes all the more powerful as the adolescent moves closer to adulthood. Here we see the oldest son working full- or part-time to help support the rest of the family and giving the mother advice when she asks or even doesn't ask for it; the 16-year-old daughter who watches the kids and makes dinner while Dad is working late; or, as with Ellen, a 15-year-old who feels, as the father did perhaps, that she has some responsibility to direct not only her younger sisters, but the right to expect that her mother will do what she wants her to do without objection.

The adolescent can be more verbal. As we will discuss later, this certainly doesn't mean that they are. But one of the main differences between child therapy and adolescent therapy is the capacity of adolescents to do more "talk" therapy, something that most small children are developmentally unable to do. Not only is the adolescent's vocabulary and comprehension greater, but so is the ability to think abstractly. Right and wrong, for example, isn't determined, as it is within the mind of the elementary school child, by whether or not someone punishes you, but by a developing internal set of values, ethics and morality, concepts that can now be asked about and discussed directly, rather than symbolically portrayed through play.

Confidentiality is more vital. While confidentiality certainly exists between young children and therapists, it must be flexible, simply because children rely so exclusively upon their parents that the latter need as much information as possible in order to help the child. As children become older and begin both to separate from the parents and to see themselves as more independent, as they no longer need to rely as much on their parents to help them solve problems, but can begin to help themselves, confidentiality becomes more absolute and important. The therapist needs to work harder to build trust and assure the adolescent that his or her confidence will be respected.

Even though child and adolescent work are clearly different, the shift from one to the other varies, of course, from family to family. There are many 14- or 15-year-olds who would rather paint than talk, just as there are some 10-year-olds who wouldn't dare play a game or touch a toy. There are adolescents who, due to intellectual or physical handicaps or limitations, are developmentally delayed and may not only play more and talk less, but may need to be managed by their parents as if they were younger. The way to find out how mature an adolescent is is to ask—about the teen's and the family's expectation; to do—to talk with the adolescent alone, together with the parents, to offer to play cards and see what happens; and, most of all, to listen and watch. By the end of that first session you should have a pretty good idea of just where the adolescent sits on the developmental continuum and how you can best join with him or her.

FALLING APART

Of course, there are all those families that you'll never see, the ones who manage to survive the trials and tribulations of adolescence not only intact, but relatively smoothly. So what distinguishes the families who do well with adolescence from the ones who don't?

For some parents, their problems with their teenagers are simply problems with their own parenting skills and knowledge. They can't make the shift from physical-authoritarian management to a verbal-negotiating one. The father who threatens to spank his six-foot-two son if he doesn't cut the grass by Friday is setting himself up to fail. The son is only challenged to ignore the father and up the ante, which might lead to a physical confrontation and blowing everything out of proportion. But if that's all the father knows, if threatening physical punishment sums up his entire repertoire of skills, his influence over his child has effectively ended.

Similarly, some teenagers have trouble because they can't make the shift to the world of adolescence. They lack the skills to make decisions or solve problems; they may have long-standing troubles getting along with peers and find it difficult fitting into the often competitive but also potentially supportive environment that friends can provide. Without peer support their emotional separation from their parents leaves them stuck between both worlds—and filled with a sense of loneliness and isolation.

Strong, rapidly changing emotions, one of the hallmarks particularly of early adolescence, can create problems for teenagers, especially those with low self-esteem and poor coping skills. Rather than verbalizing their emotions, they strike out; rather than seeking others who can provide help, they hold in their feelings and questions and get depressed; rather than finding healthy ways of relieving the pressure and stress, such as sports or creative arts, they turn to drugs, sex, acting out.

Many parents will invariably blame their child's misbehavior on friends: the group of lowlifes that he sees at school, those girls up the street who do anything that they want, that bad crowd on the corner. And they very well may be putting ideas in his or her head, leading the child astray. But what's wrong with this explanation is that it implies that if you eliminate the friends—move, place the child under house arrest, enforce a strict curfew—the child will be cured. Maybe, but often not for long. Somehow the child manages to find another group of scruffy characters in the new neighborhood or drifts back to the group once the curfew is eased.

While peers certainly shape the adolescent's choices, the parents who blame the group don't realize that the problem is less the friends and more the reflection of him- or herself that the teenager sees in them. Separating friends is only half the solution. The other half is improving the child's self-esteem, assertiveness, social skills, supports—within the family and with new friends.

When an adolescent takes on an inappropriate role within the family system, both the parents' ability to manage the child and the child's abilities to cope are stressed. A 15-year-old like Ellen, for example, who has replaced her father's role is not only filled with a sense of overresponsibility but also entitlement and power. Her "top dog" position in the family, coupled with her mother's weak parenting skills, locks the dysfuctional system in place.

Similarly, the child who has historically filled the role of scapegoat and serves as a vicarious outlet for a parent's anger, or the "good child" who secures his or her place only by complementing the scapegoat's role, become more and more entrenched in their behaviors as the gap between them widens with time. The scapegoat's behavior, once tolerable, now escalates and comes to the attention of the community, while the good child is more set on showing just how good he or she can be.

Running underneath all these adolescent potholes of skills, stress, and roles are the parent's own history and the power of this history to repeat itself. Sometimes these factors are genetically based—the son whose father has a history of bipolar illness finds himself sliding into bouts of severe depression; the attention-deficit/hyperactivity disorder (ADHD) mother finds that her son has similar problems with inattention, impulsivity, and hyperactivity. Oftentimes, however, it's the combination of role modeling, family dynamics, and environmental forces that work together to repeat the past mistakes from one generation to the next.

The mother who was pregnant at 14, finds, in spite of her constant warnings, that her daughter is pregnant at 15. The father who never went beyond the ninth grade finds himself arguing with his son who wants to quit school and work at a gas station. The mother who married an alcoholic and abuser painfully watches her own daughter endure the same fate. The father who looks back on his gang years as the start of his own descent into criminal activity and drugs feels powerless to change the power of the gang upon his own teenage son.

What drives the replaying of these scripts is the way both the family and environmental dynamics are continuously recycled. While the mother harangues her 15-year-old daughter to be careful around the boys she associates with, she isn't aware that it's the haranguing itself, and not the message, that propels the daughter into pregnancy, just as it did with her mother. Similarly, the son who feels that what was good for his father should be good enough for him finds his father's arguments to stay in school hypocritical and dismisses them. The daughter who saw her mother abused by her father not only expects men to act this way and associates intimacy with violence, but unconsciously copies the victim role that her mother modeled. The son who realizes that his own father is now in jail because of an early start in gangs also finds that he has in his community no other male role models or lifestyle options. Coupled with his adolescent sense of invulnerability, he mistakenly believes that, unlike his father, he will never get caught.

Again, it is the seeing of this replication of your life in the life of a child that often pulls the panicky parent into counseling. It's also part of what creates the ambivalence and resistance that parents display. To look at the forces affecting your child and family is to also look painfully again at the forces shaping your own past.

To talk about the life options open to a teenager and the power of history to repeat itself is to talk about the fundamental challenge of adolescence, namely, leaving home and setting a course for adulthood. Every family creates its own emotional climate, its own escape hatches, its own ultimatums that let the adolescent know how, when, and in what direction to leave. Some seem hopelessly trapped within the narrow choices they have; others work so hard not to become their parent that they don't figure out how to become themselves; and some, through a helping hand of another adult in their life, find a way to step outside the environmental and family patterns to become someone different.

If you look back on your own time of leaving home, your reactions to your parents' past, your relationships with other adults outside your family, you may find not only a clue to your own life options, the emotions that stimulate change in your life, the mistakes that you want so hard to avoid, but on a clinical level the source of your own countertransference reactions to parents and adolescents that you see.

THERAPEUTIC GOALS: THE BIG PICTURE

From the sources of problems come the solutions. Parents who are having difficulty shifting parenting styles need information about adolescent development (e.g., normal needs for privacy, adolescents' sensitivity to hypocrisy, the testing of limits) as well as coaching in specific parenting skills (e.g., detecting the power struggle and knowing when to stop, how to raise sensitive topics, giving the child permission to talk about his or her anger or sadness, when to lay down the law, how to achieve a united front). Framing the problems as problems of skill is often less threatening to the parents, and if given concrete suggestions early on, they can increase their own sense of power and control. Often this type of skill training is all that is needed.

The other question to ask yourself, however, isn't, "What don't the parents know?" but "*Why* don't they do what seems like common sense?" Parents need to find out the underlying dynamics that are shaping their child's response—take a united stand, tell Tyrone emphatically that he can't go out, go to the school and talk to the teacher to find out why Helen is failing. Here we're back to problems within the hierarchy, within the marital relationship, and among the family roles, or unresolved issues from the parents' past. Here again we are back to basics: looking for what's missing; moving toward anxiety; blocking the patterns in the room and in the home; and labeling, educating, and coaching.

When it's clear to you that problems stem from the adolescent's inappropriate role and hierarchy within the family system, realigning the system is the obvious goal. In the session process you point out when the adolescent isn't acting like an adolescent, but an adult. You challenge the parents to set limits, to act as parents rather than peers. You give the parents permission to assert their power (though not be abusive), which you as therapist along with the courts and the schools will all support. They need to know that teenagers, like Ellen, shouldn't be out of control or too much in control, but can learn to be responsible and appropriate, that the community is on the parents' side.

This message is particularly valuable for single parents who feel overrun by all-too-powerful teenagers. Your saying this doesn't make it happen—the parents still have to confront their own anxiety about changing roles and learning new skills—but your challenge and support gives them a vote of confidence. The clinician, or more often the court, serves, in fact, as the second parent, forming a united front to the child, which becomes the starting point for realignment.

But creating a workable structure is only half a solution. Parents need to provide positive attention and nurturing in order to give adolescents something to move toward, not only away from. Nurture and control go hand in hand; parents who let their kids get out of control or try to control too much too often forget that children still need love and attention, respect and appreciation. Sometimes, in fact, the best place to start regaining control is to start by being more respectful and appreciative.

But this can be difficult, especially for parents who were never nurtured themselves and have, unfortunately, learned to think of parenting as yelling, threatening, or slapping across the face or behind when a child gets out of hand, or parents who are stressed out and have little time or energy to focus on their children. The clinician's response, of course, isn't simply to tell the parents to do it, but to model it both toward the adolescent ("Mary, your teacher told me that you have been doing wonderfully the past week at school") and the parents ("From what you've told me about your father, Rochelle, it sounds like you did the very best you could for you and your sister—it must have been really tough for you").

For the teenager who's struggling with the trials of adolescence, who's depressed, overwhelmed, or has poor self-esteem, supportive individual therapy is a logical option. In chaotic, violent homes, giving the adolescent an opportunity to talk to an empathic adult, an ideal parent, can alone be a powerful corrective emotional experience. But other formats, along with or in place of individual therapy, also have advantages. An adolescent group, for example, not only provides opportunities for developing social skills in a safe environment and reduces isolation, but confrontation by peers often has far greater impact than such confrontation by a therapist. Sessions with the parents or whole family therapy can help the parents and adolescent learn to better communicate and solve problems and can provide a forum for demonstrating nurturing skills to parents.

Whatever way you choose to support a teen, it's important to be aware of the danger of usurping the parents' role. For parents who blame the child, are passive, frustrated, or tired trying to handle problems, stepping back and letting the clinician step in becomes all too easy. For the adolescent who has felt misunderstood, resentful, and hungry for intimacy with an adult, a deep dependency upon the therapist becomes a real possibility. This doesn't mean that this sometimes isn't the best course to take; it only means that the clinician needs to weigh out ahead of time the clinical implications and his or her own commitment to the teenager.

Finally, when the forces of the parents' past are being replicated in the life of the adolescent, the starting point for assessment begins with the parents' own ability to see and understand how they have helped create the dynamics that have enabled the replication to happen. Following in one's footsteps is chalked up by some parents to fate or genetics—"My cousin had a boy just like Simon who wouldn't listen and he eventually got in big trouble with the wrong crowd"—as a given over which they have little control.

Others who see the shadow of their own lives mirrored in their child find it too painful and retreat into minimization and denial. What the adolescent is doing—shoplifting but not breaking into houses, dating older men but not pregnant at 13—is different enough or doesn't seem quite so bad to them as their own past; the problem, they decide, isn't with them, but only with the child or with the influence of friends. For still others, this replication of history is all too apparent, but only creates enormous guilt and panic and little else; the forces that create them or how to change them are outside their awareness.

Your focus certainly doesn't need to be on the blame, but on helping the parents see that while their past is part of their own and their child's present, it's a present that can be changed. Parents need to know that they neither have to stay walled off by denial nor mired in guilt, but can increase their control and power by recognizing and changing the patterns and processes that create and maintain the problems. The fact that the father is emotionally abandoning his son just as his own father physically abandoned him is less important than helping the father see that his active, emotional presence within the family is what is needed to help his son succeed.

H. L. Mencken once said that most complex questions turn out to have a simple answer, but that it's usually wrong. While it's simpler to talk of adolescent problems in terms of one source/one goal, in reality, problems between parents and adolescents usually stem from several sources, all intersecting at one time—poor parenting and coping skills; an overwhelmed parent and adolescent; poor communication; and inappropriate roles and misalignments born out of the family's struggles with past losses, traumas, and environmental stress. Which you choose to focus on the most will depend upon your theoretical frame, personality, and priorities.

If you are most comfortable thinking systemically, a lopsided hierarchy is what may most stand out in the first session. If you feel comfortable in the role of teacher, or come to see many of your families as warped by unrealistic expectations for teenagers and themselves, educating the parents on normal adolescent development and appropriate skills may naturally seem the best course. If you draw from a psychodynamic orientation, your work will entail seeing the adolescent individually to unravel defenses and increase insight. Once again, there are many paths through the forest.

While theory, comfort, and family expectations are likely be what you first look to when brainstorming options, pragmatics and practicality are increasingly playing a greater and greater role. It's often valuable, especially in agencies with heavy caseloads, or for clinicians strapped by limits of managed care, for example, to do what "brief therapists" do: Think in terms of problem and solution layers, moving from the simplest and least interventionist to those more complex and long term.

For example, if a parent comes in complaining of a child like Ellen who is running the family, helping the parent tighten up his or her parenting and structure would be the first goal. If this works, and the troublesome teen settles down and starts to get attention in more positive ways, therapy can be brief indeed. If the mom has a hard time implementing the structure, or if the teen's depression over her peer relationships comes to the surface once her acting out stops and trust in the therapeutic relationship is built, a shift can be made to family work or individual work. The clinician takes on the next layer of problems only if simple solutions fail.

WALKING THE LINE: OPENING MOVES

If it seems that as a therapist you have to do a lot of juggling—between adolescents and parents, past and present, individual work and family work—you're right. Unlike treatment of younger children, working with adolescents requires walking a finer line, carefully balancing the needs of the child with those of the family.

The balancing you have to do reflects the awkwardness, in-between place, and precarious balance that comprises adolescence and distinguishes it from childhood. Even though a child may be reluctant to come to therapy, his or her parents can make him come, and rapport can usually be quickly established through play therapy. Even though the child may be under considerable personal stress, his or her sensitivity and dependency upon the relationship with the parents and the environment that they create makes it easy for the smallest of positive changes to ripple down and help the child. Even though the child may be severely acting out, he or she is unlikely to be under the gun of legal charges or decisions that can have lifelong consequences (e.g., abortion vs. becoming a teenage parent). Even though the parents may be worried about what the school says, there's a feeling that there is time to work it out.

This all changes with the adolescent. Instead of one or two adults and a child, there are one or two adults and another half adult, each side representing different cultures, with you as the bridge between them. Some therapists (especially those in their 20s and 30s, it seems) find it easy to identify with their adolescent clients and see them as the victims of rigid parents. Their efforts to get the parents to "loosen up" can quickly cause the parents to see the therapist (especially if he or she is younger than them) as siding with their teen and not them; they quickly dismiss the therapist as being out of touch with the real world of parenting.

Your fate with the teen isn't much better. Because of your age, you are also seen by him or her as "one of them"—simply offering to play a game of checkers won't automatically win him or her over. While your ability to build rapport and ease anxiety in a child can often easily be done by his or her seeing you create a comfortable relationship with the parent, this same move with adolescents can backfire. If you seem to be too much on the side of parents, working too hard for their agenda, if there is any suspicion that confidentiality will be broken, the relationship never gets off the ground.

Your place in the middle means that your opening moves are extremely important. Establishing rapport, demonstrating to the teenager across from you that you are different from their parents is more important, perhaps, than gathering information. This doesn't mean that you have to know who's the lead singer for the Smashing Pumpkins, talk only in this week's latest street slang, do card tricks or break boards with karate chops, or have a tattoo the size of Montana on your forearm; it means you do have to show sincere interest in understanding the adolescent's world. Your therapeutic contract with him or her is just as important as that with the parents.

But the parents are, to use Steve de Shazer's term, the "customers" as well. You can't leave them in the waiting room thumbing through old issues of *Time* magazine for a couple of months, wondering what's going on in there and what they're paying for. Their place in the hierarchy of the family, their anxiety, and often their problems, including the behavior of their child, requires you to include them as well.

As with the younger child, part of your assessment is figuring out just how much time you need or want to spend with each, which problem (parent's or child's) has the higher priority, which treatment format (individual, couple, family) is the best approach. As with children, as one option closes—the adolescent thinks you're a jerk and never comes back—others remain open; all is not lost.

Still, it's easy to feel like a bouncing ball if you're not careful, shuttling back and forth between the generations like some Henry Kissinger-type diplomat. The way out of this is not to think in terms of being *between,* but *above;* your client isn't the adolescent or the parent, or even the adolescent and the parent, but the family system.

Your role needs to be clear. Your job in those first few sessions is to build rapport and trust with both sides, gather information, develop a therapeutic contract with the parent and adolescent regarding their goals, and, if possible, link those goals together through your understanding of the family dynamics.

Ann, for example, is infuriated with her mother, who won't ever let her go out with her friends; her mother is furious with Ann because the only thing she seems to talk about is wanting to go out. You could help both of them not only see how they are having a power struggle and polarizing each other, but help Ann talk about how she would like to spend time with her mother, or, better yet, explore whether her wanting to go out stems at least in part from the tension and criticism she feels when she's at home. You could help Ann's mother talk about her own teenage experiences and how they may fuel her fears about Ann going out, the way she feels rejected by Ann, or how her complaining is simply her way of getting Ann to pay some attention to her. Your goal then is not to mediate how much time to spend with friends, but to help mother and daughter find positive ways of communicating and spending time together.

Similarly, when Adam complains that his parents are always on his back, and his parents complain that Adam isn't doing his schoolwork and isn't conscientious like his older brother, the problem isn't schoolwork or criticism but helping Adam move out of a scapegoat role. The parents need to know that they can help Adam with school by first seeing him as different than his brother, while Adam can be challenged to get his parents off his back by finding other ways of gaining their attention and helping them see him for who he is.

Your job, then, is to see what parent and adolescent may not, to offer a perspective that incorporates both sides of the problems. You need to say and show from the outset that you're not working for one or the other, but both. Successful adolescence is, after all, the ability to integrate into the family growing differences and needs.

While you're clear about what you'll do, you're also clear about what you won't do. Part of these limits are dictated by your theoretical model — no, you will not only do individual therapy with the teenager to fix him or her; yes, it is important that the father attend the sessions, or that the couple come in together to work on their communication and conflicts. Others are the legal and ethical limits of confidentiality — you will need to notify parents if there is suicidal or homicidal risk; you will need to contact protective services if abuse or neglect is suspected.

Some therapists prefer to define the rules of confidentiality matter-of-factly at the beginning of treatment, or may simply hand out written information at the first appointment. Others prefer to wait until the family asks, or until there seems to be a real likelihood that the situation requires breaking confidentiality. The advantage of the up-front statement is that it sounds matter-of-fact and neutral, but it can also make some families anxious and suspicious even if they feel they have nothing to hide; they don't even know you, and you're already talking about how you may turn them in. The danger of waiting until the need arises, of course, is that if and when you need to break confidentiality, the family may feel deceived, angry that you weren't up-front and clear, and that you are dishonest.

Neither approach is clearly the best. What probably matters the most is not *when* you define the limits of confidentiality, but *how* you handle it whenever you do. If you are sensitive to the family's feelings, can put into words what you think they may be thinking and feeling, can talk about your own feelings and concerns, can demonstrate by word and actions that you're willing to work to develop trust, allay suspicion, or repair the relationship with the family, potential problems in the therapeutic relationship such as these can be overcome.

In addition to defining your role, good beginnings require that you be careful to create symmetry and balance. Seeing the entire family or the adolescent and parents together at the start of the first session has the advantage of not only helping you see how they interact right away, but reducing the paranoia that family members have at being left out of the session. If there's a need to see the parent and teenager separately—to build rapport, to see what each is like apart from the other, to educate or discuss material inappropriate for the other (parents' or teen's sex lives, marital issues, details of what the teen may do outside the home)—that's fine, as long as the time is balanced and both sides have an overall sense of what's going on. The quickest way to build paranoia in a teenager or anxiety in a parent is to leave either one of them out in the waiting room for a few sessions with the magazines while the others are back in the office with you. Once you've finished your assessment, and you have discussed and come to a consensus with everyone on the type of treatment format that will be used, the balance becomes less crucial.

ASSESSMENT: CHECK IT OUT

Because most families with teenagers enter therapy in a state of war, you need to move quickly to calm things by helping everyone have his or her say, by taking both sides and helping them see what is going on in the room, how everyone bounces off of each other without even being aware of it. But once the dust has settled, you need to gather the information necessary to establish a treatment plan. The assessment of an adolescent and his or her family is not much different than that of any other family: You still want to see the patterns, define the problem, see what's missing, clarify the family's theory of the problem, and so on. However, the adolescent stage of development prompts some additional questions, especially those surrounding communication, problem solving, and rapport that you may want to ask yourself and/or the family members. Here's a quick checklist, broken down by who's in the room:

Parent(s) and Adolescent

Who's missing from the session—Father, Mother, siblings, or others? Why?

Who's the most active? Often this reflects what happens at home; sometimes it merely shows who's the most motivated or anxious.

Who's got the problem; that is, who's the customer? Mother? Father? Court? School?

What is the emotional climate in the room? Angry? Depressed? Anxious? The emotional climate is like taking the family's temperature. One of tasks for the first session may be to change the climate or uncover what can change it.

How does the adolescent respond to the parents, to you? Quiet? Argues back? Silently defiant? Again, you're wondering how much this matches what happens at home and whether it might be better to see the teen alone in order to built rapport and get a better perspective on what he or she's really like.

Can the parent(s) articulate the reason for their concern? What the teen usually hears, of course, is the criticism, the hassle, a parent on his or her back. Can you help the parents help their teenager to understand the fear and worry that underlies the parents' attitude?

Can the adolescent articulate a logical, rational counterargument? Adolescents are like novice lawyers, trying to argue the merits of their case with little experience and only the basic skills. Through the arguing, however, by trying to articulate their reasons and rationalizations for an audience, they not only develop the corners of their brains that handle abstract reasoning, they actually are forced to discover and define what they believe and think, all good life skills to have. The teen who has trouble doing this is left with a ball of emotion that spills out or gets acted out, but leaves parents and other adults scratching their heads or getting angry. One of your jobs may be to help the teen think through his or her arguments and to encourage the parents to be persuaded when they hear good thinking.

Can someone stop when things get out of control? Can the momentum be stopped, can someone stay sane, or do you have to step in and help the family learn, first of all, when conflicts are reaching the point of no return?

Are the parents presenting a united front or are they split?

Can the parents say positive things about the child? The negative is usually only bad because there's nothing positive to offset it. If kids can hear something good, they can generally respond to the bad better.

How does the family respond to you? What are their expectations of counseling?

The fact that teenagers and parents have different points of view is a given. What these questions try to uncover is just how well these differences can be discussed and resolved, how rigid or flexible the system is in terms of ideas, emotions, and roles. What you don't want to reinforce by your inactivity, especially in the first session, is the ongoing replication of the problem in the room, especially one where an adolescent who is unable to hold his or her own is being ganged up on and bashed by both parents. If the teenager sees you sitting there watching him or her getting eaten by the wolves, his or her confidence in your ability to

protect or even understand his or her point of view is severely handicapped.

Adolescent Alone

*How well and willing is he or she to articulate his or her point of
view, his or her world?*

*What is his or her theory about the problems in the home? How much
self-awareness is present, how much blame, guilt?* Again, in the theory
lies the solution. Creating rapport, developing trust, means understanding how the world and its problems seem to the teen. While developmentally most teens see themselves as victims of the adult world, they vary
in their ability to step outside themselves and empathize with someone
else's point of view. You want to know how well he or she can do this.

*How does he or she relate to siblings? What role does he or she take
in the family system? Are siblings an emotional support or a cause of stress?*

*Does he or she have friends? Is he or she a leader or follower? How
much do friends provide support? How strong and what type of influence
and modeling do they provide?* Most adolescents will tell you about their
place in the peer hierarchy without any trouble. Of particular concern are
the isolated adolescents who have few supports. They have nothing to
hold onto as they try to separate from parents; they are at greater risk
for depression, drug abuse.

*Does he or she have a boyfriend or girlfriend? What is the quality
of the relationship? How much is it a source of support or stress? Does
it follow the same pattern as the intimate relationships before? How all
encompassing is the relationship? Is there room for relationships with other
friends? Is the relationship sexual? Is it responsible? Does it replicate the
parent's history in some way, or the marital relationship?* Basically, is the
intimate relationship a positive or negative force in the teen's life? Is the
teen in that relationship a better person than he or she seems to be at home
or more of the same?

*Does he or she use drugs? What kind? How often? Is there an addic-
tion that needs treatment before any further therapy should be undertaken?*
Just matter-of-fact asking about these drugs will give you information,
especially if your tone is one of concern rather than criticism. Looking
at family history (e.g., Dad is an alcoholic) and risk for self-medication
through drugs (social isolation, poor social skills, depression, hyperactivity, etc.) should raise your antennae and give you a context for talking
to the teen about this ("You mentioned that your dad drinks a lot. How
about you—do you ever drink? Do you worry that you could become a
heavy drinker like him?"). It's not uncommon for a teen to deny drug use
at the beginning, but once he or she trusts you, to bring it up on his or

her own. Although you may use the therapy to get the teen into drug treat-ment, you can't do effective family therapy with an addicted teen.

School—an arena of accomplishment and success or failure? Are educational goals realistic? Are relationships with teachers supportive or antagonistic? Are there any apparent intellectual, emotional barriers to success? How is classroom behavior? Is work completed? Does he or she fit in with a group? Is he or she a loner? Adolescents have a home life, a school life, a street life. If the home or school feel unsupportive, guess where the teen is going to go?

Does the teenager have dreams of the future? Are they realistic? Can he or she plan the steps leading to the goal? How are the goals shaped by the parents' expectations, other siblings, the parents' own history? To put this another way, does the teen have positive vision of who he or she wants to be, and does the family support it?

How does he or she relate to you? Open? Closed? Suspicious? Accommodating? Passive? Defiant? Anxious? What is the contrast between the content and process from this session and the one together with the parents?

Does he or she understand confidentiality and its limits?

What would he or she most like to be different at home? This ques-tion is particularly important, for in it is the therapeutic contract. By ask-ing the question you are telling the adolescent that you are not just dealing with the parent's agenda, that what he or she wants is just as important. By telling the adolescent that this is the place to work on those changes gives him or her a stake in the process. Your task, of course, is to link the goals of the adolescent and parent so that one creates the other, or so both can be worked on simultaneously.

Parent(s) Alone

Can they clearly articulate the behavioral changes they want to see? Most parents say they want their child to change his or her attitude. The parents need to be absolutely clear about what they are looking for so the adolescent clearly knows what's expected.

What is their theory of the problems? Is it realistic, balanced? Do they see their own role? Is blame given to outside forces such as teachers, friends? Do they show empathy for their child? If everyone else is to blame, the parents are victims who feel that they can do nothing to fix the problems.

Is the adolescent the family scapegoat? What roles do the other children in the family play? Is there a role for the adolescent to move toward? If Mary is the smart one, Tommy the athletic one, Jane the cute one, and Eric the popular one, there may be no role for Brian except to be the delin-

quent one or Claudia to be the depressed one. Often, helping parents see
how easy it is for them to lock on to the narrowest slice of their children's
abilities and personalities is enough to start to expand family roles.

*Who is most involved with the adolescent? How enmeshed is the rela-
tionship? How appropriate? Who is more distant? Why?*

*How is the marital relationship? How is the adolescent triangled in?
How are conflicts resolved? Is the adolescent fulfilling a surrogate role?
Is there an addiction or other disability handicapping one of the parents
and the marital relationship?* Minuchin and the strucuturalists, Bowen and
the intergenerationalists would say that the bedrock of the family is the
marriage. If the marriage is strong, then the parents are united, the parental
hierarchy is in place, and there's not the need to use the child as part of
a triangle to drain off anxiety between the couple.

*How empathic can the parents be of the child? Are their goals for
counseling, their expectations for the child's future realistic and supportive?* Some parents expect a 14-year-old to act as responsible as a 30-year-
old, or they think that you will talk to their teen for two sessions and
"straighten him (or her) out." Find out what they expect.

*Is the child recreating a parent's history? How is this fueling the par-
ent's response? What does the parent think the child most needs in order
to be a success in life?* Helping the parents separate the past from the
present, themselves from their children. Children represent new potential
and a wide-open future; they don't represent a chance for the parents to
correct all their past mistakes or to live their lives over.

*What is the contrast between the presentation of the parents alone
with you and with the adolescent? What is the gap between your view
and knowledge of the adolescent and their own? What do they need to
learn most about their child?*

*How do they relate to you? What role have they placed you in? Is
there good rapport? Is there another parent or parental figure that you
need to see?*

*Whom do you need additional information from? Court? Schools?
Do they understand confidentiality and its limits between you and them,
between you and the adolescent?*

Whole Family

Who's in charge? What's the comfortable problem? You can discover
both of these answers by watching the process. Who represents the family
—the father, mother? Who talks the most or for everyone else and tells
you exactly what the problem is? Maybe the kids act up and the parents do
nothing, causing you to wonder if this is what happens at home and is
part of the problem. What problem or person does the family always return

to, especially to break a silence or when you ask an anxiety-provoking question ("So what happens when you both have marital arguments?"). This problem, that person, is what everyone is comfortable talking about. This is where the fingers point when less comfortable problems get raised at home.

How do the siblings interact? What roles do they play out? What are the coalitions and competitions? How are they joined or split between the parents? In large families the children may be broken up into camps—the boys with Dad, the girls with Mom; Kevin is Mom's favorite, Tina is Dad's. The family is split, the children have divided loyalties; through sibling rivalry the children may act out the marital tension.

What's the siblings' theory about the problems? What would they like to see changed? How do they see the adolescent differently than the parents? How do they perceive the marriage? When the children are not split into camps, they can often give a more balanced, reasonable view of the problem—"I think my parents are too tough on Jim, but he shouldn't get them mad by staying out late." This perspective gives you something to bounce off the family, such as, "Do you think what Amy says is true?" It gives you a good place to start.

How are conflicts resolved in the process of the session? How is this process different from seeing the adolescent with the parents? How are the parents and the adolescent both different with the rest of the family than they are individually? Who backs down, who is the compromiser, who sides with the mother? Is there good discussion or are there threats and hysteria? You want to know how the process breaks down so you can help them change it. What is intriguing about differences in the family session compared to the others, and why? Why does the family act differently when they are all together than when they are not?

The differences that you see may say something about the family culture, the way the children get attention, the impact of allies and divisions among the family members. Dad, for example, may sound strong and stern when talking together with his wife, but in the family session mother joins with the rest of the kids in discounting him. Simply noticing the change aloud can help the family uncover the dynamics that propel them.

Are there additional family problems that are not being acknowledged? Do other family members have goals that would help break the dysfunctional patterns within the family? Although neither the parents nor the teenager have mentioned it, you discover in the family session that the youngest son has cerebral palsy or a cleft palate. Or maybe the four-year-old blurts out that grandma went to jail last month. There may be problems lying underneath the presenting problems, family stressors that may be precipitating both the struggle the family is having and their coming in for counseling.

Do the parents see the session as valuable or irrelevant to their primary concerns? Back to expectations. Some parents wonder why you want to waste their time and money talking to the six-year-old twins when the problem is their 15-year-old. Others are surprised by what they learn from the mouths of the other family members or come to see that the problem isn't just their teenager, but their parenting or the fact that Dad drinks a lot. The way to know what they think about it is to ask.

How do you feel dealing with so many people at one time? Not only may this give a sense of how the parents may feel much of time, but also how reasonable it may be for you to do whole family sessions.

Of course, you will not have to ask all these questions—some may be obvious to you as you watch the family, some may be clear through the given background information, some may not fit your own theory and you will be substituting others instead. The point of the questions and the assessment, however, is to see how the lives of the family members overlap and stumble on each other, to find the places where functional interactions break down, to discover the ways coping mechanisms and inner and outer resources can be harnessed to solve the problems. They open the door to the treatment possibilities.

TEN

The Parent–Adolescent Struggle II

BACK TO MS. HARRIS AND ELLEN

Ms. Harris had made the appointment with the therapist at the suggestion of the school guidance counselor, who was concerned not only about Ellen's fighting and poor grades, but also her grief. During one interview with the counselor Ellen started talking about her father and seemed to the counselor to be depressed. As Ms. Harris related this during that first session with Ellen, Ms. Harris herself began to get teary-eyed and talk about how hard their father's death had been on the kids. Ellen would only look away, and told the therapist that the school counselor was making a big deal about nothing.

That entire first session was spent seeing mother and daughter together, gathering history and information. It was clear that Ms. Harris was overwhelmed by the changes that her husband's death had brought, both economically and emotionally. She spoke freely and painfully about the past year. Most of all she talked about how worried she was about Ellen, and her own guilt that she was not doing a good enough job as a mother.

Throughout all this Ellen acted stoically. When she wasn't answering a question with a grunt, it was with a simple yes or no, and she usually contradicted what her mother had said. The only change that she said she wanted at home was for her mother to not complain so much and let her do more of what she wanted ("All my friends can!"), especially take her to the mall on Saturdays. She did, however, agree to come back with her mother.

The second session was split between Ms. Harris and Ellen, to see how each was different without the other, to gather more history from Ms. Harris about her marriage, to build some rapport with Ellen. Ms. Harris was seen first, so that even if Ellen worried that the therapist and mother were talking about her, at least she wouldn't worry that the therapist was repeating what she'd just told him.

When Ms. Harris talked about her husband, her ambivalence was apparent. Once again, in that crumpled, teary posture, she described her husband as 15 years her senior, a long-standing alcoholic who was verbally abusive at times and demanding and controlling of her and the children. Ms. Harris had appeased him as much as possible, served as a buffer between him and children, swallowed her own anger, and adapted a codependent role. His sudden death knocked her off her feet. Although she had worked part-time before, she now was holding down two jobs.

While she had no trouble with the two younger girls, Ellen's behavior was compounding the stress; having never needed to take a strong role with the children, she now was struggling to reshape her role and image in their eyes. While things certainly weren't great when he was alive, now they seemed absolutely awful. What she felt most was that she had to learn to be strong for the children.

Ellen by herself continued to exude her tough air. No, she didn't think about her father that much; yes, things had changed a lot in the past year and a half; yes, school was boring; no, her mother wasn't doing a good job, in fact, she was pathetic the way she whined and complained and gave her a hard time about going out with her friends, but she was even more pathetic because she would eventually give in if Ellen pushed long enough. And Ellen was the one who had to look after her sisters all the time either because her mother was working or she was tired. She didn't mind doing it too much, but her mother sure didn't seem to appreciate it.

The therapist let her vent her fealings, and empathized with her feeling that things were unfair and that she was taking on more than most other kids her age had to. She just shrugged, but seemed to relax. The therapist talked to her about confidentiality and about therapy as a place to make some of the changes that may be important to her.

One of the traps here, of course, is to be seduced by Ellen's apparent strength and insight, to do as the mother does and give her too much power, to ask her what she thinks the mother or her sisters need most. But that only reinforces her distorted role. Her concern should only be on what she needs; it's up to Ms. Harris to be responsible for the rest.

The third session with Ms. Harris and Ellen together, with which the previous chapter opened, showed just how the interaction between them is played out. Here they were replicating in the office what happens at home. Even with the therapist's support, Ms. Harris had a difficult time acknowledging her anger and not caving into Ellen, and Ellen had a hard time not becoming angry and scolding her mother. The third session ended with the therapist talking individually to the mother about specific parenting skills.

DOING WHAT WHEN

So what do we have here? As we saw with Billy, we have another parent who is having trouble setting limits. Ms. Harris is not only having to shift gears with Ellen—from parenting a younger child to parenting a teenager—but is having to change roles within the family structure, from an ally and nurturer of the children to nurturer *and* disciplinarian. Ellen, due to her age, personality, and probably past patterns of relationship to her father and mother, has stepped into the father's role and, together with her mother, is quickly replicating the marriage, complete with verbal abuse. The heightened sense of power that she has, along with her overresponsibility and concern for her sisters, is enough to keep her in the role; what she's missing is any closeness with her mother or the opportunity to simply focus on her own life. Having Ellen to struggle against is more familiar and less anxiety provoking for Ms. Harris than making the changes in her role that she needs to make, especially since she is already so overloaded.

And so mother and daughter complement and interlock. Ellen takes charge because her mother doesn't, her mother doesn't because Ellen does. But what's holding this pattern in place? The unresolved grief? Perhaps. Ellen doesn't get sad, she (like her father did) gets angry, tough, and controlling. Ms. Harris doesn't get tough, she gets sad and helpless. Both, pulled by familiarity and pushed by complementarity, stay within their own comfortable emotion and behaviors. The anxiety, what's missing, the need for each is the same—to expand their emotional range, and move toward the underside of what they each cannot now feel, rather than depending upon the other to play it out.

What this raises is the question of timing—deciding when it's best to do what, figuring out the sequence of steps needed to learn new skills and solve problems. Issues of timing run alongside the issue of depth (moving from the least to the increasingly intrusive), alongside questions of priorities determined by the hierarchy of needs (e.g., getting the family on food stamps or helping Johnny get back in school before working on "growth" issues like understanding why you feel annoyed when your husband asks what's for dinner). The question of timing is the question of knowing when to approach a topic or task in terms of the family's emotional readiness and foundation of skills. What does the family need to do first before they will be psychologically ready to do more?

If, according to your theory, you believe that it's unresolved grief as much as anything else that is driving the emotional reactions and roles in this family, then the question and the solution lies in determining how to facilitate the grief reaction. Just like Billy, Ellen isn't comfortable approaching the topic or feelings head on; and Ms. Harris, for all her sadness, can only go so far—after a year she is still too quickly immobilized by these sad emotions, emotions that only trigger Ellen's complementary anger. Before we can help Ellen more openly grieve, we may have to help Ms. Harris get strong. To push Ellen to give up her toughness and look at her sadness while she sees her mother still wallowing in it and incapacitated may be too difficult for her. Only when Ellen knows that Ms. Harris is "on duty" and able to be more effective may Ellen be able to step down and out of her role.

Similarly, to expect Ms. Harris to tap her anger as a way of feeling stronger may be too threatening and anxiety provoking for someone who has spent most of her life suppressing such strong feelings. Before Ms. Harris may be able to work through to the anger side of her grief, she may first need the opportunity to see herself as stronger than she really is. Only with the increased self-confidence and self-esteem that comes through anxiety-approaching behaviors may she feel capable of handling her own anger and feel entitled to express it.

This way of thinking, this mapping out of sequences and deciding which holes to move toward first can seem complex but isn't. All it involves is approaching a pocket of anxiety and seeing where the resistance most arises. Ms. Harris's own history with her husband and her difficulty in mobilizing her anger within the session with Ellen gave the therapist immediate information and feedback about what may or may not work. If Ms. Harris, for example, was able to stand firm to Ellen's demands, or if Ellen was able even in individual sessions to let down her guard and approach some of her feelings about her father, these would be clues that these more direct routes may not only break the interlocking patterns between the mother and daughter, but help each move forward in healing from the loss. To push either one of them too hard so early in the therapy runs the risk of them shutting down or leaving treatment all together.

What we still don't know, however, is just how pervasive the grief is throughout the family, how entrenched both Ms. Harris and Ellen are in their roles, and the part the other girls play in maintaining the system. This is a good time to see the other children in a whole family session.

BRINGING IN THE REST OF THE TROOPS

They march in a single file down the hall, Ellen leading the way; followed by Betsy, skipping and jumping; then Marie, slouching, watching her feet; and finally Ms. Harris, once again bedraggled and frail looking. Ms. Harris dumps herself onto the couch alongside Betsy, Ellen sits by herself on the other, while Marie sits in the chair in between.

"So, did your Mom talk to you both about coming here today?"

Both Betsy and Marie nod.

"Momma, can I go over there and play?" asks eight-year-old Betsy.

Before Ms. Harris has a chance to say something, Ellen pipes up, "You need to stay here with us."

"Ms. Harris, I think Ellen spoke for you. Do you want Betsy to stay here next to you?"

"Sure, I guess. Honey, just sit here for a few minutes." Ms. Harris pulls Betsy close beside her.

"Your Mom and Ellen and I have been talking in the past couple of weeks about all the changes that have been going on in your family. It sure sounds like a lot has happened in the past year since your dad died."

"My Momma has to work a lot," says Betsy with a sigh, "and Ellen is always bossing us around."

"I do not!" snaps Ellen. "You're the one who's always bugging me, always running to Momma, always getting your way!"

"But you hit me!" And she lifts up the edge of her shorts and points to a faint black-and-blue mark.

"Girls, girls, please don't start," says Ms. Harris as she limply waves her hand toward both of them.

"Is this what happens at home, Marie?"

"All the time." She sounds bored.

"What do you do when they get into it?"

"Go to my room. Wait 'till they are finished."

"How are you and Ellen doing?"

"We get along pretty good. She tries to boss me around sometimes, but I just don't pay attention to her."

What's happened so far? We see Ellen assuming a parental role, both in the session process and at home, with little resistance from her mother. We could guess that Ms. Harris is closest to Betsy (she identifies with Betsy's helplessness?) and is openly favored by her, and that Ellen knows it, only increasing the gap between her and her mother, and her retaliation against Betsy. She and Ellen do battle where Ms. Harris does not. And Marie, just as she is seated in the room, is somewhere in between, the neutral middleman, who ducks for cover when conflict breaks out.

What we still need to know is how the family has crystallized around the father's death. After spending some time building rapport with Marie and Betsy and finding out about their relationship with each other and their mother, this is where the focus turns:

"Betsy, it sounds like you are very close to your mom. How about your dad, were you close to him?" the therapist asks gently.

"Well, sort of, I guess. He would take me to the park sometimes, and sometimes I would sit on his lap when we were watching TV."

"How did you feel when he died?"

"I was real sad, especially when I went to the funeral. Everybody was crying . . . I stayed close to Momma. . . . "

Out of the corner of his eye, the therapist sees that Marie is beginning to tear up.

"Marie," says the therapist softly, "what's wrong?"

Marie starts to cry harder.

"She feels sad," says Betsy.

"You're thinking about your dad?"

She nods.

Ellen is turned away and starts to get restless. "How about you, Ellen, how are you feeling?"

Ellen ignores the question.

"Ms. Harris, how are you doing?"

"I know this is hard on the girls. I don't bring this up at home or let them see me get upset."

"Sometimes Momma cries," says Betsy.

"And how to do you feel when you see her that way?"

"Bad, sad."

"Who do you all think misses your dad the most?"

Ellen can't handle this anymore. "This is a bunch of shit." She suddenly stands up and walks out of the office.

Grief gone underground. Ms. Harris tries to hold it within, crying secretly, hoping no one will see, making the grief itself a family secret. Marie, too, it turns out, does a lot of her own crying and missing of her father, but, like during the fights, steals off to her room. Betsy, like the little boy in *The Emperor's New Clothes,* isn't afraid to say what she sees and takes the junior caretaker role, the emotional backup when any sadness breaks out; like her mother she plays out the softer side of Ellen's anger and control. Ellen, with everyone else morose and collapsing, is boxed in with her anger. Overwhelmed with such strong feelings from everyone in the family, she has no choice but, like her dad perhaps, to leave.

And so our hypothesis is checked out. The grief is pervasive in the family, Betsy has stepped in as her mother's support and surrogate to re-create the marital tension, Marie, in many ways like her mother, is most comfortable stepping aside, and Ellen clearly is not able to tackle her own feelings of grief until the family gives her some room and helps her find a place. Ms. Harris needs to become the hub of the wheel, not to re-create her husband's role, but to include it within the new reality of her life as a single parent. Unless she can do that, the children will continue in their adaptive styles, with Ellen winding up out of the family, Betsy eventually taking care of her mother, and Marie sitting alone, depressed, in her room.

One of the biggest traps with this family, especially in the family process and especially because the therapist is a man, is stepping in and replacing the father, similar to the danger of becoming a copartner with Billy's grandmother. Ms. Harris would look to the therapist for leadership, Betsy and Marie would have someone besides their mother to rely upon, and Ellen, although she may balk initially at having her position threatened, might be happy turning things over to him, especially if she didn't have to worry about her mother anymore. All this is important for the therapist to keep in mind and to even be willing to say aloud in order to counter the possible fantasies, especially for Ms. Harris. She needs to hear instead that the therapist doesn't need to take over like Ellen is trying to do, but will support her in making the shifts she needs to make.

Ellen didn't come back in, but instead sat out the rest of the session in the waiting room. The therapist spent the rest of the time giving Ms. Harris and the other two girls some feedback—empathizing with their sadness and the change in the family, pointing out their different coping styles, including Ellen's, and their secret feelings, such as the way Betsy worries about her mother, the way Marie misses her father, the way Ms. Harris worries about the children. The therapist also gave them permission to talk about their feelings, to talk about their father openly at home, to ask questions, to bring it all out in the open. Both girls agreed to come back at another time. At the end of the session the therapist then went out and talked to Ellen; she agreed to come in and talk to the therapist individually.

As with Billy, we're at the fork in the path. Several options are open to us, depending upon your theoretical frame of reference, including staying with whole family therapy so that Betsy and Marie are not excluded. But if it's true that Ms. Harris needs to be the fulcrum of change, she may need some individual work to set her on course. Likewise, Ellen may have a easier time focusing upon her adolescent life if she doesn't have the rest of the family as an audience to ignite her role. The therapist decided to see if Ms. Harris could help facilitate grief work at home and to temporarily see her and Ellen separately.

ELLEN ALONE

When Ellen came in the following week, she looked anxious. The therapist suspected that she might be a bit gun shy from the family session and afraid that he would once again start talking about her father.

Of course he didn't. Even alone she would not have handled it any better and would only learn to dread therapy itself. Instead he asked her about her school and social life, her friends and boyfriends, and dreams about the future. Most of all, he wanted to have her talk and him listen, not about her family, but about her life as a teenager.

She did. Perhaps it was the relief of not having to talk about something more difficult that spurred her on; maybe she was feeling more comfortable with the therapist and dropping her tough exterior. It didn't matter why so much as that she was able to step out of her role, show her other side and inner life, and be supported and encouraged for doing so.

The session ended with the therapist thanking her for talking and, much as he said at the end of the last session with her mother and sisters, empathizing with the changes she and her family had faced. He worried aloud that she had taken on too much responsibility, that everybody else in the family saw her as mean and angry, but that they didn't really know how she felt or what her world was like. Of course she had to agree with him because this is what she had just spent the session talking about (explanation follows experience). The therapist suggested that he would like to help her be a better teenager and help her worry less about her mother and sisters.

She said little, but seemed much more relaxed. Essentially, she was given permission to step down. This didn't mean she automatically would or could—there was still a lot of power in her role, a need for her behavior to maintain the family patterns, and the underlying grief driving it all. But if Ms. Harris could begin to take up the slack, the new space within the family structure could be created for Ellen, and maybe then she could be able to grieve. Ellen agreed to meet alone with the therapist a few more times, think about specific things she would like help with, and meet, along with her mother, again in a few weeks.

TALKING TYPES

In contrast to those with young children, individual sessions with an adolescent are different simply because of the age difference. Whereas the play becomes the medium for Billy, the means for projecting and healing his inner world, talking becomes the medium for Ellen. Ellen's role and maturity make this easy for her.

But not all adolescents are as vocal as Ellen. In fact, adolescents are notorious for shutting down, sitting in the chair, grunting, and staring at their shoes. Those, like Ellen, who are parentified, seem to be the most willing talkers. Because they sound so much like adults, the danger is in talking to them as though they are. Doing so not only reinforces their role and defenses, but lulls you into believing that they're more mature than they really are and encourages you to gloss over their developmental struggles. Rather than letting them talk on and on about their concerns about everyone else, you need to steer teenagers like this toward their underlying, less easily talked about feelings and concerns about being a teenager.

Some teens are able to do this easily and use the therapist as a confidant. You become the big sister or brother, the good, laid-back parent to whom the adolescent can openly talk. Margaret, for example, a 16-year-old, would easily and eagerly talk about how she felt left out of the cliques at school, about feeling self-conscious about her body, about her ambivalence toward her father. Her isolation made her hungry for the opportunity to simply communicate with someone in whom she could trust, and through the process, in a Rogerian way, who could discover who she was. Her trusting of the therapist became the template for trusting others around her.

Of course, some adolescents seem to be open like Margaret, but the openness is really an anxiety-avoiding, rather than anxiety-facing, process. What they talk about is no different from what they talk about with their best friends on the phone every night. Sometimes this reflects their misunderstanding of just what therapy is about, how the conversation and the relationship is different from that with a peer. You have the responsibility to clarify your role and the purpose of the process—"Becky, I appreciate your telling me about your friends at school, but I'm not sure why you're telling me about it. What worries you the most? How can I help you with your feelings?" If it continues, then it is up to you to help the adolescent move toward what's missing in the process and his or her anxiety in order to create a new experience.

As with adults, there are important differences between adolescents who won't talk and those that can't talk, at least can't talk well. James, a 14-year-old, was referred by his school principal because he was crudely propositioning girls in his class at school for sex. He and his mother came in together for the first session and were seen by a woman therapist. James said little in the session, and the therapist thought that James was reluctant to talk because it was the initial session, she was a woman, and his mother was present. So arrangements were made for James to be seen individually by a man on the staff. Communication was still a struggle. James never initiated conversation and would only answer questions with the fewest words possible. When the therapist tried to talk to James about his sexuality ("So, James, what do you think about girls? Do you ever masturbate?"), the communication, although it didn't seem possible, broke down even more. The therapist then tried to talk about the apparent problem of talking ("James, it seems that talking about all these things seems really hard for you") but this got nowhere. The therapist felt discouraged.

It was only after the therapist received records from the school that he discovered that James had an IQ of 80. James's difficulty communicating may have reflected some of his resistance or embarrassment, but, the therapist realized, it probably reflected a communication problem on his side as well. James couldn't fully understand what the therapist was asking because he was probably talking over the boy's head. The therapist needed to talk more concretely ("Do you feel okay about touching your penis?"), and ask more specific questions ("Did you think that girl liked you?") to help James articulate what he was thinking and feeling. This painstaking process itself was valuable because it was James's difficulty appropriately expressing himself that led to the presenting problem.

But there are some adolescents who sound like James who are simply refusing to talk. They may have been dragged in by the parents, ordered to come by the court, or referred by the school, and they want no part of it. Someone else has the problem, not them, and they see no reason to be there or to talk to another adult who is going to give them a hard time.

There are several ways of approaching a grunter. One of the best is to see him or her together with the whole or part of the family. This sidesteps the grueling one-on-one struggle. By your exploration of the entire family landscape, the adolescent sees that the focus isn't only on him or her, and anxiety goes down. Better yet, usually someone in the family will say something outrageous enough to ignite some response from the teen. All you have to do is give him or her the space he or she needs to talk and be heard.

Another variation of the family session is to ask the teen to bring in a friend to the first family session. Sometimes these friends serve as advocates and help the teen speak up to his or her parents. But more often they confront the teen for keeping quiet or lying or doing self-destructive things like taking drugs or skipping school. Again, such confrontation has the effect of clearing the air quickly and getting the process moving.

Peer confrontation is, of course, the value of adolescent groups. The focus keeps moving around, and the comments of one adolescent are likely to spark responses in the others. If there are peers in the group who easily talk, and/or are familiar with the group process, they can be the cotherapists, and leave you out of the power struggle.

While most teens will generally warm up once they discover that you're different from their parents and teachers (better yet, that you have a sense of humor), are empathic to their point of view, and are interested in helping them change what they want to change, truly oppositional adolescents will cling to their corner of the ring at the slightest movement you make toward them. In that case some therapeutic aikido—"You know, if I were you I wouldn't say anything you don't want to say here, especially anything important"—is enough to challenge them to open up.

Other therapists prefer to wait the adolescent out. After they map out the terrain of therapy, it's up to the adolescent to make the first move. Their growing anxiety from the silence and the sitting usually is enough to start something. Other times it's fine to say that it's okay to be quiet here. On oppositional teens, it has a strategic effect and gets them to talk; for others it genuinely gives them a chance to settle in and collect their thoughts. What's important for the clinician to convey here is not power, but choice.

Finally, some adolescents who may clam up in front of parents or alone with the therapist (who seems like another parent) do well when paired with another sibling. This minifamily group not only gives the therapist a different perspective on family life, but the quiet adolescent invariably has another sibling who isn't. Even if he or she doesn't share enough of the adolescent's experiences, the sibling at least provides something for both the therapist and adolescent to respond to—"Your sister and I were talking about your Uncle Max last week. How do you get along with him?" This allows the teen to wade into therapeutic waters on a buddy system. Once the adolescent feels more comfortable, generally within a session or at most two, the sibling can be phased out and reappear again in whole family sessions. What you do want to avoid is the teen becoming dependent upon his or her brother or sister, allowing the sibling to be his or her voice, or reducing his or her anxiety by making the sibling the focus of therapy.

Over the course of the two individual sessions, Ellen was able to talk about specific problems at home (Betsy's constant intrusion), as well as at school (having an argument with her best friend). In each case the therapist helped her clarify both her feelings and *her* problem (e.g., Betsy's feeling bored is not Ellen's problem, but Betsy's), rather than let her feel overresponsible for the others, and encouraged her to come up with different options for handling the problem (wait for her friend to call her, write her a note). In each case she was encouraged to be assertive—with her mother and her friend—rather than suppress her feelings or get angry and create a cutoff. And she did. The next week she was able to report that she talked to her mother about Betsy, and had called up her friend and worked things out.

MS. HARRIS ALONE

Ellen's age and her ability and willingness to express herself and to think through realistic solutions to problems helped her take concrete steps at home and change the interactional patterns between her and her mother much more quickly and easily than did Billy, and than younger children usually do. When Ms. Harris was seen individually a couple of weeks later, she seemed less stressed, and reported that Ellen had been less demanding and angry and actually had come and talked to her about Betsy.

Hearing such news, it could be tempting to let Ellen initiate all the changes at home. But not only does this slow down the change process, but re-creates and maintains at home the reactive role that Ms. Harris has learned. In order for there to be long-term change in her and her relationship with her other daughters, she needs to make individual changes herself.

The therapist asked her about her relationship with her husband. Once again she sighed and seemed to collapse, but then slowly was able to talk about her loss and the first edges of her anger. His alcoholism and his violent temper overwhelmed her at times, and she retreated into a passive accommodation and made the children the focus of her concern and needs. When asked, she acknowledged feeling responsible in some way for his drinking and even his death. Perhaps she wonders if she could have helped him get sober, made sure he had gone to the doctor for a checkup. If she had, she and the children wouldn't be where they are.

There may be the inclination here to allow her to sink into these feelings, to experience them as part of working through the grief. But even though she may not have voiced her guilt aloud, these feelings were nothing new; Ms. Harris was familiar with their texture and weight; they were part of the constellation of emotions that kept her in her passive, reactive role. Instead, the therapist stepped in and did some light education about alcoholism and grief, stating that feeling guilty and responsible are normal parts of being in a family with an alcoholic and grieving an unexpected death. There was silence for several minutes, then Ms. Harris shifted gears and talked about Ellen.

Unlike before, this shift didn't feel like a retreat from these emotions, but a simply a shift in focus. The therapist followed her lead, and they began to discuss ways to deal with interactions at home. Even though things seemed better, Ms. Harris's past experience told her that they could change overnight.

Ms. Harris had never used threats to make Ellen comply. Some parents, however, particularly those who view their teenager as the problem, whose own frustrations have reached their limit, come to rely on this as the only means they feel they have of controlling their child. Over and over the message to the adolescent and the therapist is that the teen better shape up or else, the else usually being shipping the child out to foster care somewhere. Usually it doesn't work—the adolescent hears the threat and fights back, or feels the rejection and says he or she doesn't care.

Once you help the parents find other ways of responding to the adolescent's behavior, the threatening usually stops. But some parents need backing, need to know that the community, and not just the therapist, is behind them. This support can usually come through the schools, if the teen is having trouble there, or through the courts, if the adolescent is acting out in the community. The teachers, principals, or probation officers can be invited to come to meetings with the parent. They can clarify their role, their concern, their limits, and work with the parent to create a united front to the teen. The principal can stress the consequences of cutting school or offer rewards for completing work; the probation officer can let the teen know that he or she will personally bring the teen before the judge if he or she continues to ignore the parents' curfew. In many cases this is essential to keep the adolescent from splitting and undermining the changes the parent is trying to make.

But some parents, even with this backing, still lapse into threats. Even when changes are occurring, they throw out to the teen and the therapist that placement outside the home is always in their mind. This kind of talk can undermine the teen's willingness to work on changes, pull the process back into power struggles, and undermine any sense of security. These comments need to be more strongly confronted by the therapist.

The best way of handling the periodic making of such threats is to call the parent on it, that is, to take the parent's threat as a serious option. Whether you see this as a paradoxical move, a way of calling the parent's bluff, or a sincere acknowledgment of what the parent is saying and perhaps needing depends on your theoretical point of view. But the outcome is the same. Saying something to the effect of "Mr. Neal, I've been hearing you say to Tom on and off for months now that if he doesn't change, you don't want to deal with him anymore. Maybe I haven't been taking your feelings seriously enough, and we need to talk about whether we should make plans for Tom to stay somewhere else for awhile."

The message here is that what you say will be believed, rather than minimized, that it's all right to consider placement if the parents need a break. This type of stance draws out the issue of commitment and what it means to love someone, but it also clarifies ambivalence, pushes the parents to see that words need to be honest and match intent, that they need to take responsibility for their feelings and decisions. The discussion can quickly tap into the parents' own history—the way their parents managed their adolescence—and even transference issues regarding you, the therapist (Do the parents want you to shape up or get out, too?).

The net effect of this type of confrontation is to get all their feelings and intentions clearly on the table. The discussion itself will help the parents separate threat and need for control from true feelings and help them take a clearer stand. Most parents will recommit themselves to the process and stop the threats. But some may actually need to confront their emotions and sort through the possibilities of the teen's planned leaving of home. The therapist's job is to help the parent place this decision in a context and to make it a decision, rather than a frustrated reaction.

Ms. Harris never reached this point, in spite of her struggles with

Ellen. The therapist did some role playing and brainstorming with her to help her know how she could react should Ellen become too demanding or out of control. They also talked about Ms. Harris's spending more quality time with Ellen, in order to offset Ms. Harris's greater limit setting, and about the ways Ellen could help her at home, in order to begin to create a new, better role for Ellen in the family.

By focusing on Ms. Harris's parenting skills, on what she as the mother could do, rather than on what was wrong with Ellen, or her tales of victimization, the session experience was one of empowerment, the goal one of action rather than reaction and helplessness. While it's important not to move too quickly and overload her, or allow her to become too passive and merely fall into accommodating the therapist, with close monitoring of Ms. Harris's pace and her attempts to try new skills, and with change coming from Ellen, it's reasonable to believe that Ms. Harris could learn to change her self-image and come to see herself as a capable parent.

RETURN OF THE FAMILY

After two individual sessions each with Ms. Harris and Ellen, home life was beginning to calm down. Although she could easily fall back to her old ways when she was under stress, Ms. Harris had some positive experiences setting limits with Ellen and found to her amazement that Ellen, after a lot of huffing and puffing, was able do as her mother asked. Ellen spoke of spending time with her mother alone, something that she had not done in years, and didn't realize how much she missed it.

It was time to bring the rest of the family back in, to find out the impact on these changes of the other girls and to see what effect it was all having on the family's grief reaction. So in they troop again, this time Betsy leading the line straggling down the hall with Ellen and Ms. Harris walking together, taking up the rear. Ms. Harris sits by herself in a chair with Ellen on one couch next to her and Betsy and Marie together on the other. Betsy seems a bit less rambunctious than last time, and her mother asks her to take her feet off the cushion. Marie still seems quiet and depressed.

After touching base with Betsy and Marie ("How have you been?" "How was the field trip you told me about last time?") the therapist asks about how things have been going at home. True to form, Betsy immediately pipes up that Ellen has not been fighting so much.

"And you like that?" asks the therapist.

Betsy nods her head yes. Ms. Harris smiles. "And Ellen even let me borrow her sweatshirt."

"You looked like a dork," says Ellen with a smile. "It went all the way down to your knees."

"It wasn't quite her size," chimes in Ms. Harris, "but it was nice of Ellen to let her use it." Ms. Harris looks at Ellen and smiles, Ellen smiles back.

The hierarchy has shifted. Ellen and Betsy are relating more as siblings, and Ms. Harris is more in charge and positive toward Ellen. Marie, however, is still quiet.

"How about for you, Marie? Things feel any different at home? Not having to hide out in your room so much?"

"Yeah, I guess." A somewhat flat response.

"How are you and Ellen getting along?"

"Okay."

"I asked her to come to the mall with me the other night, but she didn't want to come," says Ellen.

"Marie and I talked some the other night," says Ms. Harris. "I think she is still having a hard time about her dad."

Marie's eyes begin to water.

"Is what your Mom saying true? Have you been missing your dad a lot?"

Marie nods her head.

"I bet it has still been hard for all of you." The therapist looks around the room, making eye contact with everyone.

"We went to his grave this past Sunday and brought flowers to my daddy," says Betsy. "I felt sad."

"We hadn't gone in a long time. I decided we needed to do that," says Ms. Harris.

The mother again is taking charge. Ellen so far is staying in her chair and doesn't seem to be getting anxious or angry. The goal now is to help everyone in the family stay with the process, to help the emotions come out; the content itself isn't important, it's only a medium for the emotions.

"Marie, how did you feel at the cemetery?"

"Sad." She's on the verge of tears.

"I picked the flowers," says Betsy.

Betsy is trying to distract from the emotions to help Marie. Appropriately, Ms. Harris reaches over and gently touches Betsy's knee and puts her finger to her lips. Betsy leans back and gets quiet. Ellen is staring at Marie.

"What do you miss most about your dad, Marie?" asks the therapist quietly.

"I miss going with him on Sunday mornings to get the paper." Her voice is barely audible, and tears are welling up.

"If your dad were sitting here right now," says the therapist as he pulls an empty chair alongside of him, "what would you say to him?"

"I'd say that. . . . " Marie starts quietly crying. Ms. Harris is getting teary-eyed, as is Ellen, and Betsy is sitting quietly with her head down.

"I—" starts Betsy, but Ms. Harris reaches over and touches her knee again. Betsy leans back again and gets quiet.

The only sounds in the room are everyone's sniffling and crying. The therapist says quietly that it seems that everyone has been feeling sad for awhile and missing their father, and that it's been hard to talk about, and probably making everyone feel lonely. Again, the goal is to facilitate the process, not to interpret. In contrast to the last family session, everyone is able to stay in the room together.

After several minutes, Ms. Harris speaks: "I think it would be good for us if we maybe took out the old family movies sometime this week and looked at them." Everyone nods.

"I remember when we all went out West," says Betsy.

"Do you remember that?" Ms. Harris says. "You were so young."

"I remember Dad went horseback riding with us, and almost fell off," Ellen says, half smiling.

"Yeah, he had that huge horse. My head was up to its knee," Marie says.

"I think we have movies of that," Ms. Harris says. "We'll have to get them out."

Everyone talks about things that they most remember, including Dad's temper, which Ellen brings up. The therapist merely guides the process and helps clarify the emotions, asking who felt scared when Dad got mad, if anyone felt that it was her fault that he got so angry or even that he died. Ms. Harris is able to jump in and tell the children that it wasn't, that their father drank too much, and that this made his anger worse. His drinking and his death had nothing to do with them.

Each member of the family is sorting through her grief. This session is the opening up of the process, not the end of it. This family will need to have more talks like this, more open sharing of feelings as they together and individually work through the loss. But now that Ms. Harris is empowered, she can serve as a role model of the grief process for the children; now that they feel that she can support them, rather than worrying so much that they have to take care of her, the natural healing process can follow its course.

WRAPPING UP

The family met again the following week, and again it was a mixture of emotion and substance. The family talked about seeing the family movies, and everyone related once again some past memories, but there was also focus on solving day-to-day problems—Who was going to cook when Ms. Harris had to work late one night?—with Ms. Harris taking charge. At the end of session it was agreed that Ms. Harris and Ellen would each come in individually one more time.

The session with Ellen felt like one of those termination sessions where there doesn't seem to be too much to talk about, no strong pressure to resolve anything. Ellen mostly talked about school, plans to get a job over the summer, her hope to visit Disney World with one of her friends and her family. The session ended with an agreement that she could come back by herself anytime she wanted.

The session with Ms. Harris was a debriefing of the family sessions, a review of all the positive changes she had been making, with the therapist clearly in the role of consultant. All the changes in patterns were reviewed, and ways of keeping the door open on the grief process and of supporting Marie were discussed. What was most striking about Ms. Harris was her strength, her assertiveness. She decided to stop therapy for the time being, and she was told that she could come back anytime with the entire family, with one of the kids, or by herself.

Of course, there are other avenues that this therapist and family could have followed: more individual work with Ms. Harris, ongoing monitoring of Ellen, sessions with Ellen and Ms. Harris, individual work with Marie to help her with her sadness, continued family sessions to help them unravel their anger as well as sadness and to solidify the changes in the family structure. All these options, no doubt, have merit and might have helped this family.

But therapy can and often should end with significant but modest changes. This family had moved beyond the place they were stuck. They are on a solid, more developmentally appropriate path. They learned some skills (particularly the mom) that they should be able to use as they individually and together face the changes and challenges to come in the next few years. If after these sessions they were still lumbering under their grief, if Ms. Harris was unable to develop more power in spite of the therapist's coaching, if Ellen remained angry or shifted her anger to another arena (e.g., started fighting at school or ran away), if Marie or Betsy stepped in to take Ellen's place as the I.P. and began to have severe symptoms that Ms. Harris could not help them with, more work would obviously be needed.

Some families are content merely getting to the other side of a crisis; others want therapy to leave them with a firmer sense of stability and some new skills; still others, building on the momentum of the initial changes, want to continue in order to maximize the family's potential. Where the end is set is determined by their expectations for therapy and yours. What you don't want to leave them with is a feeling of fragility, or a wanting and needing more help and not getting it, of resolving one problem perhaps, but left staring at the one or several that have taken its place.

Why did this case turn out seemingly better than that with Billy? Probably because the trauma was not so great, because Ellen at her age was able to verbalize her feelings and direct her behavior more deliberately perhaps, because Ms. Harris's level of depression wasn't as great as that of Billy's grandmother's, and she did not feel as isolated. And the therapists were different, in their personality, their clinical strengths and weaknesses, their ability to join with the family—a hundred and one variables that affect the course and outcome of a case that are beyond anyone's awareness or direct control. This, of course, is part of what makes for the art of therapy and the challenges that come with each new case.

LOOKING WITHIN

Adolescence is a bridge between two different worlds. During those few short years we consolidate and build on the lessons learned in childhood, about ourselves and life, and we are forced to look ahead to our future and our "grown-up" selves while struggling to discover who we are in the present. How well we master the challenges of adolescence and learn the lessons that it needs to teach us often becomes the template upon which we shape our adulthood for years to come. As you do these exercises, think back and remember your life as a teenager.

1. Think about your own attitudes about adolescents. Should they, in general, be given more freedom, more discipline? What does your answer tell you about what you believe adolescents need to learn most?

2. How could a therapist have been helpful to you when you were a teenager? How would have individual therapy been useful? Family therapy? What would have been your attitude toward each? How would have your family reacted?

3. In what situations, with what types of problems, or with what types of families with teenagers are you apt to overidentify, project, resist?

4. How might have a psychoanalyst, a Rogerian individual therapist, and a biological psychiatrist handled the case of the Harris family differently? What do you see as the major advantages or disadvantages of each?

5. Comparing the contrasting cases involving younger children and teens, which do you feel more confident about? What specific skills do you most need to develop?

6. How do you privately decide just how good a job you are doing with a particular family?

ELEVEN

Getting to the Core:
Couple Work in Family Therapy

The room seems empty, and quiet. It's just you, Eric, and Cathy. No kids, no fighting over blocks, Play-Doh, or puppets; no stretching out of a parent's arm to rein in one child before he has a chance to go clobber his brother. You're wondering what they did with the kids (or to the kids?) to come alone, but then you decide you really don't want to know.

Your mission: to help this couple gain some control over the bedlam at home. With four children between the ages of four and 12, two of them at any one time are fighting in some sort of a tag-team arrangement. Actually, this should be pretty simple: Find out where things break down, help the parents clarify their rules and their responses, make sure they are working together as a team. Straightforward child management.

"So how was your week?" you casually throw out to give yourself time to grab your coffee cup behind you and settle in.

"I sent him to his room, didn't I? I specifically told Danny to stay in his room for 10 minutes." Cathy has pushed her eyebrows together into a glower.

Whoa, did you just miss something, you wonder, as you barely swallow your first sip of coffee.

Eric, nervously pulling at his tie, apparently knows what Cathy is talking about. "Then three minutes later he's out there in kitchen with me, telling me that *you* told him his time-out was over!" Frail, quiet Cathy of last week suddenly is sounding angry and tough. She's now scowling at Eric, who is taking a deep breath and getting ready to swing into his defense.

"I thought you were being too hard on him, I—"

"But you do this all the time, Eric, ALL THE TIME!" She's getting hot.

"No, I *don't* do this all the time." Eric's cranking up, too. "You're the one who always lets Allison off easy, but do I say anything about it? No, I don't, because—"

"Don't give me that. I don't treat her any different than the boys. I'm the one—"

So much for a quiet, peaceful session.

Just as it is helpful to create for yourself and the family a vision of how they together would want to be, it's helpful to create your own vision of how the couple ideally needs to be. Good communication, respect, flexibility, good problem-solving and decision-making skills, a united front with the kids, ability to compromise, a commitment to each other and their parental relationship, an ability to separate out their issues as a couple from those of the children, an ability to see themselves as the building block, the central core of the family—all these readily come to mind. Basically, when the couple is sound, the rest of the family is sound.

But when they're not, things begin to fall apart. When the rules become unclear or contradictory, the children wind up either constantly testing them as a way of defining them or ignoring them. When the parents aren't united, the children quickly learn to split them—bypass the tough one and ask the easy one, or appeal to the other if you don't like what the first one said. When problems are never solved or communication is poor, the household is in a state of tension as the same problems come up over and over again. When the parents are always battling or struggling with each other the tension is magnified, and the kids have to learn to lean on each other for support, withdraw or escape, or, especially young children, blame themselves for what they believe is happening.

DANGEROUS STRUCTURES

When such patterns become part of the fabric of the couple relationship, when the battles are not just simple differences of opinion, but relentless struggles for power, or, worse, when tensions are never openly expressed, but instead are driven underground, the entire family structure becomes warped and distorted. This distortion can take various overlapping forms, varying in their toxicity and effect on the children.

The Child-Centered Family

Child-centered is a term that is used by those in the therapy field to describe families where the hierarchy has broken down or become blurred. The parents do not have a viable relationship as a couple, and instead the children become the glue and focus holding them together.

But it's important to keep in mind that this dysfunctional pattern wherein the parents are filling in holes in their marital relationship with children is very different from those families wherein the parents together choose to make the children their primary focus. The parents in these families are usually following core values of their culture (e.g., Jewish or Latino families), which essentially imply that children come first. Such families can be healthy and happy because the parents can have a good relationship with each other even if they spend more of their energy on the children than we as therapists or we as the mass American culture feel comfortable with.

In the dysfunctional, child-centered family there has been an erosion of the couple relationship. Imagine the start of marriage being like moving into a new, large house. There's room to explore, places to decorate and make your own, space to move around. But over the years the rooms become dusty and dirty and slowly filled with junk—resentments, half-finished arguments, unexpressed needs, memories of hurt. Rather than getting up the courage and cleaning these rooms out by talking about what is difficult to say, one by one the couple simply shuts and locks the rooms. Over and over this happens through the years, until the once beautiful and large house seems narrow and cramped as the partners find themselves living in the hallway by the front door. And so the only safe topics are the weather and that no-good supervisor on the job, and the only safe focus at home is the kids. Even though both may occasionally look at each other and shift their eyes upstairs, they just as quickly glance away. The partners silently make a pact to be good parents, if not good lovers.

There are two dangers that arise from this structure. One is that the children of such parents will by default use this as a model of their own couple relationships and families. Even though they have a strong model for parenting, they lack one for adult intimacy. As a couple they may think they are doing the right things, but wonder why they feel empty or awkward when they are alone without children. Essentially, how they wind up feeling is just the same as their parents did, but which they as children were never aware of. They have failed to learn that being an adult in all its roles and forms is something valuable in its own right.

The other danger is that anxiety, even panic, can set in as the children begin to leave home and the parents face the prospect of being alone with just each other. They may either undermine the children's leaving ("Why don't you go to the college right here in town, dear?") or scramble to find other replacements, such as adopting children, acquiring pets, becoming workaholics, and so on, to fill in the holes.

Separate Lives

At the next level of distortion, the split between the partners becomes wider and the parenting pact collapses. The problem of intimacy is not solved with children but with distance. In many families one of the parents is *the* parent (often the mother), while the other is somewhere else (at work, outside in the garage, out with friends). In other families the parents take turns: One minds the kids certain days or parts of days while the other is off, and then they switch. There isn't so much conflict as emptiness, deadness. The children are involved with one parent, the other is gone, and rarely do they have a chance to see how they are together. In their own couple relationships as adults the children re-create these patterns and struggle with the same emotions.

The Surrogate Partner

Of course, a parent's intimacy needs can also be met through one of the children. There are certainly times when parents and children can have a very close relationship, and this closeness ranges on a continuum from okay to not okay. In its most extreme not-okay form we find physical incest, where a parent literally co-opts one of the children to be his or her mate. But to varying degrees there can be emotional incest, such as when the parent starts complaining to his or her child about the other parent or uses the child as a confidant of his or her money troubles or relationship with his or her latest boyfriend or girlfriend. What makes these situations not okay is not that the parent and child are too close, but rather that there's a blurring of the parent–child boundary. The child is treated more as an adult than a child, and plays out an adult role in the parent's life.

When this type of blurring occurs, what we often wind up with is a child or teenager with a distorted sense of power, an overresponsibility for a parent or the family, and a loss at some level of his or her own childhood as he or she is forced to support the parent as much as be supported. We also potentially have three people in leadership roles, which creates confusion for the other children and competition and resentment among the three. Rather than struggling for his or her place, the other parent may physically leave the relationship or emotionally leave it by essentially taking on a role of one of the kids or forming a coalition with the rest of the kids against the other parent and the favorite child.

Ganging Up

Coalitions and collusions with children by one parent against the other aren't driven by lack of marital intimacy as much as by anger and destructive power. Rather than acknowledging each's separate sphere of power (e.g., work vs. parenting), or, as in the child-centered family, accepting at some level the lack of a relationship, the marital struggle is unending, with the children always triangled in. The mother becomes the ring leader of the children against mean old Dad; Dad heads the gang of boys in the family against Mom and Sally. Arguments may be over parenting, but it is all projection ("Stop picking on Tommy; let him do what he wants!" rather than saying, "Let me do what I want"). The conflict may be open or subtle, but, regardless, the effect is one of splitting the family into camps with each side against the other.

Fighting by Proxy

Of course, parents can lead from behind the scenes. When parents decide to fight by proxy, we have never-ending sibling rivalry. Some sibling rivalry is natural—not only do children get irritable with each other just as adults do, but every child also wants to feel special in the eyes of the parents and so at times inevitably feels jealous or resentful of the other sibling. Generally, children can learn to work these conflicts out on their own. If the parents interfere too much in their squabbles they can inadvertently reinforce them; the children learn that one way to get the parents' attention is to start a fight.

In families where the parents openly argue the children may take sibling rivalry one step further. With the parents as models of interaction, the children copy what they see the parents do and argue and fight most of the time. The parents may do little to stop it because they are so caught up in the marital conflict, or they may foster the children's fighting by taking sides.

When the parents fight by proxy, it is the children who do the fighting for the parents and express the anger and conflict that the parents cannot. It usually starts with one of the parents subtly favoring one of the children (perhaps one who looks like him or her or who shares a similar personality) or encouraging the child to stand up for him- or herself against the siblings. The resentment and conflict is stirred, and rather than stopping it or leading the coalition, the parents do nothing. They may complain to you about the children's constant battling, they may even make jabs at stopping it, but their own inability to work together as a unit, and their own frightening anger that lies just below the surface keep them from getting clear and organized enough to be effective.

The problem and the patterns, like most negative patterns with children, continue because essentially everyone wins: The children have emotional outlets and means of gaining, if not positive attention, at least negative attention from the parents; the parents have vicarious outlets for their own anger, as well as a comfortable, familiar problems around which to focus their anxiety.

All of these patterns—the ganging up, the children as surrogates, the child-centered marriage, the fighting by proxy—distort the parent–child relationship by placing children in inappropriate roles that threaten their security and trample their development. These patterns so easily come about, of course, because of the malleability of children themselves. The children's dependency on the parents and the pliancy of their personality enable them to take on habits and roles that re-create the parents' own pasts or fill holes in the sinking marital relationship in exchange for some attention and sense of purpose. Through the interlocking of patterns within the family system, it's just as easy for such patterns to become entrenched. Even if one of the parents attempts to change the nature of the family relationships, he or she not only may run into a power struggle with the other parent, but with resistance from the children, who become anxious from the change.

SEPARATING ROLES: ASSESSING THE COUPLE

Resistance doesn't mean that one parent (or even one child) can't bring about change in the family; they can because a shift in one pattern will ripple through the others. But such one-person change takes both enormous time and persistence. When there is a stable couple relationship on which to build, when the parents can separate their problems as a couple from those problems as parents, when they can work together to present a united front to the children, changes can occur more quickly and be sustained more easily.

In order to help the couple learn how to distinguish needs and concerns as a couple from those as parents, you need to shift through and separate the roles and emotional dynamics that make up their relationship. Here's a quick checklist of questions to ask yourself and/or them:

Are couple problems defined? Some couples openly complain about each other and clearly state that it's their relationship that's creating problems in the family. This gives you their permission to directly focus on these issues and improves the prognosis. But more often, when the I.P. is a child, such problems are at best alluded to in side comments or joking remarks—"He's got a temper like his father"; or, "Of course, I don't get any help with this!" If you pick up on these comments—"Do you feel you need more help from your wife? or, "If your wife helped more, do you think it would help Joey do better?"—the couple often won't agree that there are problems in the relationship worth discussing.

You need permission from both partners to bring up the marital issues in the therapy, but how do you do that when they don't agree? Since the disagreement there in the session probably reflects the larger conflict between the partners, you can sometimes start with that—"It seems like you have a difference of opinion about whether this is important enough to bring up. Sam, maybe you can tell Mary why you think that is?" or, "Mary, Sam's bringing up things that you'd rather not talk about, and that seems to bother you. Does this happen a lot?"

However you choose to ask the question, your goal here is to open the communication between the partners. By doing so in your presence they are both defining the emotions and qualities of their relationship and finding out as it unfolds within the process that by your supportive response it's safe to do so in front of you. In effect, they are moving toward their anxiety and learning that it is okay to do so. Once this is done, using the principle of explanation follows experience, you can then link this inter-action to their concern about the presenting problem—"It sounds to me like you both feel that the other one totally disregards what you say. I wonder if Joey can sense this and uses the split between you to try and get his own way?" The link between the couple issues and parenting issues now seems more clear, and the couple is more motivated to explore their problems.

What emotions are presented and how are they handled? Sarah is seething throughout the session, while her husband, Carl, scarcely responds and seems depressed, or perhaps both are flat and detached, and the children do all the talking.

You assume that the process you see in your office replicates to some degree what happens at home. You want to notice not only the mood of each partner, but the mood in relationship to the other and perhaps the children. Does Carl always seem depressed and unresponsive, or is it his way of coping with Sarah's anger? Does he cope through alcohol or drugs, or does one of the children act out his anger? Does Sarah get angry be-cause Carl is depressed? Is it her way of trying to get him to respond, or is it some internal response independent of Carl or anyone else? How else does she manage her emotions—through drugs, eating, having affairs? Are the parents detached most of time, letting the children at home essentially take care of themselves or endlessly try to find better ways of getting their parents to respond to them? How does any of this possibly tie into the presenting problem? For example, does Carl's depression make it easy for Michelle to walk all over Sarah? Does Jeff boss the other kids around be-cause he feels like the parents aren't going to parent?

This type of brainstorming is a way of trying to link the emotional lives both of the individual parents and of the couple as a unit with the rest of the family and the presenting problems. These questions can then be directly asked and explored with the couple—"Sarah, you seem angry. How do you feel about the fact that Carl is saying nothing back?" or, "Carl, you seem depressed. Do you sometimes feel this way at home? Sarah, is this how Carl seems to feel around you at home?"

As you do with the whole issue of problems in the marriage, your immediate goal is to open the communication, explore the emotions and their outlets, the emotional flexibility each partner shows and has, the ways the emotions bounce off each other and drive the behavioral patterns (e.g., Carl is depressed and withdraws, Sarah feels overwhelmed by the children and gets angry, causing the children to run to Carl and drag him back into the family's interactions) and fuel the presenting problem (e.g., Jeff acts out Carl's anger toward Sarah). This exploration and tracking early on helps you see where emotions need to be expanded (e.g., Carl needs to get in touch with his anger), where emotional triggers can be used by the couple as signals of a dysfunctional pattern (e.g., when Sarah starts to get angry Carl needs to step in rather than ignore her), and to help the couple once again see how their moods spill out over each other and the rest of the family.

How has the relationship changed? Explore changes in interaction (less affection, more affection, more arguments), changes in one person (she's more bitchy, he's controlling), changes over time (how different from when they first met), changes in the family (environmental, situational stress).

There are two elements to explore in these questions. The first is understanding how the needs of each partner for the other have changed over time. The developmental view of relationships, the seven-year itch, and the like, presents the model that relationships naturally change over time because the people naturally continue to grow. Problems arise because there is not a way of changing the structure of the relationship with its rules, routines, and roles, as the people change. The woman who married someone who was in charge like her dad may need less control 10 years later. The man who married a woman who desperately needed him now feels weighed down with responsibilities and begins to resent her dependency. While this struggle over changed needs may surface as problems over children or acting out (e.g., affairs), the underlying issue and challenge is the need to bring the relationship up-to-date so that it can better represent the individuals within it.

The second notion is that relationships are changed not only from the inside but the outside. Even the strongest relationships have been toppled by the serious illness or death of a child, financial stress, or even the building of a new house. Although it's tempting to see these stressors as only pushing on cracks already established in the foundation of the relationship, it's also reasonable to believe that a reduction of stress can get the relationship back on course.

Often it's helpful not to just ask these questions, but to follow the answers with your explanation of your thinking. For example, if the wife complains that her husband has always been somewhat controlling, but that it's been driving her crazy recently, you might talk about how individual needs change over time, and how it's common that what was once attractive (he seemed so confident and powerful) over time turns so negative simply because the people have changed and they no longer need what they did before. Unfortunately, the new needs do not fit easily within the old structure and patterns of the relationship. Their task then is not getting him to be less controlling or her to be less bitchy, but for both to talk about what they need from each other right now.

How are decisions made about children, money, household chores, and sex? Most couples have evolved rules and roles for making decisions between them without discussing them or even being aware of them. To ask questions about decisions is, in the language of Haley, Madanes, Watzlawick, and other strategic therapists, second-order questions, questions not about what is ultimately decided, but how the decision-making process itself works. Such questions ask the couple to talk about power in the relationship, to define who's the boss of what, to acknowledge who has the last word. Questions about parenting, money, sex, and household chores are in particular often the ones that readily become the power issues in the family, where finding a fair or effective solution ("Why don't you pay the rent from your check and I'll pay the child care from mine") often gives way to battles over whose way is going to come out on top ("It's my money and you aren't going to tell me what to do with it").

Needless to say, these questions can arouse anxiety in the session and in the couple, and some therapists may argue that it's best to wait until the partners bring up these issues when they are ready, rather than confronting and raising their anxiety too soon. This certainly is good advice if the couple is wary or hostile of therapy itself, clearly untrusting of or uncomfortable with the therapist, or already so anxious that any more stress is likely to make the couple head for the door or shut up. It's also probably not a good idea if such confrontation goes solidly against the grain of your own personality style, values, or theory.

But bringing up issues that the couple doesn't is an active way of helping the couple understand the family structure and how it may contribute to the presenting problem. The proactive stance helps keep you from becoming inducted into the system and being lulled into accepting only what is presented. By raising these questions regarding how decisions are made or how disagreements end (someone gives in, someone walks away and it's not discussed anymore, someone becomes violent) you, and the couple, define the limits of anger and ability to compromise, the underlying power structure and struggle, and the emotions that fuel them. Resentments that have been tucked away within these issues and which warp the family structure are often exposed. More importantly, perhaps, by raising these issues and their anxiety you're testing the waters; you're able to see right there and then how this couple will respond to the anxiety of change itself—where they may resist, how quickly or carefully you may have to go.

What is the role of children in the patterns of the couple? How child-centered is the couple? Are children pulled into arguments literally or figuratively? Are the children divided in their support of the parents? Is one child a surrogate partner? What parent spends what time with what child? How is the hierarchy skewed?

Again, by asking yourself these questions you are mapping the ways the children may become part of the couple's conflicts and solutions. By asking the partners some of these questions—What do the kids do when you argue? Do any of the kids join in and take sides? Which of the children do you think feels closest to your husband, to you?—you are once again beginning to link the couple's dynamics to the children's behaviors, helping them see where the children may be inappropriately being brought into their relationship.

How does the couple need the presenting problem? The presenting problem can stabilize not only the entire family system, but the couple's relationship. Martha's drinking, for example, becomes the focus and reason the couple stays together, or her behavior creates enough of an ongoing crisis and distraction that their marital problems never have time to come to the surface, or the partners argue about how to handle her rather than arguing about the ways they treat each other. The answer to this question tells you what you may need to work on in the relationship if the presenting problem is to change (e.g., the couple needs to acknowledge the conflicts; they need to find positive rather than negative ways of interacting); and clues to the answer often lie in the session process, such as when Martha acts up and distracts just at the point that tension arises between the couple, or the way one partner switches topics to complain about the other when you ask a sensitive question about the relationship.

How severe are the relationship problems? Have there been separations, divorce action, abuse, arrests, affairs? The answers to these questions tell about the chronicity of the problems and patterns, the prognosis for the relationship, and the need to focus on these issues before expecting any lasting change in other family patterns. Some couples will be up-front about this information, but many won't. Obviously you can't initiate asking these types of questions directly if they don't bring it up—the couple will get too anxious and probably lie to end the discussion. But once the couple is talking about arguments or problems in the relationship, you can ask something like, "And what is the worst that your arguments have ever been? Has anyone ever gotten hit, have you ever thought about separating or divorcing?" Your sensitivity, gentleness, and sense of concern, rather than judgment and investigation, are most important in approaching this delicate area.

All these questions are similar to those you used in assessing the entire family. Basically, you are looking to find out whether there is both fluidity and structure, whether problems have a way of being solved, whether change, even though difficult, can be accommodated, whether emotions have appropriate outlets, and whether the partners see that their relationship is different from that of the children and that they both have a commitment to it and each other. By asking yourself these questions, you can begin to separate out the couple from the family; by asking the couple some of these questions you are letting them know that their relationship is important and linked to the problem; by their response you can discover just how open they are to such exploration.

CHOOSE YOUR FORMAT

What you do with what you discover once again depends upon your own theoretical frame and the expectations of the family. For example, the Bowenian use of genograms is a powerful way to learn about the couple's history and family patterns (e.g., divorce is rampant as a solution to marital problems; grandmothers and granddaughters are close, but mothers and daughters are not) and for the couple to see how larger patterns take hold within their relationship. Many therapists matter-of-factly start in this manner: "I've found that sometimes parents have trouble making decisions (or handling a particular child, or getting along, etc.) because they have learned through their families different ways of approaching problems and relationships. I'd like to take a few minutes in this session to better understand some of your family background and what you've learned about parenting and solving problems. I'm going to ask you a few questions about your grandparents and parents and draw a map of it, which we can then look at together and compare." The process of doing the genogram, as well as the product itself, allows them to step back and adopt a larger, less personal view of their problems as a couple, as well as helps them step back from their anger and frustration in the session process to look at what is occurring more objectively. Rather than each one feeling that the partner is out to get him or her, they become curious about the way they are both helping history to repeat itself.

On the other hand, a communications perspective looks not to history but to the skills the individuals need in order to express without attacking what they want their partner to know. The couple is taught how to make "I" statements, to discuss feelings rather than use rationalizations, to say what they want rather than what they don't like. This works well not only when communication is clearly poor, but when the less threatening idea of "learning communication skills" can make the couple less anxious and more motivated.

An especially effective approach is the use of a problem-solving model supported by the historical material of a genogram, and an emphasis on good communication skills. If a couple, for example, is constantly fighting over the limits that should be imposed on the children (they have to finish their homework before dinner vs. doing it whenever they want provided they get it done), you could do a genogram to help them see how their families and hence their expectations and models of parenting and decision making are different (e.g., mothers decide such issues or the couple talks it out). You could then help them clean up their communication so that they are less likely to trigger arguments and power struggles that undermine their ability to solve the problem, and lead them through the steps to resolving the problem. For example, help them brainstorm creative options, encourage them to make compromises rather than just giving in, help them recognize when they are reaching an impasse or falling into a power struggle and that they need to talk about those feelings or take a break and cool down. By doing all this in the session process, you stay aware of exactly how things break down and can help the couple be successful. This success ensures that they are more apt to try to practice the skills at home and to see therapy as an effective process.

Similarly, it can be helpful to use the psychodynamic view of marriage as a layering of projections. Each person doesn't see the real person before him or her, but one disguised with all the unresolved issues from the other's past. So Mary sees her husband as harsh and brutally critical just like her father, even though in reality he's not. Or Fred hasn't resolved the desertion of his mother when he was young and spends much of his energy "being good" and repressing most of his anger so that his wife won't get angry and leave him. Your task becomes one of exploring the past (perhaps with a genogram) and helping the individuals separate past and present issues and emotionally resolve unhealed wounds through interpretations or experiences (e.g., having Fred write a letter to his mother expressing how he feels, or having Mary imagine her husband sitting next to her in an empty chair and telling him how she feels when he criticizes her). As the projections are peeled away, the real person can be seen and the overreactions can stop.

Finally, you may want to start your couple assessment with the "mir-

acle question" of brief, solution-oriented therapy: "How would your relationship be different if the problem of Arnold's truancy, your sexual
problems, Betty's whining, whatever, was miraculously gone tomorrow
when you woke up?" Even if you decide not to use a solution-oriented
approach (e.g., helping them imagine how they would act if the problem
wasn't there), the couple's answer can give you a clue as to the centrality
of the problem in their lives, their motivation for changing it, or even the
ways things might get worse (e.g., they may admit that they may have
nothing to talk about).

Whatever approach you use, however, your choice will be pragmati-
cally overshadowed by the couple's expectations. We're back to the question of who has the problem. For some couples, the children have been
so much a focus of their attention, either because the couple is child centered or because the children's behavior has created the most problems,
that any discussion of their relationship, by you through your questions,
or by them through their own initiation, is too fraught with anxiety. The
message clearly given is that they are there to help the children and everything else is hands off.

At the other extreme are those couples who drop the subject of children within a few minutes of the first session. When you ask them why
they think the presenting problem is happening, they immediately begin
their tales of woe and rage about each other. The children, it turns out,
were merely the ticket of admission into the therapy system. The focus
from the start is upon the relationship.

Unfortunately, some therapists, especially those trained only to work
with adults, are quite happy to shift from the children to the marital relationship, never coming back to work on the children issues. This is a mistake on two counts. While it's true that in the long haul children will
generally do okay if the couple is doing okay, one or two of the kids may
have developed individual problems (e.g., encopresis, extremely aggressive behavior) that need specific parental and professional attention. To
ignore such behavior or assume that they will automatically get better may
result in the children only continuing to do worse, or the couple becoming dragged back into their old patterns. Similarly, even if the problem
with the children isn't severe, the couple needs to be able to apply their
improved relationship skills to parenting. If they don't, or if you as the
therapist aren't sure how well they can, parenting issues may remain the
couple's Achilles heel and eventually erode the gains that they have made.

One step back from those couples who declare from the outset that
their relationship is the problem, and probably more common, are those
cases where an individual parent comes in because of a problem with a
child, but then quickly switches focus to the other parent—"I think the
kids are having so much trouble these days because me and my wife have

just not been getting along." The parent leads the way into the relationship and you can decide to invite the other parent in, coach the parent on ways of talking at home to his or her spouse about problems, work with the parent individually to increase insight into his or her role in the relationship and problems, help him or her become the change agent in the family, or offer to help with the child's problems and refer the parent to someone else for individual or couple work. What option you choose will again depend upon your theory and the client's expectations.

In between these positions of staunch resistance and open acceptance of marital problems are the infinite degrees of variation from the willingness to explore the relationship only as it pertains to the I.P. child, to the possibility that improving communication may help coordinate parenting, to some agreement that yes, the couple's issues probably are affecting the rest of the family and couple therapy might be helpful. Your initial task is to close the gap that lies between your view of the family problems and that of the couple. If you believe that the children and family cannot get better unless this couple gets better, you must persuade them by education, by underscoring the dysfunctional process in the room, by exploring the ways that emotions spill over to the children, and by tracking and highlighting the distortions in the family structure that their relationship, in spite of what they assume, is not separate from the world of their children, but the hub onto which everything else in the family holds.

Eric and Cathy, for example, the couple we met at the beginning of this chapter, were by the second session openly acknowledging their divided approach to the children, and the breaking of the sibling group into father and mother camps. The fact that both were so quickly and openly arguing about it makes it easy for you to talk about their relationship and the struggle they are having not only with the kids, but with each other. They may easily decide that they need to leave the children at home for a few weeks so that they can sort out some of these marital issues. The three of you may then decide to bring the children back in and do total family sessions to translate the couple skills into the parenting structure, or let them do it on their own at home and simply check in with you.

If, however, Eric had refused to talk with Cathy about her concerns, or denied there was any difference in their parenting styles and kept the focus only on the children, you would have had to create a new starting point for discussing the relationship and linking it to the children. You might, for example, have asked Cathy how she felt about Eric's minimizing of her complaints, and have wondered aloud if this happens at home as well. Or you may have turned to Eric and asked if he's heard this all before, or if Cathy seems to always find problems where he feels there are none. These questions, this empathizing with each partner's feelings, would, you hope, encourage the couple to talk about their relationship in a broader way and help them to talk more openly to each other there in the session. The process that emerges between them could then be used as a springboard for talking about parenting and the problems the children are having—for example, "I notice that the more impatient you seem, Cathy, to change what the kids are doing, the more, Eric, you say that there's not that much of a problem. I wonder if the kids hear the same thing at home, pick up the split between you both, and wind up playing one of you against the other in order to get their way?"

Of course, it's possible to work on the relationship through the family work. Tina and Marcia, for example, a lesbian couple raising two of Tina's children from a previous marriage, came in with the children because of minor behavioral problems with the oldest boy, Tim, age 6, at school. Although the couple had been together for several years, it quickly became clear to the therapist at our clinic that Marcia's role with the children was not clearly and consistently defined. At times Tina would be upset because Marcia would not take an active disciplinary role with the children, while at other times she castigated Marcia for doing precisely that. When the therapist tried to explore the issues of control and decision making between them, both quickly became resistant.

Rather than pressing the issue, the therapist asked the boy to describe his view of the problem, which highlighted for the couple his confusion about knowing whom he should turn to for permission. She then asked Tina and Marcia to work up some guidelines that Tim could use in order to clarify communication and ease the boy's confusion. They were both willing to do this.

The next week Tina and Marcia reported just how difficult the process was and how they both felt that there was a power struggle going on. Working within the problem context, the therapist then used the session to help them develop guidelines right there and then. She helped them recognize when they were starting to get into a power struggle and, by focusing on their communication and encouraging them to compromise, helped them come up with boundaries that both of them could live with. These guidelines and the negotiation process itself became the foundation for helping Tim with his school problems and making other decisions about the children.

Another therapist might have taken a different path, wanting to explore, perhaps, Tina's unresolved past marital issues; the children's own response to Tina and Marcia's relationship; the stresses of being a same-sex couple; or spending play therapy time with the boy to uncover his inner struggles, loss, or adjustment to the family transitions. All these are valid and possible, and may be met with more or less resistance that the therapist would need to negotiate.

Are there times when it would be beneficial for the children to be part of the couple work? Some therapists would say that as soon as the focus shifts to the couple's relationship the children should be out of there. This exclusion of the children helps demarcate for the couple the boundary between couple and parenting issues. This becomes even better advice when the interaction between the parents is openly hostile and destructive and the children will not understand what is happening, or when the process only reinforces a blaming of the children (even hearing their name mentioned a lot is enough to cause little kids to think what is happening is their fault). And, of course, if the topics to be discussed are clearly adult topics—sex, money, adult relationships—or the parents feel inhibited or too easily distracted around the children, or you feel you can't manage all those people in one room and you can't get a cotherapist, make it easy on everyone and send the children out.

The other side of this issue, however, is that there is value in the children, especially older children, seeing how adults can communicate and work out problems. The work between the partners may be good modeling for the children of communication and problem solving in relationships, or the process can help the children see the underside of the tension in and between the parents and can come away with a more balanced view of the parent (e.g., Mom isn't just angry all the time, but is worried or sad about Grandma). They can discover or see right before them that they are not to blame for the family's problems, but that problems lie elsewhere, and with your direct blocking of their interruptions, can learn that they don't need to take sides and try to fix what is happening, but can let the parents work it out themselves. Your decision to include children or not ultimately rests on your confidence that the session will be positive, rather than hurtful for the children, that you will not be inadvertently re-creating the problem in the session (pulling in the children and triangulating the couple's relationship rather than helping the partners work out their own problems), and that your approach fits both your values and operating theory.

Similarly, whatever way you decide to integrate couple work into the family work, it's best that it be integrated both with the other issues in the family and your own view of the system. What to do about the couple is part of your assessment of what to do about the family and the problem. You don't want to replicate the problem (e.g., ignore the couple issues the way the couple does) or become swept up in the dysfunctional patterns and roles (e.g., giving into the husband just like his wife does). Remember, you're in charge of the therapy.

TWELVE

Couple Repair

So what do you do when you see that the couple's relationship needs some work? The easiest way to think of couple work is to see it as a smaller version of family work. You are still dealing, after all, with patterns and process. Here are the guidelines and goals for family work translated into couple dynamics:

Improve communication. There's a lot to be said for simply getting two people to stay in a room and talk. There are the basics of Therapy 101—facilitate the process so that they can learn to take turns, so they talk about themselves rather than just blaming or criticizing the other person, so they talk about their emotions and not just their ideas and rationalizations, so they talk about what they haven't talked about before. You can see your job as a coach or traffic cop, a teacher, a role model, or all of them. Give them communication exercises (have each repeat what he or she thought the other said before saying something else), teach them about "I statements," educate them about the differences between male and female communication styles (e.g., men tend to want to come up with solutions to a problem and be done with it, while their partners want them to listen and discuss the problem together), have them communicate nonverbally—each taking turns positioning themselves in a live sculpture of the relationship, drawing pictures respresenting their relationship when they first met and at the present time. Help them experience intimacy by communicating what they have never communicated before.

How much should you control the communication between the couple? It depends. Initially you want them to talk to each other so that you can see just how well they can communicate—see where things go well, notice how and where communication starts to break down—and so they don't get into the habit of directing all their communication through you; this only makes them too dependent on you and anxious about talking to each other at home. Once you've figured out their communication patterns, you can begin to block and change the patterns ("Hector, you're blaming Teresa and she's having hard time not getting defensive. Try telling her how you feel and what you want her to do.").

Obviously, if their communication is really destructive you will need to take more control over the process and perhaps ask them to talk to you rather than the partner in order to decrease the verbal and nonverbal triggers that set the other person off. But as they improve, give them more leeway and enter the conversation only enough to keep them on track and keep the communication open and honest.

There are two common mistakes that therapists make in teaching couples how to communicate better. One is that they don't match their teaching with the couple's expectations. For example, doing formal communication exercises (e.g., starting a series of statements with "I feel . . . ") may effectively teach skills, but will be met with resistance if the couple desperately wants to talk about their child or the argument they had Thursday night, or if the husband sees this as confirming his worst fears about the stupidity of therapy. Your teaching needs to match the couple's needs in terms of timing and content.

A more serious mistake is moving too quickly with angry couples. Couples who cannot yet communicate well or who only intellectually understand good communication skills but haven't practiced enough yet in their sessions to be able to integrate them into their everyday communication shouldn't be encouraged to discuss topics, especially sensitive ones, at home on their own too soon. Without your protective presence the communication falls apart, the outcome is emotionally or even physically destructive, and their confidence in you and the therapy is broken.

Stop violence. With the increase in couple violence, you need to be sensitive to its presence even when it's not openly discussed. Ask them matter-of-factly to tell you about their worst argument so you can get some idea of just how bad it can get. Be clear and firm in saying that emotional or physical violence is the product of other emotions and problems, as well as their own interaction, but that they individually need to be responsible for their behavior and that violence has no place in their relationship.

One of the keys to violence prevention is the couple's ability to realize when the argument is crossing over the line and becoming destructive. If you ask the couple, they can usually identify the triggers themselves ("We do fine until she starts bringing up things from the past." "I can stay calm until he raises his voice and starts shaking his finger at me."). You can also identify the verbal and nonverbal triggers in the process of the session and clearly stop and label them so that the couple can begin to do the same. In the beginning it's a good idea to have them "save" arguments from home (e.g., write down complaints on a list during the week) and bring them into the session where you can help them talk them out.

You can also have them sign a nonviolence contract to emphasize their self-responsibility, and help them come up with nonverbal signals that either one can use when he or she feels the conversation is getting too hot and needs to stop. (I once saw a video of one of Jay Haley's students who was working with a violent couple. The husband decided he would drop his pants as a signal when conversations were getting out of control. Obviously, you can use simpler methods like waving a handkerchief.) If you feel the emotions are just too volatile and the situation is too dangerous, don't be afraid to recommend that the couple temporarily separate until they and you can get things under control. Once you've helped the couple stop falling into the violent patterns, you can begin to focus on the underlying issues and emotions generating the anger.

Educate them about relationships. "What you both are experiencing is something that happens in most couples after six, seven, eight years of marriage." Talk about the normal changes in a relationship, help them see that all relationships change over time simply because people naturally change over time. Having a developmental context for their struggle helps them feel less guilty or overwhelmed.

One of the best ways of developing this context is to ask the couple what each of them needed most when they got married or met. Looking back, how were they different people than the way they are now? How did their partner help fill those needs? Then ask them to talk about what they need now, for themselves, from the relationship.

You can then weave these answers together, highlighting that they're both saying that they've changed over the years, that what they needed at the beginning they no longer need now because they have each grown, in part due to the help of their partner. But the current needs and current people don't fit within the box that the marriage has become with its set patterns and silent rules, and so they complain, or blame or argue, or have fantasies of getting divorced or having affairs. But the real goal is to create a new relationship that better represents who they are today.

Couples get angry or disappointed because they feel that the other person has changed in some negative way. It helps them to see that the change they see is only one manifestation of larger, normal changes within the relationship.

Help them recognize when and how the children are a solution/distraction. As mentioned several times earlier, you need to help the couple see the link between the children's problems and their relationship. The couple needs to see how and when the children are being triangled into the relationship and the way the children's problems can become distractions from their own. This point of view in effect makes the children's problems barometers of the couple relationship. When the kids start arguing more than they were, when Tommy's grades start dropping off once again, it's a signal not only that they need to intervene together to help the children, but that they need to look at something that they may need to work out in their relationship.

Teach problem-solving skills. You don't want to help them solve one problem, but learn the skills they need to solve other problems in the family as well. Good problem solving involves a combination of all the above — good communication, a realistic view of the way relationships work, an ability to know what the problem really is.

Ask the couple to bring their problems and arguments into the session so that you can help them learn better ways of handling them. As you work through the problem with them, identify the skills, help them generalize the process ("You both did a good job talking about Jane without getting angry. What did you both do that made it easier this time?"). Look at your role as being more of a coach fine-tuning what they present, rather than a lecturer merely dumping out a lot of information.

Help them recognize the power issues. Just as with good communication with adolescents and with violence prevention, it's important to know when problem solving turns into power struggling, when who makes the decision or who gets the last word has become more important than what the decision or word is. Couples shouldn't only know what topics are potential land mines for them ("We realize that we can't talk about my mother, your drinking, the affair I had two years ago") and which they need help to discuss productively, but more importantly, they should recognize when these topics are being used as ammunition in arguments and the conversation has emotionally escalated, is no longer productive, and needs to stop. Again, you as the outsider, as the therapist, are the one to set the pace on this; you are often the first to clarify the process and emotions that accompany the power struggle.

Create a united front / support the underdog. Not only is there the selling of the idea of working together to be accomplished, but also helping the couple make the transition and do it. Sometimes therapists don't adequately map out with the couple exactly what they will do at home, and their anxiety and uncertainty makes them fall back into their old patterns and leaves the therapist erroneously believing that they are being resistant.

If Ms. Smith, for example, has always left the discipline to her husband, or has taken sides with the children, her shift to a stronger role will be a difficult one. Help her say what support she needs from her spouse —

"I need you to tell me that I've done a good job"; "I need you to stand next to me when I tell the kids to go to bed"; "I need you to tell Rachel to ask me if she can go out to play" — in order to help her from becoming overwhelmed by the children, in order to give him a new role and task, in order to help them both avoid easily slipping back into the old patterns. Whatever strategy is developed, it needs to be specific and well-planned ahead of time.

Create positive interactions. Affection anyone? How about a night out without the kids? As you help push the children back into their appropriate roles, as you cool down the conflict, something needs to fill the space or it will just fill back up again. Couples who have gone for years living with distance, children as buffers, and/or conflict instead of positive interaction need not only to learn to stop what they are doing, but gradually to learn to feel comfortable with intimacy and support.

Pacing is the key here, and it's important not to move too quickly. The couple that hasn't been out on a date for 10 years is going to have an anxious time when they do. They could easily wind up talking the entire time about what Johnny did wrong this week, or arguing at the restaurant about whether the bill is too expensive.

You can begin by increasing intimacy and risk within the session — helping them to talk about each other rather than the children, about what they like rather than what they don't. You can help them plan together some small exercise in quality time (watch a video together after the kids go to bed that they want to see, rather than always watching kid movies) and normalize the anxiety they may feel. Again, you need to be sensitive here and walk that fine line between approaching their anxiety, and opening up communication and intimacy (go ahead, casually ask them about their sex lives) and scaring them and causing them to back away (Okay, maybe that wasn't a good idea — go back and ask them how they feel about your bringing up sexual issues). As they get more positive experience with each other, and you, they'll be able to move on to bigger activities and challenges.

Block the patterns. The couple work is like the family work. Stop the dysfunctional patterns and see what happens.

STEPPING INTO THE QUAGMIRE

Yes, the couple work isn't much different from the family work, but it can seem more difficult for several reasons. By seeing the couple alone you are by definition creating another awkward triangle. Instead of the children, it's you who's in the middle, and like them you may feel tempted to form coalitions, to be a buffer or distraction between them, or to not take sides so no one gets mad at you. As with family work with children, the easiest way to avoid the tension of such triangles is to define them as they arise, in the room and in the process, in order to keep the focus on the couple and their anxiety.

But before you step into the room you need to be aware of your own sensitivities and needs, the way you may be seduced into playing out a role, identifying with one side over another not only because of their needs and patterns, but yours. When focusing on children, when seeing several people in the family, it's fairly easy to step back, to see the patterns and the dysfunctional process, to emotionally maintain a balanced view. But with couple work it can all get too close. How you are doing or not doing in your own relationships can easily color what you see before you in the room.

If, for example, you've just been arguing with your husband about his doing more work around the house, or his taking off every Saturday to play golf or watch football with the guys, you may find yourself identifying with the woman across from you who complains that her husband "doesn't do a damn thing except sit in front of the TV," or with the husband who says he hates the way his wife stays on the phone talking to her family for what seems like 12 hours a day. It's tempting to use their process to vicariously express your depression, your loneliness, your anger—"Doesn't that make you angry, Helen? Why don't you tell Alan just how angry you feel." You may even encourage the couple to play out your own desire for a divorce. Through rationalizations and values we easily see so much of what we need to see.

The subtlety of this countertransference–transference process is enhanced if you choose to see the partners individually. The man who flirts as a way of coping with his anxiety may successfully re-create with you the affair he has had, is having, or that he and you fantasize about. The woman who "just would like to meet with you alone next time to discuss some personal issues" may help to create the friendship, the intimacy that she, and you, don't have in your current relationships. Each person becomes a blank screen for the other's fantasies and projections.

The solution, of course, is awareness, asking ourselves the hard questions: What do I need from my personal relationship that I'm not getting? What do I need most from my clients? How can I tell when I'm overidentifying with a client, or when I'm encouraging clients to do what I have trouble doing myself? It also helps to have people around (e.g., supervisors, trusted, experienced colleagues, your own therapist) who will help you practice what you preach and separate your personal issues from professional ones.

LONG-DISTANCE FEUDS

Mark comes in to see you with his 10-year-old daughter, Maggie, of whom he has custody. Maggie has been "wild and disrespectful" for three or four days after her visits with her mother two weekends a month. Mark knows what the problem is; his ex just "lets Maggie do anything she wants, and basically neglects her." He says he wants help in managing Maggie after these visits, and, by the way, he's thinking of going back to court to stop the visitations altogether and is wondering if at some point you could consider writing a letter giving your professional opinion about this.

Just as there are infinite points along the continuum of the ability of a couple in the home to own their relationship problems, the same continuum can be found in long-distance conflictual relationships between separated or divorced partners and parents. Doing couple work where there is no couple, where the child is still triangled and caught in a cross fire between two warring parents is not uncommon, and not easy.

Just as the couple or ex-couple is blurring the lines between themselves and their pasts, and themselves and their children, it can become easy for your role to blur as well. The best defense in these cases is a good offensive, namely, defining for yourself and the client as quickly and clearly as possible just what you will and will not do, what you see as appropriate goals and what are not, what is considered therapeutic and what is a legal matter. In order not to get sucked in, you need to do what this couple apparently cannot.

With Mark, for example, it would be important to clarify exactly what he needs help with in relation to Maggie. Is he asking for management techniques or an expectation that you will see Maggie alone to help her work out her tumultuous emotions following the visits? Is he asking for a formal evaluation of Maggie for court testimony or is there an unspoken expectation that through your individual contacts with Maggie you will gather information from her that he can then subpoena to use in court? If your client seems to be trying to corner you into making a legal recommendation, don't hesitate to suggest that the client contact his or her attorney about this, or request that the attorney make a formal request. Make it clear, get it out on the table; be sure once again that you know who has and what is the problem, and who is your client.

If your initial impression is that the problem is less the child than the ongoing battle between the parents, you can say this. The next step is then to invite the absent parent in and help the parents work together. This may involve helping come up with some mutually agreed ways of managing the child (e.g., both agree to enforce the same bedtimes), moving deeper and helping them resolve their continuing issues, or farming the whole thing out to trained mediators or other marital therapists. By having both parents in front of you, you avoid getting sucked in and triangled into an ongoing battle between the parents.

Some therapists will refuse to see the case unless they can actually see both parents together; others don't necessarily have to see them in the office, but want to have at least telephone contact with the other parent (e.g., when the other parent lives out of state) so that they can hear both sides of the story, clarify what the child may need and encourage the parents to work together. Again, the goal is to avoid taking sides and replicating the triangle that already exists with the child.

Of course, you have some responsibility to advocate for the child if you feel that there is a basis for worry. If, for example, you learn from Maggie that she is being neglected, is being placed in unsafe situations, talks about potential or real emotional, physical, or sexual abuse situations, you have a responsibility to notify the proper authorities, usually social services, so that they can pursue a formal investigation. There may be times where there is a fine line between your sense of what may be happening to the child and what the child may feel pressure to report by the parent. If the parent reports to you that he or she thinks the child is being abused or neglected, but you have no firsthand evidence yourself, you may want to contact your local protective services to clarify their protocols and tell the parent to make a formal report as well.

If you have any doubt (and in cases like this there may often be doubt), contacting the proper authorities (and your supervisor, if appropriate) is the best approach. They have the mandate to do the investigation, and your role as therapist, rather than investigator, stays clear.

As with other couple work, these long-distance conflicts have a way of emotionally pulling you in, particularly if you have similar unresolved issues yourself. Hearing only one side of the story, seeing the poor child caught in the middle, it's easy to emotionally join the bandwagon against one or both of the parents, easy to overidentify with the child.

Clarity is the antidote—with the client, with yourself through self-reflection, and supervision. Bring someone else to work the case with you; have someone else see the child; have a team behind the mirror observe the session process; gather court records to find out if there is a court order and legal mandates; talk to the guardian ad litem, a court-appointed advocate for the children, to clarify roles and gather background; do what you need to do to prevent yourself from becoming swept up in already emotionally sweeping family dynamics.

COUPLES AND CONTEXT

Parents share two relationships—the one as caretakers of their children, the other, their relationship as a couple. While they often enter therapy with the line between these relationships blurred, or with their focus only on one and not the other, your job is to both distinguish between them and to show how each is connected.

As has been said throughout this chapter, this is important in order for the family to remain structurally and emotionally healthy. It's hard enough being a child without having to get dragged into acting like an adult or taking the heat for problems that the adults aren't handling. It's easy as a parent to turn to your children for support or distraction when you feel overwhelmed or overlooked in your relationship with your partner.

Because the couple's relationship is made of the same basic building blocks of patterns and process as the family's, your other family skills will serve you as you begin work with them. Keep in mind the basics, don't be afraid to move against their grain and yours, and, once again, above all, be honest.

LOOKING WITHIN

Again, the biggest difference between couple and family work isn't the number of people in the room but your own reactions to what the couple presents. These exercises encourage you to become aware of your own professional and personal biases.

1. What is your own theory of couple work? How is it different from and similar to total family work or child therapy? What are your basic assumptions?

2. What are your personal values regarding relationships, commitments, the line between the couple's problems and the welfare of the children? How open should the couple be with the children about the couple relationship? Who, when, has higher priority: the partner, the child, the self? How do you personally decide?

3. What did you learn from your parents about the way relationships are, how they change, what to expect from them? What did you learn about how problems in the relationship should be solved? What mistake(s) did your parents make that you would most like to avoid?

4. Think about your current or past intimate relationships. What does your partner do that you hate? What power struggles, impasses do you or did you have? What role does or did sex play in your relationship? How do any of these issues create countertransference problems for you when doing couple therapy?

THIRTEEN

The Power of One: Individual
Work in a Family Context

Ann talks with a slow whine, each word barely limping ahead of the one before. She looks drained, and she tells you how she spends hours in the middle of the night pacing up and down, just sitting at the kitchen table, or lying in bed staring up at the darkness. To her everything seems gray; even things that used to excite her—an evening with friends, a new project at work—seem now like another burden, another responsibility. She sighs, one of those long, heavy sighs that stretches out and fills the room.

Major depression? Dysthymia? Adjustment disorder with depression? Bereavement? Whatever you call it, it has DSM-IV written all over it. Individual therapy, here we come.

But if you're a family therapist, you may feel, or think you ought to feel, uncomfortable with this. Not only is the room a bit too empty, but you feel a flutter of hesitation at the thought of plodding into that swamp of individual pathology and internal dynamics.

Don't fear. In this chapter we'll explore together how to work with individuals and still consider yourself a family therapist. Family therapy, after all, isn't about how many people you can cram into a room, but about how many people you can keep in your mind. Family therapy isn't as much about what you do as how you think—looking at problems and people in terms of their patterns and interactions. With it you can help others change one person or help one person change others. They're both sides of the same fence.

IS IT ME?

But clients don't usually look at their problems in this interactive way; from where they sit the problem and the coin only has one side. When they show up alone in your office they will generally talk about their problems as being caused by themselves ("I am the problem") or by others ("My mother is the problem"). Whatever way they present their problem doesn't really matter. What's important is that you offer them a perspective that they don't have.

We're talking again about seeing what's missing and moving toward their anxiety, about giving the client a different theory and problem to replace one that has become too familiar and comfortable. If Ann, for example, only talks about all the awful things she feels she did in the past, goes on and on about the way her husband is always screwing up her life, or laments about her mother who never really cared about her, she's not wrong in her view, simply stuck—stuck with only half the story. You will need to start by hearing and acknowledging her perspective, the half that makes up her problem, but then you want to encourage her to look at the other side of the coin, to focus on what she's not seeing.

Instead of only the past, you want to know about the present; instead of blaming her husband or mother, you want to help her draw lines of responsibility between herself and them, help her separate her issues from theirs. By helping her recognize what she can control and what she can't, by encouraging her to talk in new ways about new topics, you are helping her mobilize her energy and resources in a new and potentially more positive direction.

Systemic thinking can give Ann a new way of organizing and expanding her assumptions. By recognizing the way she has been shaped by her interaction with others in the past and present, she may come to see her past decisions in a less self-accusatory, but more responsible light. Appreciating how her mother and husband are individuals influenced by their own psychological networks of others doesn't excuse their actions, perhaps, but casts them as less villainous and more human.

It's this wider, more dynamic perspective that allows Ann to see both sides of her problem, to understand, examine, and possibly change her interactions. Rather than being cornered into thinking only in terms of bad and good, blame and guilt, Ann has a more complete view of her relationships and problems that can give her a greater sense of mastery and serve as an antidote to depression.

The answer then to the question, "Is the problem me?" is "Yes, at least in part, if you don't think it is," and "No, maybe not, if you feel absolutely sure that it is." In either case, the value is in learning to expand your thinking beyond either/or dichotomies, to think that you are not the victim or the persecutor, but often both and neither, that you affect and are affected by those around you.

COME ON IN:
USING THE FAMILY TO HELP THE INDIVIDUAL

The best way to learn about the interactional nature of life is to see it and experience it. Bringing in all those individuals who interact and intersect around a problem is, of course, the tried-and-true approach to family therapy. But even if you or the client decide that switching from individual to some form of ongoing family therapy isn't reasonable, there are still ways to enlist others to help you engage the individual.

One is to bring in significant others for one or two information-gathering sessions. For example, when Cassandra talked about her guilt over the abusive way she felt she had treated her sister when they were teenagers, the therapist suggested that she invite her sister to one of their sessions. She did, and the time was spent with Cassandra, with much hesitation and anxiety, simply monologuing about the way she felt about those times past. Cassandra had the opportunity to say what she could not say, to put into words what she had only grieved inside for years. The proclamation, the confession, was itself therapeutic.

Having the right audience made it even more so. Her sister did what often happens in such situations. She acknowledged what Cassandra had said, acknowledged how she had felt both hurt and confused by Cassandra's behavior, and how her memories of that time continued to strain their relationship in the present. But then she turned the corner and talked about her regret and guilt for not understanding how hard their parents had been on her and for walling her off over the years. But most of all she talked about her appreciation for all that Cassandra had done for her—the offer to take her in when she was having a difficult time in college, her reaching out with consolation and support when her daughter had died several years before.

Healing occurred because Cassandra not only repented and was forgiven, but because the distorted memories were corrected; she discovered through her sister a new way of viewing herself and her actions that would have been difficult to achieve in therapy without the feedback of this family member.

Other times the focus is less on healing of the past and more on problem solving in the present. David had just started dating Jill, but was already struggling with what he thought were her expectations over how much time they should spend together. Because the relationship was still new, David didn't feel comfortable starting any ongoing couple therapy, but did think it was a good idea to have Jill come to one of his individual therapy sessions just to discuss the topic.

She did, and the session and the dialogue enabled David to deal with his feelings and concerns in a much more direct way than he had in the past. Rather than remaining silent and ruminating, he was able in the session to be assertive; rather than assuming he knew what Jill wanted, he took the risk to ask her. Jill came away with an honest picture of the kind of person David was, and David had the opportunity to start a new relationship with a different set of patterns.

Sometimes the motivation of having others come into individual therapy is more yours than the client's. One disadvantage of any individual therapy is, namely, that—it is individual and hence limited in its view. While there are ways to expand this view (as we'll discuss below) by actually talking to a parent, sister, brother, wife, fiancé, you may want others to come in to provide a more complete and accurate picture of the past or present, or another view of the interactional patterns that have occurred or are ongoing.

Additional people thus serve as consultants. The process is less of the client using the session as a forum for solving problems or disclosing long-held secrets, as much as your using it to uncover what you think is important. The client listens, and in the listening can step back and perhaps hear what couldn't be heard before.

For example, in the course of her individual treatment, Molly talked about the ways she felt favored by her alcoholic father, while he seemed to ignore her other brothers and sisters. The therapist asked if she would talk to her brother who lived in town about coming in for a session. He did, and in contrast to Cassandra's session with her sister, it was the therapist who asked questions of the brother. She asked how he viewed his father's relationship with Molly and the other children, and she asked what sense he had made out of his childhood years.

Not only did the therapist gain a different and more rounded view of the early family life, but Molly, sitting quietly in the corner, heard reactions and feelings and answers to questions that, because of her own blind spots, anxiety, and assumptions, she would never have been aware of. Because the session focus and process wasn't on her, she was able to really hear what her brother was saying, and, like Cassandra, was offered a new vision of her past.

While bringing others into individual therapy is clearly a good way of reshaping the past and present, it needs to be carefully planned. The people invited need to know why they're there. No doubt they're already anxious about what might happen and may have all kinds of fantasies about the session turning into an interrogation or trial. They need to be welcomed and treated as guests, and, either before the session or at its start, need to know exactly what you are planning. By being both respectful and in command you can offset their fear that the session will turn into an emotional free-for-all.

You also want to be in charge to support your client. Because you don't really know the guests, you don't know what they may or may not launch into. Cassandra's sister, for example, might have tried to dominate the session from the moment she sat down, or spewed venom at Cassandra as soon as she stopped to take a breath of air in the middle of her monologue. While getting things out in the open and working through the process are all valuable, no one should wind up feeling emotionally trampled.

One way to ensure that this doesn't happen is to leave sufficient time and space for debriefing. By inviting collaterals in for a limited time you're taking on some responsibility to see that there's some closure to the experience. This doesn't mean that they might not walk away with questions, doubts, concerns that the discussion may have stirred up, but the process should be balanced.

Cassandra shouldn't just deliver her monologue and leave; David shouldn't just say what he wants without hearing what Jill expects; Molly's brother shouldn't just open his own emotional can of worms and then be thanked for coming. Make clear to the guests that they have a choice — to talk or not to talk, to stop, to ask questions. Pay close attention to the process and leave time at the end of the session to debrief, clarify, and support. Offer to have the people come back again, if necessary.

You need to judge whether your client is ready to handle a live confrontation or confession. You need to assess whether his or her assumption that this would be a good idea really is a good idea; you have to decide whether this is something the client genuinely wants to do, or whether he or she is merely trying to please you by going along with what he or she thinks you want. In the process of both making these decisions with your client and bringing in others to help solve a problem, you want to be sure that the problem isn't unwittingly being replicated.

You also need to be honest with yourself that you're not bringing in others as a way of coping with your anxiety or sloughing off your responsibility. Just like the college professor who fills his course with guest speakers as a way of avoiding having to actually teach the class, you can fill therapy sessions with all kinds of significant others who you think can do the therapy work you should be doing yourself. Again, good family therapy doesn't take place simple by inviting more and more varied grouping of people to session.

As the therapist you must know what you're trying to accomplish and push hard to have an effect. Having a variety of people present sometimes facilitates this effort, but is no substitute for it. Bringing someone into the session because you don't know what else to do or to dissipate the anxiety that the intimacy of individual therapy can create serves your purposes, not the client's. Be clear who's got the problem.

IN LOCO FAMILIA

When family members can't or won't come in—they live too far away, the client doesn't want them to know that he or she's in therapy, they think therapy is only for neurotics—there's always the opportunity to reach out and communicate long-distance. You can suggest to your client Ned that he call up and talk to his brother about how disappointed he was that his brother didn't come to his son's wedding, or encourage Alice to write a letter and mail it to her boyfriend, putting into words what she would have said if he could have been there in the session.

Such long-distance methods are often easier for the client than the face-to-face meeting. The client may feel less intimidated and less on the spot—Ned can write down what he wants to say before he makes the call; Alice can shape the words in a letter with more consideration.

Your job is to counteract the limitation of each medium—the absence of nonverbal feedback, the one-sidedness of the letter. Coach the client on talking or writing completely, making sure he or she says what he or she thinks the other may be thinking or feeling, addressing the other's unspoken but suspected concerns.

Here, for example, is a letter that one woman wrote to her father, who was dying of cancer:

> Dear Dad,
>
> I've wanted to come see you and I'm sorry that I haven't been able to do so. I hope to come at the end of the month.
>
> I've wanted to write to you for some time because I guess I need to get some things off my chest. When I look back on my teenage years, those early years of my marriage, I still get filled with anger and regret— anger that you left, regret that you weren't part of my life for so long. For a long time I blamed myself, blamed Mom. Much of the trouble I got into, some of the bad decisions that I made, I thought would have never happened if you had stayed.
>
> Slowly I'm beginning to see that you didn't leave because of me but because of you and Mom. I wish we hadn't lost that time.

This is a pretty clear letter, but she needed to talk more fully so that her father could better understand why she was saying what she was saying. Here is the revised letter that she wrote after she and I talked more about her feelings about her father and what she hoped the letter could convey:

> Dear Dad,
>
> I've wanted to come and see you and I'm sorry that I haven't been able to do so. I hope to come at the end of the month.

I've wanted to write to you for some time because I guess I need to get some things off my chest. I've been doing a lot of thinking lately about some of the decisions I've made, about my time growing up, trying to understand my past better so that I don't make the same mistakes in the future.

When I look back on my teenage years and those early years of my marriage, I still get filled with anger and regret—anger that you left, regret that you weren't part of my life for so long. For a long time I blamed myself, blamed Mom for your leaving. I used to think that somehow you were the reason I got into so much trouble, the reason I made some bad decisions. If only you had stayed, my life, I believed, would have turned out so much different.

And maybe it would have, but I also know that I need to take some responsibility for the life I've led. Finally now I'm beginning to realize that you didn't leave because of me, but because of you and Mom.

It's taken me a long time to figure this out. I'm not writing to make you feel guilty or to hit you over the head with the past. I know you've got your own regrets. I just want to let you know that I'm sorry I've pushed you away for so many years when you did try to come back in my life. I'm sorry that we lost that time between us. I just want to let you know that I love you.

When connections with family are not possible, others can step in to facilitate the change process. Both the systemic notion of interactional patterns and the concept of transference tell us that while people are unique, our relationships with them are not. Each of us re-creates over and over again the same patterns across relationships. By changing the patterns between friends, coworkers, bosses, even strangers, these changes can flow out to change other family members, and flow in to change the client.

This, of course, is the basis of group therapy, where the group members project on each other unresolved emotions and re-create the dynamics of their past relationships. Over time the group becomes a surrogate family. As the interactions are played out, challenged and changed within the group process, so too are the individual's cognitive and emotional responses that held the patterns in place.

When formal group therapy isn't possible, you can create a minigroup. Have friends, roommates, coworkers, cousins—anybody whom the client feels comfortable inviting—come into session with him or her. By focusing on the process, rather than the content, by looking for replication of patterns—the way John is just as unassertive with his roommate as he is with his sister; the way Cynthia holds back how she feels when her friend hurts her feelings, just as she does when her mother does the same—you are tackling the same problems from a different angle.

Again you need to be clear—about the expectations and goals for the session or sessions, about confidentiality, about the role of the guest. You need to be in charge, be sensitive to the process, and leave time to debrief so that there are not any loose emotional ends left dangling.

Finally, there are cases where neither family nor family surrogates are available. How else can you expand the client's perspective to include the viewpoint of others and create individual change? Some change will naturally come about from your relationship with the client, through your tracking of client's transference, as he or she projects on you significant others from his or her past.

But it's also possible to expand the client's perspective by bringing others in through the client's imagination. Use experiential techniques, such as letter writing to those who are deceased, complete with their expected or ideal response back to the client; empty chair work (having the client role play both sides of a dialogue between himself and another from his past or present); guided imagery (helping the client imagine a conversation between himself and his old mentor, or the dialogue he wished he'd had the last time he saw his mother, or imagine his life as a play with different periods of time—childhood, adolescence, early marriage—as specific scenes on a stage). These techniques and any other that you can create increase your understanding of the client's inner and outer world and expand the therapeutic ground that you both have to work on. Through the experiential process you are providing opportunities for catharsis, closure, and healing to take place.

THE FIFTH COLUMN

Frank comes to see you, saying that he wants his wife, Suzanne, to stop crabbing at him all the time. At her first appointment Jane states that she wants to get her 14-year-old son, Todd, to stop talking back at her and to come in on time. Tamisha complains endlessly, it seems, about the way her mother stirs guilt in her every time she calls. She wants her mother to just stop doing it. What do you say to these people?

You might say you can't help them—"I can't change them, I can only help you to change. I can see you individually and help you sort out your reaction, your problems, one of which right now happens to be this other person. If you want to get them to change, get them in here. I don't do marital work or fix adolescents or mothers without seeing them."

If this is what you believe, this is a reasonable stand to take. You're defining who has the problem, drawing lines between what you (and they) can change and what you cannot. You may coach them on how to talk to the others about coming in, you may even offer to call the other persons up and invite them in, but you are clear about what you will and will not do.

You may also decide to help Frank and Jane and Tamisha to do exactly what they want, to help each of them solve their problem and help change the behavior of Suzanne, Todd, or Mom. This is the other side of the individual/family equation. Not only can others help us as individuals change, we as individuals can help others to change. This is the application and implication of the systemic notion of interaction. If Frank changes what he does, not only will Suzanne change, but so too *must* Suzanne. Frank, by deliberately planning to change what he does, becomes the therapeutic agent, the fifth column in the family system.

This is what Billy's grandmother and Ellen's mother were doing as parents—changing their parenting approach in order to affect change in the children. But obviously it doesn't stop there. You as the therapist can coach the client to become the change agent within the family; you can help him or her create change by getting the client to change the patterns at home.

Basically, you teach the individual how to think systemically. Patterns of interactions are tracked down and mapped out, and strategies are developed to specifically change them—"So, Frank, what would happen if you didn't snap back when your wife starts complaining?"; "Tamisha, when your mother calls on Sunday and starts her usual spiel that makes you feel guilty and angry, try telling her how you feel, rather than staying quiet or trying to change the topic"; "Jane, if Todd doesn't come in on time Saturday night, what do you want to do about it? What kinds of consequences can you set that are different from what you have done before?"

The "different from what you have done before" is the key to changing the patterns. Just as you would do in a session, you're pushing the individual to do something against the grain, to do something that stirs his or her anxiety, which in turn will stir the anxiety in the other. In order to help sustain the change you must think ahead and help the client anticipate what he or she can do in the face of the other's resistance and opposition—help Frank envision how Suzanne may react, help him decide what he can do when she becomes even more irritable or angry, what Tamisha can say if her mother switches roles and begins to sound guilty herself, what Jane can do when Todd blows up or ignores her when she says he's grounded the next two days.

This type of change making is a slower process than total family or couple work because you're only able to work with one side of the interaction. Your primary job is going to be helping your client stay the course. Maintaining a new stance over the long haul is where the change process usually breaks down. Frank or Jane or Tamisha may do fine the first week and be amazed at just how easily and seemingly quickly the patterns changed, but keeping this up in the face of other stressors—the double-

and triple-teaming by others in the family fighting the change, the client's own deeper ambivalence about the problem arising from his or her possible need for it, the vacuum created by the problem's absence—all require that you model what you preach.

Just as the individual needs to hold a clear vision of what he or she wants and stay committed to it in the face of the resistance, you need to hold a clear vision of what your role and task are. When the client starts to waver, you need to make sure you don't.

INDIVIDUAL DANGERS

This one-person approach to problems and family change can all start to sound pretty simple, too simple perhaps—give me any problem, any individual, and I, as the therapist, can coach him or her into getting what he or she wants. Yes and no. Yes, you can help stimulate change by helping your client change, but no, you and the client can't absolutely direct its outcome in others.

But the bigger issue is that there is a bigger issue. The goal isn't only to change patterns and behaviors in another, but to create change in a relationship for a purpose, because there are unmet needs that aren't being addressed. At some point down the line, the shifting of patterns runs out and the individual and family need to be honest. At some point Frank doesn't need only to stop overreacting to Suzanne, but needs to be clear with her about what he wants, what he needs from her and the relationship, so that she can do the same. At some point Jane needs to ask herself why Todd seems so angry at her and how she and he can have a better relationship. At some point Tamisha needs not only to teach her mother not to trigger her guilt, but to leave enough room in the conversation to tell her mother how she needs her.

Without this honesty, this bare-bones declaration of who and what is really needed, wanted, and most important to the client, strategies for stopping dysfunctional patterns become nothing more than a new way of sidestepping the problem in order to keep the other person off balance; the individual may feel in control, even feel omnipotent, but without self-responsibility, commitment to the relationship, and caring for the other person, he or she is being manipulative. The shifting of patterns merely becomes another form of dysfunctional interaction.

But this type of honesty can sometimes be difficult to bring into the individual therapy because of the blind spots that the process itself so easily creates. Just as couple work becomes more difficult than total family work because the couple's issues can more easily tap into our own personal weak spots and the triangling can press us into collusions and compromises, individual work can pull the net even tighter.

Individual work often creates an intimacy that can make the therapeutic relationship more important than the change you're trying to establish. Rather than helping Frank look at what he needs from Suzanne, there's the danger that Frank and his therapist will join forces in seeing her as a problem. Rather than helping Jane expand her relationship with Todd, the therapist and she may spend session after session spinning around the problem so that they have a reason to keep their relationship the same. At some point the therapeutic relationship, while seemingly working to change family patterns, becomes another way of replicating them.

These powerful countertransference issues are what make individual therapy so different from other formats. Just as bringing people into the therapy can become a crutch for the therapist to avoid the anxiety of doing the therapy, excluding the people can be the rationalized trap for getting your intimacy needs met through your clients.

And if the potential intimacy isn't enough of a seduction, power can be. The dependency of the individual client on the therapist, even when the therapist is helping the individual to change his or her relationships, is still great, and greater still can be the therapist's need for the dependency. Again, it's not that this collusion can't happen in other formats; it can. It's the subtle way the process can be so easily distorted through the more narrow, less distracted focus of the individual therapy. Even though the goal may be problem solving, the problems somehow never seem to end; the dependency may be recognized, but is rationalized as a necessary step in reparenting.

The push for brief and short-term models may offset the danger of much of this. But even if it doesn't, the fact that the danger is there doesn't mean that individual therapy isn't valuable; it may even be the approach of choice in its own right. What it does mean is that you as the therapist need to be alert, need to be clear from the outset about your values and role, need to be as sure as the client must be about the line between fostering positive changes and engaging in outright manipulation for manipulation's sake, between helping the other in order to mostly help yourself. At the bottom line, it's you, the clinician, who most needs to have and demonstrate that rock-bone honesty.

BACK TO ANN

So where does all this take us with regard to Ann's depression? Here are some possible therapeutic options open to her:

- Bring in family members to solve the problems that she's having difficulty solving, to increase their support, to help her be more assertive and more powerful within her relationships, to educate them about depression, to discourage whatever blame or guilt they may be heaping on her.

• If she is relatively isolated, bring in nonfamily members or have her start in a therapy group to increase support around her, to develop her social skills, to help her unravel and change the patterns that undermine her power, maintain her stress, compromise her decision and problem-solving ability.

• See her individually to help her see how she can change, rather than be victimized by the forces and people around her. Coach her on changing interactional patterns, help her draw clear lines of responsibility around her problem and those of others, between what she can change and what she cannot. Serve as morale booster, an emotional cheerleader for promoting change in her life patterns.

• Refer her for antidepressant medication, coordinate services with the physician, monitor the results along with the physician; be responsible and see if there's a need for more intensive services, such as hospitalization or increased supervision; once she is stable, negotiate with her about her goals and needs for further therapy.

• See her individually to help her learn to apply cognitive-behavioral principles. By helping her track her self-talk ("I always screw up") and change her own catastrophizing and self-deprecation ("It's never going to get any better; I'm just a basket case"), she can alter the emotions these statements and this language creates.

• See her individually to resolve unresolved issues with people from her past and present; use experiential techniques to help her use the therapeutic relationship to learn to take risks within the session, to gain that unconditional sense of caring and acceptance, to experience intimacy, all the while being careful as the therapist not to replicate past patterns or put your own needs for the relationship above her goals.

All these and probably more are possible paths to take. The choice, once again, depends upon the severity of the symptoms, Ann's stated goals, her perception of her problem, and her expectation of therapy, as well as your own framework for viewing the problem, your values, comfort, and skills with various approaches, options, and formats. Once you decide on a particular approach, try it and see what happens.

If Ann isn't getting better, try something else. If you start to slow down, feel helpless, feel like your options are getting narrow, if your world is taking on the same hue as Ann's, it's time to get some supervisory help to pull you out of the therapeutic quagmire. Most of all, listen to your inner voice and teach your client to do the same; respect your intuitions and trust your and the client's creativity.

LOOKING WITHIN

1. What are your reactions to, your values regarding, the notion of helping others become change agents? When is it therapeutic and when is it manipulative? How do you know?

2. What are your own countertransference issues when working with individuals, the emotional dangers that can undermine the therapy you are seeking to provide? How do you resolve for yourself the issue of the therapeutic relationship as the primary arena for change versus the client's relationships with others?

3. Does your focus on the past, on inner dynamics, change when seeing an individual rather than seeing a family? Why or why not?

4. Imagine your intimate partner were to come to your individual therapy to present his or her view of a major problem between you both. How do you think you would react? How might it help or hinder your solving of the problem, your relationship? How do you feel about bringing in others to the sessions as consultants? What would make you hesitate about doing this?

FOURTEEN

Staying Sane:
Survival Tips for Therapists

The basic notions underlying all the clinical material throughout this book have been simple: that family therapy rests on certain basic assumptions and principles, which are effective and relatively easy to use, and that there are many therapeutic roads to the same end. The key to good therapeutic work lies in being clear about your goals, flexible in your approach, creative in your thinking, pragmatic in your philosophy — and having the humility to make mistakes and the courage to just do it.

Fine, but how do you do all these things besides simply doing them? How do you stay creative in the face of endless tales of abuse, despair, chaos, frustration? How do you stay sane and committed, rather than numb, bitter, cynical, or even hostile?

The answer is, of course, that you simply push yourself to learn and do, just as the family members have to push themselves in order to make changes in themselves, their families, their world. The therapeutic buck stops with you. But that doesn't mean you can't get help and support along the way.

In this chapter, a catalogue of sorts, we'll consider the idea of self-care for the family therapist, ways to keep your creative juices flowing and your options open, ways to stay grounded and sensitive without becoming emotionally overwhelmed. We're talking about doing for yourself what you want your families to learn to do for themselves.

STAND BY ME:
THE SUPERVISOR–CONSULTANT CONNECTION

Clients come to you for help with their children, their marriage, themselves. You go to your supervisor for help with the assessment, to develop strategies, to help you become less emotionally entangled. The parallel process is obvious. A good supervisor or consultant isn't there to solve your personal problems, perhaps, but like a good therapist he or she is there as a support, a parent, a teacher, a sounding board, a brainstormer, a coach, a cheerleader, a storyteller, and a friend, who can, nonetheless, provide a similar powerful buoying up. Like a therapist, how the supervisor is as an individual is probably less important than how he or she interacts with you. It's not the person, after all, that helps you, but the relationship you both create together.

The best kind of supervisors are those who have skills and knowledge that you lack. But they are more than walking textbooks or catalogues of therapeutic skills, only interested in filling you up with information. The job of the good supervisor is not just to educate, but also to help you take all that you learn and shape it into a professional self.

Learning to do therapy is in many ways like learning to speak a foreign language. Competence isn't measured by the ability to memorize a list of words or clinical interventions, but by the ability to use these tools — to *think* in the language of therapy. The challenge is to meld the theoretical concepts and techniques that you know into a therapeutic style that will be effective.

In order to do this you need a supervisor who appreciates your learning style, whether it be learning by watching your supervisor in action, first; planning, preparing, and mapping out your sessions with your supervisor carefully in advance; or jumping right in and asking questions in supervision later. Only by supporting your way of learning can your supervisor help you to develop your own approach, your own voice, your own unique weaving of personality and skill.

A good supervisor also needs to be sensitive to your level of professional development. He or she should know, for example, that the novice will need more direction and straight-ahead information than someone more advanced; that the performance pressure of the beginning may give way to the therapist's true dependence on the supervisor, and this may, in turn, eventually lead to an adolescent stage of testing, questioning, and separating from the supervisor's own model before the therapist can reach a more integrated self. A good supervisor is flexible; as you grow as a therapist and your needs for supervision change, your supervisor should not only be able to address your developing skills and interests, but change the supervisory process so that the supervisory relationship can change along with you.

This is where good supervision most emulates good therapy, that is, in the supervisor's recognition and appreciation that the relationship is organic, that it will and must change over time to accommodate the shifting needs of both. More importantly, perhaps, the good supervisor, like the good therapist, knows that it's through the process itself—the negotiating and sorting and solving that goes on between you and your supervisor—that the growth occurs. He or she believes that in the development of the relationship between the two of you comes the development of the professional self within you both.

Bad supervision or consultation is the opposite of responsiveness and collaboration—it's supervision that becomes snarled in empty patterns, where the pressure is not on developing individuality but on cloning, where difficult topics are avoided rather than approached, where learning follows a rigid format that the therapist quickly outgrows, and is resented by the supervisor for doing so. Bad supervision is like a bad job, a bad marriage, bad therapy. It not only stifles you as the therapist, its negative effects eventually ripple through all your other relationships.

It's your responsibility to make sure you get the supervision you need, supervision that both supports and challenges, that helps you to learn and helps you to use what you learn; supervision that teaches not only how to correct mistakes, but helps you learn the lessons that they hold and gives you the permission and courage to make them.

STEPPING BACK: SELF-SUPERVISION

If you imagine supervising yourself, more likely than not your mind heads for all that's critical—there you are, mentally wagging your finger at yourself for being so tough on that mother; there's the scowling face of your father, your mother, your old mentor with hands on hips telling you that you totally ignored the signs of that father's depression and there's no excuse for it; there's that small, snarly voice saying, "Caught you!" whenever you get off track and seem confused.

This is a harsh, critical-parent image of self-supervision that some claim can keep us on our toes. Others in the field counter with the argument that the danger isn't that we'll be too hard on ourselves, but too easy. The blindspots, rationalizations, and contradictions in what we do are impossible for us to see, let alone change, by ourselves. We have no business trying to supervise ourselves; we need someone else, someone with a different perspective to help us see what we're doing.

In between the dangers of being too easy and too hard on ourselves is the view that self-supervision can be a means of reflecting, of stepping back and away from your work in order not to scold but to discover; to follow the path of your anxiety and emotions to cast new light on your assumptions; to look at the patterns of your practice in much the same way we encourage families to look at the patterns in their own lives—to recognize in them the themes that run our living and our work.

Sit down with some of your colleagues at lunch one day and listen to each other describe his or her caseload—the problems, the assessment, his or her plan of action. If you can avoid getting swept up in the details of the families' lives, or bickering over the right diagnosis, but can just listen carefully as the stories unfold from each one, patterns will begin to emerge. Tom, you realize, almost always struggles with resistant fathers "who need to be more responsible"; Nancy sniffs out "fragmentation in the family structure" and is set on getting everyone back and in their proper places; Arnold finds that many of his clients have "suppressed anger" that needs to be expressed in order to increase their personal power; Joy uses a genogram like a road map to invariably track down some "unresolved grief," some "unspoken trauma."

The themes and patterns stand out before you. Your colleagues may or may not be aware of them, and the fact that the patterns are there doesn't make their clinical assessment invalid or the work ineffective. Their impressions are, after all, wrapped around their favorite theories. The pause comes only in questioning why the theory seems so true, why the clients so clearly have such consistent underlying problems and needs. What is it that your colleagues see in others that may tell them what they may need to repair in their own lives? These are the questions that help keep the projections down, that keep the therapy from being twisted and becoming a vicarious outlet for the therapist's own unexpressed emotions.

Most therapists, especially after they've been doing their work for awhile, get in the habit of not thinking much about their sessions once they are over. If the session has been a difficult one, there's more the inclination to breathe a sigh of relief or to passively ruminate about it for awhile, but to do little else. Maybe it's the pace of the work; maybe it reflects exhaustion and burnout; maybe it merely involves falling into set work patterns and clinical routines that we're inclined to leave alone. Whatever the reason, stepping back, mulling over a case in an active way, and learning from the process itself isn't something that we all readily do.

But taking the time to reflect on your work has its rewards. It helps you slow down and see each family more clearly. Rather than the family turning into the "the two o'clock appointment with the ADHD kid," you have time to sort through your wider impressions and reactions. You have a chance to step back and evaluate how you are responding to everyone in the family, rather than just getting caught up in "getting the parents to set some structure." Small cracks in your approach, such as your failing to get the father consistently involved, can be noticed and fixed before they develop into something larger, like the father starting to undermine the structure.

Self-reflection also enhances your creativity. The creative process is one of thinking—stirring the pot, so to speak—and then letting go, allowing the bits and pieces of impressions and images to settle and sit where they may. As they simmer, they combine in their own unique combinations. Through this process, new insights, new approaches, develop. When you cut this process off by shutting off your thoughts at the end of the hour, your work is more likely to reflect your clinical habits and formulas rather than a novel approach.

Finally, self-reflection helps you recognize your own countertransference. Often, your pushing the session out of your mind after it is over is a way of pushing away uncomfortable reactions and emotions. By taking the time to dwell on them in a deliberate way, you may discover exactly the problem that's causing you to feel stuck.

How you make time for self-supervision depends upon your working style. Some therapists take time when they are writing up their session notes to look back over the work on the case so far. Others set a time aside each week, an hour perhaps, specifically to reflect upon their entire caseload. Still others focus only on difficult cases, or ones where they sense some resistance on their part—the slight feeling of dread they have at the start of a session, for example, or the way they put off sending a follow-up letter. However you ultimately decide to approach this task, make a specific time for it when you first begin practicing it. Like any other change, once you do it consistently for a few weeks, you'll feel more comfortable doing it.

Look back over your own caseload or, better yet, read through your own case files of a year ago. What patterns do you see and hear? What common assessment, struggles, goals? What kinds of clients do you seem to hold onto, while others fall away after a few sessions? How flexible is your own style and approach, how rigid? How has your perspective changed now? What developmental issues of yours—breaking away from parents, becoming a parent, establishing one's own sense of mastery, dealing with death, becoming a wise man or woman—are reflected in your work, coloring your perspective, changing the shape of your practice, recasting your values?

Tap into your emotions. So you are frustrated with Mr. Jones, angry for some reason at Mrs. Wilson. Go ahead, imagine him sitting there upright, stiff as iron, across from you in the chair; see her in that flowery dress that she always wears with that half-smirk on her face. Tell him what you are thinking; tell her how you feel. Now switch chairs. What would he say back? How would she translate that smirk into words? Switch back again; respond back. Switch again. Notice how the conversation has changed, how you are feeling less frustrated and angry, perhaps, and more depressed or compassionate, how he or she looks less critical and more helpless. Who else from your past or present could you put in the chair that reminds you of these people, this dialogue, these emotions?

Write a brief short story about those clients you're having a hard time with. Use them as characters, making them as dramatic and sympathetic as you can. See what you learn about their motives, their dreams. Put yourself and therapy in the story. What can the fictional process tell you about the real one?

You're sorting out your countertransference, you're owning your projections, you're separating yourself out from the family. Use those lagging emotions, that afterburn following a session to discover something about you and them. Self-supervision can help you recharge yourself and the therapy.

TRAINING AND EDUCATION

Want to learn how to work with sexually abused children? Trying to integrate psychodrama into your group work? Need new techniques for working with violent teens? Interested in learning how to apply paradoxical directives in marital therapy? Then get yourself to a conference, a workshop; get some training.

Short-term training opportunities obviously help you increase your skills, keep you on top of the latest and maybe greatest developments in the field. They also provide the side benefits of getting you out of the office, taking you to a city where you haven't been before, giving you a chance to meet and re-meet colleagues whom you would probably never see otherwise. When you are feeling burned out or discouraged, short trainings can recharge you by helping you see that there is more that you can do, that there are ways to overcome the places in your practice where you feel the most stuck. And sitting in a room with hundreds or thousands of other therapists validates not only that you are not the only one struggling, but that you in fact belong to a larger therapy family.

Should you desire to delve even deeper into any subject, there are always extended trainings—the three-week or one-month variety. Rather than just a taste of a particular skill or approach, you can get a whole meal. Beyond that, there is ongoing training, usually leading to some certification—the three-year program in hypnosis, the yearlong study of strategic therapy, the two-year investigation of object relations. Here the commitment of time and money is obviously greater, as is the commitment to that approach. You need to be clear about your objectives: What is it that you most want to learn? Why now? How does it fit or conflict with your values? How does it fit with your internal image of whom you want to be?

The questions are important because the answers, which on the surface seem so transparent, quickly turn murky with a bit of reflection. If, for example, you are burned out on what you are doing, or are at that stage of development wherein you are beginning to outgrow your supervision and feeling restless, the feeling that you want something else, something more—increased energy, a new perspective that cuts through your hodgepodge of techniques—may be strong, but undefined. It's tempting to grasp onto something that at least points a direction, that provides some structure, some activity, some release from the tension or depression that you feel.

The program may do just that—catch you up in something that's new, that gives you a new sense of defining yourself and what you do. But it also may be a mistake if you're not honest with yourself about what you are really seeking and feeling. The restlessness or burnout may merely be a symptom of a larger problem and not the problem itself.

Often the best course is to wait, rather than jumping in, to sit through the transition period and see what happens, rather than becoming impatient and grasping onto something just to have it to hold onto. You may discover that the problem has nothing to do with your professional practice and more to do with your personal needs.

Once you've clarified your clinical needs and goals, however, such extended training can indeed help you feel more grounded, solid, and expert in your work. In contrast to a conference or workshop, the immersion that the more intensive training format provides becomes a good way of soaking in the new ideas and skills. As you apply the new approach to your practice and begin to integrate it with your past skills and style, you replace the bits and pieces of models that you relied upon before with a strong, cohesive foundation on which you can lean.

Like good supervision, long-term training should challenge you to discover a deeper level of yourself than short-term training usually does. At its best, extended training shouldn't only give you a few more details about what you already know, or reconfirm what you already believe, but push you to look at what you're doing with fresh eyes, help you to see yourself in a new context and discover what makes you tick. In fact, any good, rigorous course of study, even if it is outside your field— literature, mathematics, music, rock climbing—can be worthwhile if you come away from it intellectually and emotionally stretched.

TEACHING

The learning process can be divided up into four stages: (1) You know what you don't know; (2) you don't know what you know; (3) you don't know what you don't know; (4) you know what you know.

In the first stage, as a beginner, you're filled with anxiety because you're only aware of your incompetence, what you don't know. Much of what you do feels like you're barely keeping your head above water. You mistakenly believe that others see your incompetence as well and are not mentioning it only in order to be polite.

In the second you've gained ground, you've learned more, but pieces of what you've learned remained scattered in your mind—you don't know what you know. You haven't been able to bring them together to give you a solid framework from which to practice. Instead, you often wind up winging it—pulling out bits of theory here, samples of techniques there—and feeling once again like a beginner.

In the third stage your knowledge and skills consolidate and your sense of confidence and power grows. In fact, like an adolescent, you're aware only of your power and you see only what you know—your way is the best way. You feel on top of things, but in this haughty frame of mind, you don't realize the limits of your knowledge and experience—you don't know what you don't know. Your vision is myopic; you're often not aware of the subtleties of your approach; you can easily ignore the larger implications and effects of what you're doing. Your sense of self-importance, your uncritical loyalty to your beliefs, may make you take unnecessary risks.

In the final stage you come back down to earth; you're more humble about your skills and knowledge. Like everyone else, you have your own strengths and weaknesses—you know what you know, but you're less cocky, more flexible. There isn't one way, you realize, but many. There's always more to learn, but you also know you can trust the foundation of knowledge and skill that you have worked hard to acquire.

In all of these stages, the challenge is in defining and using what you know and believe and honestly admitting what you don't. But doing this obviously isn't simply a matter of glancing over your shoulder and tallying up what you have and what you don't. Learning to be a therapist involves bringing together all the aspects of who you are; when you're in the middle of it it's hard to know exactly what is happening and where you stand because everything is in flux. It's an ongoing, developmental climb of building up and peeling away, of supporting and confronting, of giving yourself the break and looking yourself squarely in the eye.

One useful way of clarifying what you know from what you don't, of ferreting out the gaps in your knowledge, is through teaching, formally (the classroom, the seminar, the short course, the writing of a journal article) or informally (the brown-bag lunch topic, the two-hour staff development for colleagues, the taking on of a student in supervision). In order to tell someone what you know, you first have to figure out what you think. Teaching forces you to consolidate your bits of knowledge, to pinpoint and name your hunches and intuitions, and shape them into something more integrated, more substantial. In the process of sorting through for others what is important to learn, you have to sort through for yourself what you already know.

The teaching process is also a great antidote to the feeling that you're intellectually treading water. It's easy to become dulled by your own practice, to feel that you "just do what you do." You need the opportunity to rediscover your uniqueness, to reconfirm for others and yourself that what you do works, that your approach represents a unique blend of personality and skills. Teaching, and the feedback that others give about what you say, can do this. Even if others don't gain vast amounts of new information from you, they gain the opportunity to compare and contrast their own style against yours, which helps them rediscover themselves.

Arrange to have a regular staff development time where each therapist presents his or her own unique approach to helping families. Think about a case or technique that was particularly successful and expand upon its implications. Do a literature review, define your own unique perspective or application, and write it up for a journal. Contact your local university and see if you can serve as a field instructor for graduate students in social work or clinical or counseling psychology. See if they need adjunct lecturers. Offer to teach a course on marriage and family at the local community college, or one on parenting through the county continuing adult education program. Make up a flyer of the topics and workshops that you can teach and mail them out to all the Departments of Social Services and Family Courts in your state. You may be surprised by how much you have to offer.

THE QUICK AND EASY: MISCELLANEOUS SURVIVAL SKILLS

Finally there are everyday antidotes to therapy's wear and tear. Here are a few:

Diversify. A caseload filled with 20 hyperactive eight-year-old boys may help you refine your skills, but may also drive you insane. If at all possible, diversify your caseload — a mix of families, problems, and personalities, a stable core, perhaps, of what you do best, along with one or two cases that lead you to learn something new. Whenever possible, be in charge of your own scheduling — seeing four depressed clients in a row on a rainy Wednesday afternoon may leave you feeling dull and empty. Put a couple of those hyperactive kids in the middle of it all, see a couple after doing some play therapy, an individual adult after three teenagers. If your clients start to sound the same, you'll start to react the same.

Don't be afraid to diversify your work responsibilities as well. Take part in a community assessment or treatment team, help with public relations and marketing, do follow-up research on your clients' satisfaction. These additional activities can break up the grind of doing back-to-back therapy and can give you another perspective on work.

Control your time. This is relatively easy to do in private practice, though, of course, even here some of your time is going to be generated by client demand. In agency work, however, where others may schedule your appointments, you could wind up with the most chaotic family at the time of day when you are most sluggish and least able to manage them. You know how the case flow over the course of the day affects you; you know when you are at your best, when you need a break to regroup. Set your own schedule.

Make an effort to spend time with colleagues. Therapy is isolating. Offset this by scheduling a regular time to have lunch with a colleague upstairs, have a weekly meeting with everyone in the practice every Thursday morning just to check in and touch base, or have an informal supervision lunch meeting on Wednesdays twice a month with a group of folks whose work you respect.

Make your work space as comfortable as possible. Is that rickety chair driving you crazy? What about the drawer that always sticks, the bland beige walls, the couch with the dark stain and the sagging cushions that you feel embarrassed about every time a new client sits down in it. You spend a good amount of your time in one place, so try to make it your own.

Try to make it attractive as well. Take a look at the offices of friends and colleagues to give you creative ideas. How about a nice picture on the wall that reflects your personality or the mood you want to create (skip that painting of Pickett's Charge)? Get a small aquarium and a few fish. Shut off the overhead florescent lights and get some attractive lamps. Put down carpeting, or throw down a small Oriental-looking rug over the grayish, industrial carpeting that's there. Set up the toys on a bookcase, rather than heaping them in a cardboard box. Bring in some plants, even fake ones, to help the place look less sterile. Use your imagination. Make it look more like home and less like an office.

Do something that helps you feel centered. Because therapy so easily pulls you into others' lives, it important to have something in your life that can pull you back out, that helps you feel centered, that activates another portion of yourself. Meditation twice a day, running, cooking dinner, playing the piano, writing a novel, rafting, gardening, singing—

whatever it is, find something (preferably legal and nonaddictive) that puts you somewhere else, that lets you drop the day's events from your mind, that makes you feel competent, healthy, powerful, or positive about who you are and what you do.

Take vacations. Not working vacations, but real vacations that either help you relax or stimulate you, but that certainly are different from your everyday life. Go to the beach for a week and bring novels, not journals. Go to Pennsylvania, but instead of going to see your mother or Aunt Rosie, stay in Philadelphia and take in the sights. Or go see your mother and Aunt Rosie, but stop off in Philadelphia, anyhow.

Have a balanced personal life. Easier said than done, of course. But if you want to avoid the dangers we have been talking about—the vicarious acting out through your clients, the need for their intimacy, all the ways that therapy can be distorted because you have come to personally need more from it than the rest of your life provides—you need to discover and stay involved in the rest of your life. If you need to do therapy more than your clients need the therapy, everyone is in trouble.

Have realistic expectations. Like any other craft or art, it takes time—8 to 10 years is probably reasonable—to hone your skills and style, to begin to master the subtleties of practice, to feel confident in what you do. Some therapists, often the most sensitive ones it seems, give up too quickly. They get so frustrated and critical of themselves in those early years over what they're aware that they don't know, that they leave the field before they have a chance to develop their skills and get really good. Be patient with yourself and don't box yourself in with unrealistic expectations.

These survival skills, along with good supervision, training, and opportunities to teach what you know can help you stay sane, stable, even steadily enthusiastic about your work over the long haul. The overriding theme here is one of balance and diversity—of putting your emotional eggs in several baskets so that you don't have to clutch too tightly to just one, of finding many ways of expressing yourself, working, and discovering what lies within.

Finally, it's also important to find balance in your therapeutic role. One of the important and often subtle shifts that I think good therapists make as they continue to work is in seeing their responsibility less as fixing the presenting problem that the family brings in and more as helping the family fix it themselves. Therapy and the therapist don't solve the problem, but instead provide a forum for doing so. The therapist can help the family understand how and why the problem came about, point out what they're doing to each other and themselves, and speculate on how it might be connected to their concerns, as well as give them a place for and a way of talking about ideas and options, and supporting them in what they decide to do. But what they ultimately do is up to them, not you, the therapist. As was said in the first chapter, therapy is only one way of approaching problems. Your sanity and satisfaction, and that of your clients as well, comes in accepting and appreciating your limits.

LOOKING WITHIN

1. How do you learn best? What do you need most from supervision or consultation? How have your needs changed over the past year? What would be most difficult to talk about in supervision? Why? How can you repair/expand that relationship? Change it to better meet your clinical personal needs? How can you make time for self-supervision of your work?

2. List all the reasons you give yourself for not taking advantage of some kind of extended training. How much would it be worth to feel 50% more competent as a therapist? How can you overcome the obstacles?

3. What can you teach? What can't you teach but would like to? What's stopping you? Make a list of all the possible teaching opportunities in your area.

4. How can you change your work environment—physically, socially, emotionally—to make it less stressful?

5. Be honest—how's your personal life? How is it affecting your work life? What can you do to change it?

FIFTEEN
The Lessons of Therapy

Therapy is a way of thinking. What you do isn't as important as how you think about what you do: how you sort and shift, making one fact more important than another or one sigh mean more than whatever is being said, organizing what you hear and what you ask into a picture that you then hand back to the family.

This is what I see, you say, and they pass the picture around and turn it this way and that. They tell you that you've made them look funny, or misshapen, or have left out something important, or that they can't recognize anything in the picture. But in a way it doesn't matter. The picture you offer them helps them begin to think about themselves in a new way.

Therapy is an approach to life. Even before anything is said in the office, before the client makes that first phone call to you, before the shuffling through magazines in the waiting room, there's an understanding—about problems, about relationships, about the way both can change. There is the shared belief, even faith perhaps, that through others, even strangers, through talking about what is painful, confusing, frustrating, depressing, it can become less so. Living, we agree, isn't a solo act, nor is it smooth and easy. It's a bumpy road where we fall and skin our knees and where we sometimes get lost. We need others to help us get up, to point the way, to walk beside us.

We—you and I—started this exploration of family therapy by stepping back and looking at its assumptions and foundations. In this chapter we will swing back around and look once again at this thing we call therapy, but with a wider perspective, in a broader context, namely, that of our own personal work lives and everyday living.

What we're looking at and for this time are those places where what you do and what you believe clash, where your values are trodden on by the pace and pattern of your everyday life and lost, where what you do and what you feel are disjointed. It's in these spaces of neglect and contradiction and disparity that the seams and eventually the structure of your work, your life, are most likely to weaken; it's here where your professional and personal selves begin to drift off course, where you suddenly find that the difference between who you are and what you do has become wide indeed.

As we move through this chapter, try to step back and look at your work life in its entirety, and see how well therapy and your work represents the larger self that is you. Look for the gaps, places where important parts of yourself are ignored, where self-honesty is clouded by rationalizations and routine.

THERAPY AS TEACHER

The lens of therapy is capable of focusing upon the smallest, most elemental, concentrated forms of our psychological lives. But what do we see when we look? What does therapy teach us, not only about itself, but about the process of life itself? Some ideas:

It's not individuals who help us to heal, but relationships with those individuals. We talked about this in the context of supervision; we saw this validated in the stories of Billy, the boy traumatized by the murder of his brother, and Ellen, the teenager struggling to replace her deceased father. It's not the rider or the horse that wins the race, but both working together; it's not you fixing someone, nor the family necessarily fixing themselves; whatever positive or negative that happens in the session happens in the smallest of psychic spaces between you and them. It is this therapeutic alchemy, the mixing together of elements from each other's worldview and living that makes something new.

We constantly re-create our past. From each new vantage point in the present we look back on our past and see it anew. As the research on trauma and false memory suggests, our past, rather than being a granite-like foundation on which we build our present and personality, is instead a shadowy and fragile thing always connected to our present. As I enter middle age, for example, I also find myself reentering my adolescence. I feel at times impatient and rebellious as I did then, I want people to get off my back, I want to pursue now the paths that I turned away from back then.

As I create and discover my present, I rediscover and re-create my past, which in turn shapes my present and future. As therapists you and I use this interrelationship of time in the therapeutic process. By helping to create changes in one dimension of time—for example, by asking everyone about good memories of the past—we stimulate change in the present and future.

Symptoms and problems are interchangeable perspectives. When have we really reached the core problem? When are presenting issues the center of our focus and when are they just smoke and dust, distracting us and the family from what lies beyond? When is a problem not really a problem but a mere symptom of something larger, less defined?

Just as the past continually comes alive to become the present, problems and symptoms are fluid landscapes that shift and sway in the eyes of the beholder. What we call problems aren't things out there that are solid or permanent, but rather are our attempts to capture and name for a moment the emotions, memories, and needs flowing within which are too difficult to name and hold. The name we choose is less important than the process of naming. Our purpose in handing our picture of the family back to them to look at isn't our way of trying to shake them and make them see once-and-for-all the problem that's right there in front of their faces; rather, we're trying to open the door and invite the family to look at and step into the pool of memory and emotion from which it comes.

Life is made up of patterns. Once we step into the process that makes up the problem, we and they can see the patterns that make up the process. It's these patterns that we map and follow in sessions with our clients.

But it's not only our clients whose lives are built this way, of course. Like the stone blocks of a house, our own lives are made up of the patterns that we created long ago as children, to survive. They keep our lives stable, but they can also become outdated, no longer representing who we truly are, and ineffective, limiting our power as therapists.

While I learned, for example, to accommodate rather than confront people who seem to intimidate me, both my feeling of intimidation and my fear of their reaction to my challenge are based upon childhood fears that in effect keep me a child. And so I hold back at times in my personal life, falling into habits and responses that help me feel safe, but often resentful. When I do the same in therapy I risk replicating the dysfunctional process in the family, overidentifying with the victim, or inadvertently encouraging someone else in the family to fight my battle. I am less powerful, less able to put what I know into practice, less a good role model. We need to be able to confront and change the patterns that make up our lives as we internally change.

Self-awareness is the ability to step out of the patterns, to adopt a different perspective. Many of the families that we see feel they have no control over their lives because they are swirling around in the middle of them. Our job in the therapeutic process is to offer our view as an outsider—a different look at the relationship, a new slant on the past. The newness of what they see through our eyes can pull the family out of their life current and onto the shore for even the briefest period of time.

From this different place not only can they catch their breath, but they can stand still and see the flow of the current they were in the middle of; these become the "Aha" experiences, the spiritual moments.

We need to be able to do the same, to step outside our own lives periodically in order get away from the craziness we feel, to see the bigger picture and our place in it. But knowing we need to do it doesn't make it easy to do. Sometimes we think we come close to seeing our lives and our work when we find ourselves measuring ours against those of our clients. But like our clients, real self-awareness usually comes when we're most in the thick ourselves, most sensitive to what we don't have and want, most in doubt, turmoil, and pain, most ready to really listen to people around us when we ask, "What do you see when you see me?"

We live the visions of our own lives. We are all mystics in our own way. We live out our visions, our pictures of how life goes, and if they are bad or painful, so will be our lives, unless the vision can be changed. The new pictures created by our experience, garnered from our self-awareness, and offered to us by caring others become the template of a new future, the foundation of hope.

Creative living means moving toward the unknown. Pick up a book of fairy tales—the brothers Grimm, Hans Christian Andersen, tales from India or those of Native Americans—and read a few of them. You'll begin to hear the same theme, see the same pattern running through each one. The hero, usually timid and naive, wishes for something (gold, a home, loving parents), or wishes to be different (to be able to fly, to touch the sun, to become a king).

The wish fills him and fills him until it pushes him out the door of his cottage and into the strange, enchanting, frightening world around him. He begins his quest, confronting the forces of darkness and the voices of doubt; he challenges and is challenged. If his heart is good, his courage strong, he prevails—the king, the gold, the power, the home—is his.

New visions of our professional and personal lives are the starting point for change, but not the end. What the fairy tales tell us is that the next step to growth is action, moving away from the familiar, well-known path toward the one we don't know. Our task is not to be fearless, but to keep going in spite of our fear. We only discover we're brave by acting brave; we only become what we envision by actively doing it.

Life is process. Life is a verb, not a noun. It's in the movement within the moment, the processes that compromise life and work, where relationships live, where the visions and pictures are created, where the stepping back occurs, where the anxiety is felt; the content is always secondary. As the research on adult development suggests, reaching an accomplishment—marriage, earning the college degree, becoming the CEO—quickly fades and leaves us empty; what gives us a sense of purpose and sustains us is the active creating of the accomplishment. To put it another way, the moving toward is more important than the arriving.

These are some of the notions that I see woven in the therapy process. You may discover others. The purpose of such sifting through the therapy process isn't necessarily to discover truths, but to help you to define the values and assumptions hidden within your work. By stepping back to ask what therapy teaches you about life, you see mirrored in the answer the framework of your world.

LIFE AS WORK

The life of the artist has always been an enticing, alluring image—Mary Cassatt struggling to capture on the canvas the vision that fills her brain; Mozart and Beethoven, driven to translate the melodies, the feelings inside, into notes on a page so that others may hear the sounds and experience the emotions; Virginia Woolf, dedicating five years of her life to create the perfect novel, one that carries the reader away into another world. We're drawn to this way of life in part because it's so unstructured, compared to the nine-to-five routine into which most of us feel wedged. But mostly we're drawn to it because it's so *committed,* so *creative.* It's a different approach to work than that of 15-hour-a-day, performance-driven workaholics; unlike them, the artist isn't working because he or she feels compelled to get through the stack of papers on the desk; the stack of papers are on the desk because the artist is working.

This is work that flows from the inside out, rather than from the outside in, work that soaks in all of who and what you are. It is work that goes beyond the boundaries of a "good job" with its means to other ends, or the career, that track that we follow leading to anticipated accomplishment and publicly recognized success. No, we're talking about a calling.

Hold on, before you start to think that you have to hear the sound of celestial choirs and see beams of radiant light falling down on you from above. Take it easy, you don't. A calling can and often does begin with only a whisper of some inner voice telling you that this is something you should do. It may start as only the flicker of an image across your mind that gradually, over time, grows into a vision, a vision not unlike the one you create in the therapy process, which pulls you forward. A calling is realized when you step back from what you are already doing and sense that this work is something that you are not only good at, but were meant to do. You have found a medium for expressing who you are; you do the work not because of what you might get for it at some time in the future, but because of what it does for you in the present.

So what is that calling for you? Why do you do therapy or want to do therapy? What does it offer you as a medium? How does it actualize your values and beliefs, your sense of purpose and creativity? Why do you need to do it?

If you are not sure that therapy is your calling, then what is? What is it that you can't wait to do when you wake up in the morning? What do the dreams, the visions, the fantasies that you have tell you about what you need to do most?

Yes, this doesn't sound practical or realistic. Yes, you need to have a job for money, to have a place to live, to pay off the college loans, to survive in the real world. But unless you have the courage to periodically ask these bigger questions, the gap between your work and yourself will gradually widen. You will feel cynical, tired, and burned out, frustrated and fed up. You will find yourself one day in the middle of a 20-, or 30- or 40-year crisis, filled with fantasies and ready to run away toward dreams that have only become more desperate and powerful by your neglect. If you don't build your work around your life, you can easily wind up building your life around your work.

LIFE OF INTEGRITY

Actually, building may be the wrong word. Do we really build our lives? Many would say yes, especially considering the society we live in. Each of us has incorporated within us the images of our American pioneers, those self-sufficient, hard-working, brave frontier men and women who created their lives out of nothing more than hope and sweat and guts. We have, we're told, roughly 40 years—from 20 to 60 years old—to do the same, to grab hold of our lives and make something out of it. At the end of the time, you and everyone else will take stock and look at just how much you've accomplished, how well you have done, how successful you are.

But there is another point of view, another way of looking at our relationship to living. Rather than building our lives, we discover them. This is the image of life unfolding, the sense that our lives are led, moving always just two steps ahead of us, gently waving its hand, urging us to follow. It's an image that tells us that by staying close to ourselves, with our ear pressed tight against the ground of our lives, listening—to our intuitions, our emotions, our fantasies—we will discover our purpose, our calling; we will live the life we were meant to have.

The split between these two notions is like that of context and process, two sides of the same reality. Building at its worst becomes a left-brain-driven march to succeed and accomplish. Discovery at its worst lacks grounding; weightless visions and fragile dreams float forever within our heads but never enter our lives. The best is the combination of both, where discovery becomes the thin lines on a sheet of blueprint paper and building becomes the nailing of rafters and beams into the solid structure that we call our life.

Both are important, but like its sister, process, it is discovery that leads the way. To give credence and respect to this side of our lives is only to do what we do with our families—help them to give full voice to whispers and nods, help them to step aside for a moment from the pain that their problem may be creating in order to hear what their problem is telling them about what they need to learn, ask the "miracle questions" to help them draw out the answers within them that they didn't know were there. Even when they feel victimized and battered by life, we say to them that life, their life, is ready to give something back to them if only they have the courage to open their eyes and live it.

When we scrape down to the bottom of this way of thinking, we find ourselves resting once again on assumptions, values, even faith—a faith that we can not only find our purpose, but that there is purpose; that problems not only have solutions, but lessons to teach us; and that once we learn them, the problems miraculously disappear. This is not the calm, sedentary faith that reassures us that everything will turn out all right, but the wild, robust faith that comes from living by the seat of our pants.

If you are able to live this way, to wait and listen, then go to work to make your inner and outer life the mirror of each other, then your life is filled with gut-sure honesty, with true integrity. It will be a different life than the carefully built one that keeps discovery locked away, that sets its marker early on and moves steadily forward. To bring faith and discovery and honesty into your life, into your work, is to walk out on a trail on a crisp morning following the sound of the hawk flying above rather than the painted sign on the tree. You may suddenly find yourself sitting out on a limb or looking over the edge of a cliff and not knowing why or how you got there. You may look down and feel afraid, but if you look inside you will find courage; if you look up, you will see visions.

LOOKING WITHIN

1. Draw a picture of your life. Get crayons, pencils, paint, a large sheet of paper and write at the top "My Life." Let your unconscious lead you—follow the images that come to mind, the memories that may be stirred up, the feelings that you have. Give yourself about 15 minutes. Let the picture sit for a day, then look at it carefully again.

2. What do your recurring problems tell you about what you need to learn? How can doing therapy or your clients help you learn those lessons?

3. How do you look back on your past now, compared with how you did 5 or 10 years ago? How has this image changed your sense of the present, the future?

4. What did you want to be when you grew up? How have you incorporated those characteristics into your current work?

5. How close is the gap between your inner and outer world? What would it take to bring them together?

Suggested Readings

FAMILY THERAPY CLASSICS

These are the texts by the grandmothers and grandfathers of family therapy. Each offers its own particular theory and slant on the systemic process.

Ackerman, Nathan W. (1995). *The Psychodynamics of Family Life: Diagnosis and Treatment of Family Relationships.* Northvale, NJ: Jason Aronson.

Originally published in the early 1970s, this was one of the first books to chart the course into family therapy waters. You can tell from the title that Ackerman was coming out of the psychodynamic, psychiatric school.

Bowen, Murray. (1978). *Family Therapy in Clinical Practice.* Northvale, NJ: Jason Aronson.

Theory, theory, theory, said Bowen. If you had a good theory you had the lens through which you could see and understand any family. Here's his theory—the world of undifferentiation, the influence of history, the start of genograms, the therapist as coach and change agent.

Haley, Jay. (1991). *Problem Solving Therapy: New Strategies for Effective Family Therapy* (2nd ed.). San Francisco: Jossey-Bass.

This new edition describes the beginnings of strategic therapy. Learning to think not only in patterns and circles, but from different heights. Understanding how solutions turn into problems. Telling a client that he needs to wax his floor on his hands and knees before he goes to bed each night. If nothing else, just learning to think the way Haley does can open your mind to new possibilities.

Minuchin, Salvador. (1974). *Families and Family Therapy.* Cambridge, MA: Harvard University Press.

The original book on Structural Family Therapy, which first described those enmeshed and rigid families with diffuse boundaries, distant parents, unresolved marital issues.

Minuchin, Salvador, and Fishman, Charles H. (1981). *Family Therapy Techniques.* Cambridge, MA: Harvard University Press.

Minuchin's sequel—how to put into operation all the theory of his first book.

Satir, Virginia. (1994). *Helping Families to Change*. Northvale, NJ: Jason Aronson.

The grandmother of family therapy, the person to bring out the softer side of the family therapy movement, the first to write in a consumer-friendly way. This new edition of her classic provides useful, practical information about communication and emotional patterns in families.

Whitaker, Carl, and Bumberry, William M. (1988). *Dancing with the Family: A Symbolic–Experiential Approach*. New York: Brunner/Mazel.

Carl Whitaker, the crazy uncle of family therapy who seemed to be always fooling around but wasn't. His summary of what all the fooling around was really about.

OTHER FAMILY THERAPY BOOKS

The newer generation of family therapists—some offshoots of the classics, others combining various approaches into one, still others food for thought from other schools that you can apply to your family work.

Anderson, Carol M., and Stewart, Susan. (1983). *Mastering Resistance: A Practical Guide to Family Therapy*. New York: Guilford Press.

Practical is definitely the defining word here. The book clearly lays out various types of client resistance, with concrete ways to offset each one. It makes you feel that whatever the client throws at you, there's nothing you can't manage. Which isn't bad as long as you don't get too cocky.

Assagioli, Roberto. (1993). *Psychosynthesis: A Collection of Basic Writings*. New York: Penguin.

Assagioli was popular with his theory of psychosynthesis in the late 1960s and early 1970s, the heyday of the growth movement in therapy. Instead of Freud's harsh superego, Assagioli postulated that we all had a more benevolent, higher self to guide us. Even if you don't buy his theory, his use of imagery techniques is excellent.

de Shazer, Steve. (1982). *Patterns of Brief Family Therapy: An Ecosytemic Approach*. New York: Guilford Press.

In the light of current managed care and the push for brief therapy, this book now seems almost prophetic.

Efran, Jay S., et al. (1990). *Language, Structure, and Change: Framework of Meaning in Psychotherapy*. New York: Norton.

Heard about contructivism but aren't sure what it is? This book will fill you in.

Elkin, Michael. (1990). *Families under the Influence: Changing Alcoholic Patterns*. New York: Norton.

The alcoholic in the family. If you work with families who have a member who has trouble with alcohol addiction (and who doesn't have such clients?), this book gives you a way of addressing the addiction in the family process.

Kerr, Michael E., and Bowen, Murray. (1988). *Family Evaluation: An Approach Based on Bowen Theory*. New York: Norton.

Michael Kerr was the designated heir of the Georgetown Program, picked by Bowen several years before his death. Here they teamed up to present the heart of Bowen's theory. A bit dense, but a good source of Bowen's ideas.

Lankton, Stephen R., and Lankton, Carol H. (1986). *Enchantment and Intervention in Family Therapy: Training in Ericksonian Approaches*. New York: Brunner/Mazel.

Milton Erickson was a master of using hypnosis to create what we see now as ingenious strategic and paradoxical interventions. Unfortunately, he didn't write about his work, but he was lucky enough to train people who did. Another book to expand your thinking.

Madanes, Cloe. (1991). *Strategic Family Therapy*. San Francisco: Jossey-Bass.

Madanes's work with Haley enabled her to build on Haley's original ideas. A good broadening of the strategic approach.

McGoldrick, Monica, Giordano, Joseph, and Pearce, John K., eds. (1996). *Ethnicity and Family Therapy* (2nd ed.). New York: Guilford Press.

The newly published second edition of a classic. Each chapter describes the culture and attitudes of various ethnic groups (Irish, Jewish, Italian, African American, etc.) toward family structure, problems, and use of outside help. It sensitizes you to the cultural elements that are always interacting with your work, but which all too easily get overlooked, as well as providing plenty of practical information.

Minuchin, Salvador, and Nichols, Michael P. (1992). *Family Healing: Tales of Hope and Renewal from Family Therapy*. New York: Free Press.

It's good to see that Minuchin didn't stop writing after his initial works. A reader-friendly book describing his actual work with a variety of families and problems.

Napier, Augustus, and Whitaker, Carl. (1988). *The Family Crucible: The Intense Experience of Family Therapy*. New York: HarperCollins.

Another reader-friendly book, one that is in many ways a better presentation of Whitaker's work than his other book is. Good description of the family process and the layers of problems. `

Nichols, Michael P. (1995). *The Lost Art of Listening*. New York: Guilford Press.

As the title says, this book can make you look again at the power and practice of good listening.

Nichols, Michael P., and Schwartz, Richard C. (1994). *Family Therapy: Concepts and Methods* (3rd ed.). Needham Heights, MA: Allyn & Bacon.

If you didn't have to use this in graduate school, it's a good basic text, now in its third edition. Plenty of practical information as well as theory.

O'Hanlon, William, and Weiner-Davis, Michele. (1988). *In Search of Solutions: Creating Context for Change*. New York: Norton.

A good book on solution-oriented, brief therapy.

Palazzoli, Mara. (1990). *Paradox and Counterparadox*. Northvale, NJ: Jason
    Aronson.

The start of paradoxical therapy, taking Jay Haley another step. The use of
teams behind the mirror, paradoxical letters to families telling them why their
daughter should keep sacrificing herself for the good of the family. Another mind
stretcher.

Scharff, David, and Scharff, Jill S. (1992). *Object Relations Family Therapy*. North-
    vale, NJ: Jason Aronson.

If you're not sure how to apply an objects relations approach to family therapy, here's your answer.

Waters, David, and Lawrence, Edith C. (1993). *Competence, Courage, and
    Change: An Approach to Family Therapy*. New York: Norton.

Work with the family's strengths, and take the positive approach, say these
two authors. An uplifting book with good case examples.

White, Michael, and Epston, David. (1990). *Narrative Means to Therapeutic Ends*.
    New York: Norton.

Theory and practice of narrative therapy.

Zinker, Joseph. (1994). *In Search of Good Form: Gestalt Therapy with Couples
    and Families*. San Francisco: Jossey-Bass.

Since Fritz Perls's early development of Gestalt therapy in the 1960s it has
continued to find applications in all phases of clinical practice. This is a good book
that helps you use Gestalt theory and techniques, such as empty chair work, in
your family practice. A good adjunct perspective.

MARITAL THERAPY

Many of the books above include marital work in the context of family therapy.
These books specifically focus on couple therapy and theory.

Gottman, John M., and Silver, Nan. (1994). *Two-Part Harmony: Why Marriages
    Succeed or Fail*. New York: Simon & Schuster.

Gottman has tried to do for couple relationships what Masters and Johnson
did for sexual relationships. He brought couples into a lab, hooked them up to
wires, put them on videotape, and tried to find out what made some relationships
last when others fell apart. What he found out is interesting, and much of it counter to the usual marriage counseling assumptions. Written for the general public,
this is a good book for you and your clients to read.

Guerin, Philip J., Fay, Leo F., Burden, Susan L., and Kautto, Judith D. (1987).
    The Evaluation and Treatment of Marital Conflict: A Four Stage Approach.
    New York: Basic Books.

A good, practical book on doing marital therapy.

Gurman, Alan S., ed. (1991). *Casebook of Marital Therapy*. New York: Guilford Press.

As the title says, a good book of various approaches to cases.

Martin, Peter A. (1993). *A Marital Therapy Manual*. Northvale, NJ: Jason Aronson.

A manual with a psychodynamic bent.

Nichols, William C. (1988). *Marital Therapy: An Integrative Approach*. New York: Guilford Press.

Another example of the integration of approaches into a coherent model.

Paolino, Thomas J., and McCrady, Barbara, eds. (1978). *Marriage and Marital Therapy: Psychoanalytic, Behavioral, and Systems Perspectives*. New York: Brunner / Mazel.

Unlike William Nichols's book which tries to integrate approaches, this book helps you clearly see the differences between them. A basic text, used for many years in graduate programs.

PLAY THERAPY

These books focus on the ins and outs of play therapy—theory, techniques, even equipment to buy. A mix of therapeutic approaches.

Ammann, Ruth. (1991). *Healing and Transformation in Sand Play: Creative Processes Become Visible*. Peru, IL: Open Court.

There's a whole school of practice regarding the use of sand work. This will get you started.

Gil, Eliana. (1994). *Play in Family Therapy*. New York: Guilford Press.

Now you don't have to wonder what to do with the little kids in family therapy. This book will help you make good use of them.

Kissel, Stanley. (1990). *Play Therapy: A Strategic Approach*. Springfield, IL: Charles C Thomas.

How to keep your strategic family therapy and play therapy consistent.

O'Connor, Kevin J. (1991). *The Play Therapy Primer: An Integration of Theories and Techniques*. New York: Wiley.

The basics, from an integrated approach.

Schaefer, Charles, and Cangelosi, Donna, eds. (1994). *Play Therapy Techniques*. Northvale, NJ: Jason Aronson.

This book covers the gamut—storytelling, drawing and art, board games, dollhouses—all the ways to play and learn from children.

Index